WILLIAM KITTREDGE

The NATURE of GENEROSITY

William Kittredge is the author of *Hole in the Sky; Owning It All,* a book of essays; and the story collections *The Van Gogh Field* and *We Are Not in This Together.* With Annick Smith, he edited *The Last Best Place: A Montana Anthology.*

The NATURE
of GENEROSITY

The
NATURE
of
GENEROSITY

WILLIAM
KITTREDGE

Vintage Departures

VINTAGE BOOKS

A DIVISION OF RANDOM HOUSE, INC.

NEW YORK

VINTAGE DEPARTURES EDITION

Copyright © 2000 by William Kittredge

All rights reserved under International and Pan-American
Copyright Conventions. Published in the United States
by Vintage Books, a division of Random House, Inc.,
New York, and simultaneously in Canada by Random
House of Canada Limited, Toronto. Originally published in
hardcover in the United States by Alfred A. Knopf, a division
of Random House, Inc., New York, in 2000.

Vintage is a registered trademark and Vintage Departures and
colophon are trademarks of Random House, Inc.

Owing to limitations of space, all permissions to reprint
previously published material can be found on page 279.

Library of Congress Cataloging-in-Publication Data
Kittredge, William.
The nature of generosity / William Kittredge.
p.   cm.
ISBN-10: 0-679-75687-6
ISBN-13: 978-0-679-75687-3

1. Kittredge, William—Journeys.   2. Authors, American—
20th century—Biography.   3. Social ecology.   4. Human
ecology.   5. Altruism.   I. Title.
PS3561.I87 Z472 2001
813'.54—dc21
[B]
2001026038

Book design by Virginia Tan

www.vintagebooks.com

146684614

Contents

The NATURE
of GENEROSITY

Introduction

The Imperishable World

SOMETIME in the early 1880s, a medical doctor named Israel Wood Powell, superintendent for Indian Affairs for Coastal Indians in British Columbia, collected a raven rattle from the Tsimshian Indians. He sent the rattle to the American Museum of Natural History in New York City, where it remains today.

A percussive musical instrument used in elaborate ceremonial dances, this simple rattle resembles the ones we all shook in childhood, except that it is carved into the form of a mythological raven caught in the act of stealing the sun back from captivity, carrying the little red ball of the sun in his mouth, preparing to spit it back home into the heavens.

This is a striking idea, but not half so remarkable as the beings we see riding on the raven: a human figure reclining in a posture of sexual openness, and a frog crouched over, as if preparing to mount. Their tongues, in a slender red arc, form a single tongue as it reaches from human to frog and frog to human. In this vision, we share tongues with animals in some perfect sexuality while our trickster raven redeploys the sun.

See, that raven rattle says, this is how we are, inextricably one with everything, however tricked, riding, in fact, on the back of trickiness itself.

JUST ABOVE Elliott Bay in Seattle, in the public market, farmers wash leeks and radishes. Fish merchants sell crabs from seawater tanks. The air stinks of loam and oceans, the stench as wholesome as musk from a bed where a baby is at its mother's breast.

North of here, on the British Columbian coast, Prince Rupert is a colonial town with wide, clean streets and European gardens like something out of the nineteenth century. When I was there, a great storm rolled in off the Pacific. My true companion, Annick Smith, and I walked the beach beside the red cedar forest, a cold mist spraying over us from the dark rocks as ravens danced along on the power lines above the totem poles, mocking us—as if trying to tell us that the world makes sense without us, in ways we are unlikely to understand.

Dempsey Bob, when we met decades ago (I know nothing of his life since), carved and sold traditional masks of great-eyed bears and ravens. He showed us how he did his work, uncovering a face hidden in the sweet red wood with one precise incision and then another. When I asked how he knew when a mask was finished, he said, "When they start lookin' back." This had the sound of a line tailor-made for tourists.

Reefs of wild roses bloomed under the cottonwoods. Upstream on either side of the Skeena River, which at that high-water stage looked wide as the Columbia, the stony, snowy peaks stood like boundary markers. Beyond lay the unroaded rain forests where Dempsey Bob had come to believe in his masks (if he really did and wasn't just kidding). At twilight, traveling through thickets of aspen along a feeder creek, we came to the village of Kitwancool, where we first saw the door pole called Hole in the Sky, which was thought to mark an entry into that particular heaven in which all the people we loved are still alive and somehow kicking.

Alongside it was a pole called All Frogs, erected in celebration of a native clan. Here, the carvers had re-created the beginning of things, a world of great frogs, four of them leaving the hands of a deity who revered them, the mother at the top and her young climbing down the red-cedar pole toward earth.

Meanwhile, all over the earth, frog populations are dying after surviving extinctions that killed off the dinosaurs. Maybe the cause is solar radiation leaking through our infamous holes in the ozone layer, or parasites—or both, or neither.

The point is, not many people have the will to care. The Greek word *tragos* means "goat," and *oide* means "song." Tragedies are goat songs, hymns to our fate as animals on earth. But many of us despise our animal natures. Many of us think it's too late for nature, and others think that dying out is what we deserve. Maybe we should pull up our socks and just dance those blues away.

IN LATE SUNLIGHT on a hot May afternoon, I sauntered (à la Whitman) down Broadway toward Prince Street in Manhattan's SoHo district and was struck by happiness. The streets were crowded by people seeming to represent every racial mix and continent and subcontinent, many of them talking in tongues, so far as I could tell, sometimes singing in any one of a multitude of languages I couldn't place. So much humanity, with the old boy, myself, idling among them in the maze of ornate brickwork walls, the heat rising from the reach of Broadway to the south. I wanted to think that one silver-haired young couple in matching lavender shorts were Icelandic; maybe they'd come to this city in search of glory—or sin, having had enough of glorious, silent ice fields.

In the 1950s, as I grew up in the backlands of the American West, we didn't believe in escaping to cities. Since our people had gone west looking for some version of freedom, we learned to despise cities as the native homes of injustice, or so we understood; yet look at me now, at ease with myself in this urban mix.

I was happy inside this downtown, our ancient, thronging situation. Every story adds to the stock of metaphors that is our actuality. This is why our lives seem so double- and triple-hearted—at least that many hearts, given so many stories. We are creatures who have evolved with other creatures, whether ants, calling birds, charismatic lions, milk cows, gorillas, or one another. Nature and neighborhoods are versions of the same thing, our common homeland.

But the frogs and the 60 million North American buffalo and the thundering herds of wildebeest and elephants are dying out. Twenty-five or thirty thousand species each year, at a rate of around three an hour, like the entirely lost passenger pigeons, are vanishing forever. More are going while we lament their passing (maybe we should mount a great electric sign down the side of a New York skyscraper, on which the names of creatures flash in lights as they cease to exist).

It's our fault. Too many humans, too many conflicting needs, heedlessness—we all know the reasons. In a branch of the Nature Company on Broadway, the Eocene fossil remains of some kind of long-tailed bat-fish preserved in orange sandstone was on sale for $2,200, and a beautifully detailed little carved elephant for $595, whereas the white rhino was a mere $495. As a Westerner who walks in forests anytime he wants, I was tempted to dismiss their merchandise as virtual and unnatural. But that was only a cheap try at feeling superior. The Nature Company helps people answer a hunger for intimacy (though lately, it has been replaced in this Manhattan location by a branch of Victoria's Secret).

Across the street, there was a market whose tables flowed with mangoes and glowing blood oranges and Spanish lemons and shiitake mushrooms and Holland orange bell peppers. Display cases were loaded with Portuguese linguica sausage, Black Forest hams, double-smoked sides of bacon, old-fashioned brine-cured belly lox and extra-aged farmhouse English cheddar (dark and moldy and waxy brown), as well as catfish and Manila clams—guilty pleasures all. How can we disdain a civilization that provides us with such things to eat?

Around the corner, a monk in reddish robes sat on a stack of what I took to be prayer rugs, fanning himself in the heat in a tiny Tibetan store that sold singing bowls, brocade-adorned Bhutan woolen fabrics, and, apparently their speciality, fox-fur hats crowned with raw silk, elegant enough to be chic anywhere in winter. Was he a practiced dreamer, I wondered, yearning to pass from life into the energy that is light?

All the stories in the world surround us. We all have to deal with the run of metaphor loose near Broadway and Prince. It's possible to think of that as part of our good fortune.

STORYTELLING is a technique we have long used in our efforts to determine our true situation. We define ourselves with two fundamental kinds of stories: cautionary tales, which warn us, and celebratory ones, in which we acknowledge what has announced itself as invaluable. We try to protect ourselves with one and heal or calm ourselves with the other.

Defining stories, whether called metaphors or paradigms, work like filters or lenses, determining what we are capable of experiencing (or, more exactly, what we are capable of noticing that we have experienced).

The commonsense notion that we share patterns of perception and behavior with other animals is plainly evident in ancient stories. After watching animals, and seeing versions of themselves, humans were increasingly capable of judging their own conduct. The wolf and his three little pigs all live within us. Pets, grazing herds, and wilderness carnivores were the singular mirror in which humans first saw themselves reflected. Stories about animals, our companions, were a tool early humans used in their efforts to understand themselves. And they still are. Places come to exist in our imaginations because of stories, and so do we. When we reach for "a sense of place," we posit an intimate relationship to a set of stories connected to a particular location, such as Hong Kong or the Grand Canyon or the bed where we were born, thinking of histories and the evolution of personalities in a local context. Having "a sense of self" means possessing a set of stories about who we are and where and with whom and why.

Our stories also remind us to love ourselves, one another, and the world. My own sense of what's valuable was defined in a swampy valley ringed by high deserts, and it centers on families, intelligent horses, deep, fragrant peat soil, flocks of waterbirds traced one above the other, calling in the silent morning sky. Trying to fathom myself, I've written about the yard in front of the house my father built in that valley, and of tasting sour springtime in the early-morning air, with those birds above me, in flight and calling.

Each morning, we wake and start telling a story about our

lives, an act almost as involuntary as breathing. We listen as long as we live, and if we're lucky, we discover terms that make us feel whole and safe, even useful.

A society capable of naming itself lives within its stories, inhabiting and furnishing them. We see this process in the songlines of the Australian Aborigines and in Saint Augustine's *Confessions,* in Saint Teresa and Sam Johnson, in Shakespeare's young Hamlet and old Lear, who talk and think themselves toward fresh versions of who they are.

We ride stories like rafts, or lay them out on the table like maps. They always, eventually, fail and have to be reinvented. The world is too complex for our forms ever to encompass for long.

Storytelling requires continuous reimagining. The process of reinvention is often formalized, as in the call and response in blues music—statement and confrontation, improvisation and play, then the introduction of new elements. If our willingness to think freshly deserts us, or if we refuse outright, we are left adrift.

In childhood, we begin discovering the legend we will come to inhabit. Some things are frightening, others reassuring. Down with the measles, maybe five years old, confined to my bed on a summer afternoon while soft rain fell into apple trees outside the open window, I listened as my mother read me stories like *Little Black Sambo* (its injustices terrified me) and the one by Kipling about how the elephant got its trunk, until I could hear nothing but the consolation of her voice and fell asleep. I will never forget the falling, into perfect ease. Who and what I am began taking shape in those moments. Even as children, as it is happening, we know, dimly but not entirely unconsciously, that we are engaged in the central business of our lives, gone off on a voyage, setting out along our personal songlines.

THE POINT of this book can be suggested by pairing metaphors and examining how they resonate against each other: tricksters and jazz next to manicured gardens in Kyoto, walled cities against wilderness, and island empires that evolve into commodified carnivals, freedom against containment. This is a book about attempting to discover answers to questions about what work to attempt. It proceeds, as it must, from my own travels—real and metaphoric—and begins with what in retrospect seems to have been the sweetness and constraints of a childhood paradise that evolved into a family-built entrapment.

The northern reaches of the Great Basin, where I grew up—marshland valleys under fault-block ridges along the boundary between Oregon and Nevada, expanses of alkaline sagebrush desert—is to me the holy land. My father's ashes were scattered over the rimrocks of Hart Mountain, where you can gaze out over lakes named Stone Corral and Bluejoint as they evaporate under the black-lava escarpment of Poker Jim Ridge.

In Warner Valley, the great horses ran the hard, dry hay fields in summer before daybreak, their hooves echoing on sod as I herded them through mists toward the willow-walled corral at some hay camp. I could see myself in those massive creatures. If they loved this world as they seemed to, on those mornings when our breath fogged before us, then so did I.

Hard-handed men with their cases of beer, drifting through Sunday afternoons on the front steps of the Adel store, talked on and on about quick little roping horses and big-horned mule deer bucks leaping through the juniper on the opening day of hunting season. To them, this part of creation was beloved and obviously holy (in my usage, the words *sacred* and *holy* denote the invaluable—beyond which, I cannot think how to explain it).

Acknowledge what you value most, what you actually love, I tell myself. Think of the child you were, of what that distant creature thought he might become, how his future would work out, how he came to imagine that particular version of what would come next, and next.

Years ago, I should've written a book called *Jo and Oscar*, in which to parade the enormous advantages my parents gave me with the example of their good spirits and humor. My mother and I understood my father in separate ways, which allowed us to express our profound regard for each other, and our lives were more significant because of it, and also, of course, because of my father. He had a genius for friendship and high jinks, an affinity for poker, nights on the town, hunting trips and any general wandering, conversations conducted while leaning against a pickup truck with a bottle of beer in his hand, studying the sunset. This caused my mother endless consternation. To quiet her, he would take me along when he was just going, as he said, for a drive. Without plans having been made, we would sometimes stay out overnight.

When I was about eight, he took me to the Cedarville Rodeo, where he ran into Butch Powers, a convivial Surprise Valley rancher who later became the lieutenant governor of California. After the rodeo was over, when we were supposed to be well on the road toward home, we ended up in the Golden Hotel. An old two-story frame building under cottonwoods on the main street, it also served as the primary Basque eating establishment. I recall bright faces in that yellow-painted room, families crowding the tables. They all laughed when my father said, "Sure, go ahead, have a glass of wine like the other kids."

Later, I woke up disoriented in the wood box beside the black ironwork stove in the kitchen. A cook was washing the last of the dishes, up to her elbows in soapsuds. The dining room was alive with the talk and laughter of men who were playing cards, my father among them. His face shone in the lamplight as he laid down his cards and rubbed the top of my head, looking around at his friends, and the child I was—even sick and disoriented—saw how they loved him and therefore me.

What I did was pile some coats on a bench and go back to sleep. I don't know how we got home, but I do remember that my mother thought it was all right this once, since we'd been at the Golden Hotel, a family place, where nothing could go wrong.

AN EARLY spring morning, my mother and my father in their rumpled bed, which smelled of them, waterbirds heading north toward their breeding grounds on the tundra when I wandered out onto the lawns around our house—these memories constitute parts of the best world I expect to know about. My ideas of perfection connect to our great landlocked valley just at the time World War II was beginning. One summer, we moved into a new house, which was fresh and clean and smelled of sawdust. From the screened veranda, we could see over the wild-hay meadows and willow-lined sloughs of the Thompson Field and beyond to swamplands my family was draining and preparing to farm. This luminous world was populated by my fair-armed mother and my gray-eyed father, my baby sister in a white blanket and my little brother, by Ada and Clyde (a country couple hired to look out for us), and by the cooks in the ranch-hand camps and the occasional cowhands.

The late 1930s were like the last years of the nineteenth century. What I want to convey is our isolation. We were thirty-six gravel-road miles over the Warner Mountains from the little lumbering and rancher town of Lakeview (2,500 souls, tops). Warner Valley was not en route to anywhere.

The way in was the way out. Sagebrush deserts on the high and mostly waterless plateaus to the east were traced with wagon-track roads over rimrocks and salt-grass playas from spring to spring, water hole to water hole, but nobody ever headed in that direction with any idea of heading toward the future.

Looking toward the sunrise from a ridge above our buckaroo camp beside the desert spring at South Corral, I studied the snowy highlands of Steens Mountain, where, at least in legend, the whores from Burns had camped in summer with the sheep herders at a place called Whorehouse Meadows, where nobody but wandering men ever went, men who would never be around when you needed them. And beyond, in Idaho, more desert. Beyond Idaho were the Rocky Mountains and the Mississippi, the Empire State Building, the Eiffel Tower, and the pyramids of Egypt, places I read about in schoolbooks, where nobody I knew had ever gone or ever would go. We were not wandering people. We were concentrating on our properties.

In what I persist in thinking of as the innocence of boyhood, not old enough for school, I tried to walk silently, listening, tracking rabbits, attempting to be sure of foot and move without thought, while paying absolute attention. Tracing animal trails through wild-grass meadows, I crawled into nests of willow on the banks of the sloughs, into grass-walled chambers where raccoons had bedded and which reeked of their fierce lives. I listened to some voice in my mind predicting I was on the verge of unimaginable discoveries.

Now I wonder if it would be possible to find those trails, or trails like them, even crawl into the brushy hideouts where creatures feast and breed, and again try to be part of the thrumming world, a child in a narrative about quail running the brush and conjoined iridescent dragonflies. Waterbirds in their comings and goings, and rivers, lead me to intuit that such flowing cannot be in disorder. We work at our stories, and reawaken as we make them.

The summer I turned four, my father began catching an old gelding called Moon, lifting me to the saddle, then leading me to the plow ground along the irrigation ditch at the head of our garden, where he would instruct me in the arts of staying horseback. If I came unseated, he'd knock the dust off my shirt and lift me up again. Childish crying was unthinkable. Coming to understand what it meant to act like a horseman in our part of the outback West involved a lot of great pretending. We learned theater at an early age.

In the 1930s, the work was mostly done with the help of horses. It was easy to love horses moving in herds, running the meadowlands, and the waterbirds in calling flocks, and the antelope flaring across the alkaline playas on the deserts out east of the valley, and the white-faced calves left to rest in the shade of tall sage along a draw while the mother cows walked dusty miles to water.

Before I could read, I learned to revere horsemen and cow horses and pay attention to cookhouse manners. Once in a while my own-the-ranch grandparents on my father's side would take us all down to what was called the Buck Shack, the buckaroo cookhouse, for a Sunday meal concocted by one of the snoose-spitting old hands who was so worn down by his life on horses that he was reduced to cooking for the chuck-wagon crew. On perhaps the first of these expeditions, I was instructed that I had to eat everything I took on my plate or the cook would be insulted. After everybody had finished, I was still there, a child who felt abandoned by his family (and at that moment, he hated them), a humiliated little boy worrying away, bite by bite, at a piece of tough beefsteak. The old cook swept my plate away.

"Shit, kid," he said. "You don't need to eat that son of a bitch." Then he served me a slice of rhubarb pie sprinkled with sugar. My wising up to the world may have begun there, in noontime light that fell at an angle I can still see across that rough table, with that old man, as I was flooded with gratitude.

By the time I was seven, I was riding with a sort of cruel Spanish spade bit, the silver-mounted side bars shaped to the form of a woman's thigh, knee, and calf. I could draw blood from my horse's mouth with that Spanish bit, but I caught hell if I ever did.

That child, in that absolutely formative time, is who I want to think I am. But there was another boy. The silences of the linoleum-floored rooms in my grandparents' white-painted house always left me ill at ease. Out on the lawn, under the Lombardy poplars, I'd flip my jackknife to stick in the ground, over and over. That boy wanted to walk around swatting at dragonflies. He didn't want to be the useful type.

ONE OF MY FIRST successes (as I understand it in hindsight) came on an evening when my father took my brother and cousins and me on a fishing trip to Bidwell Mountain. We camped beside a little branch of Deep Creek that had cut a twisty channel through the roots of an aspen grove, then ran into a sod-banked set of turns through the summer pastures of a place we called Big Valley, where I think I recall wild lilies in blossom.

My timing—what we called luck—was dead perfect that evening. I caught more fish than even my father, who responded by pouring bourbon into his coffee at sunup and laughing as he cooked up those trout for our breakfast. I went home sure that one key to making myself happy involved fishing. Days like that drove me to consider trout, as they flashed in the fluttering light over heavy gravel in some silvery stream, to be enormously valuable. They were beautiful and quick, difficult to catch and to kill—the entire double-bind streamside enactment was unfathomably important. The killing, which should resonate in fishing literature but rarely does, the audible cracking of a spine over the thumb, was nothing but the occasion for a flinch of regret, as I learned to pretend by watching adults. The death of a fish didn't seem to matter. An important element was victory, over the fish and maybe, as psychiatrists surely would suggest, over my father. As much as anything on earth, for a lot of years, I loved casting a fly to water where there might be a trout, and the rise, the hit, and the setting of the hook, and, more than anything else, the truly sporting part, as I saw it, playing those brilliant fish through riffles into the pools, letting them run. I was always surprised by their strength as the bamboo rod flexed and brought them back. Then cooking them up with spuds and onions over a little willow fire on a sandbank, bare-fingered eating. But most important was wading out into water rippling with light around black basalt boulders, balancing against the current every summer evening if you were so moved, the only killing sport I ever loved.

SUMMERTIME THUNDERSTORMS almost never broke until twilight, when great hammerhead clouds materialized above Bidwell Mountain. Slants of rain fell miles away over the meadowlands, illuminated under the clouds by a sun lying just at the dark reef of mountains that formed the western horizon. Lightning would strike nearby (one evening, it ran down the telephone wires right into our house, flaring in a yellow ball of something we could only call fire, just a doorway away from the table where my father sat across from one of his friends, drinking scotch). Thunder went off like artillery, a sound so numbing that to truly remember it was impossible once it was gone. The air would hang entirely still, mosquitoes whirling above us in complex spirals as the edge of a storm blew along the valley toward us. Willow leaves flashed along the sloughs in the Thompson Field, in the valley below our house, and a throng of children would run trails through the orchard like happy animals (as I think of them, able to trust utterly in impulses that run their nervous wiring like waves—I think we often float like birds in the updrafts of what comes to us).

Rain pattered in the dust, a drop on your flesh, and at last the wind was there as we ran for the house, soaking wet before we got there. We stood dripping and awed, up close to the window glass as the lightning flowered, the trees shook in the wind, and, more often than not, the rain fell steadily through the night to a cloudless daybreak.

After the electric storm ended, I would go to a steaming shower and dry myself on one of my mother's huge towels, then fall into the sweetness of a quiet bed and rain on the roof. Lately, I sleep under a white down-filled comforter. After bathing, I go to rest beneath it in the breathing darkness. I listen for rain on the roof, and imagine my mother smiling at my foolishness.

My father, because I never gave a damn about hunting, thought I was repudiating one of his ways of revering the world. Horses and trout weren't enough. When my father stood still for a photograph, the occasion usually had to do with hunting—Oscar carrying an orange crate full of groceries into the line shack at Ackney Camp, where he would hole up with pals, hunting mule deer in the draws from sunup until dark, drinking whiskey and dealing poker hands through the night. There he is on a winter day with friends, all of them dead a long time now, out back of the house where we lived, breath hanging in the cold air, twenty-nine Canada geese, killed that day, on display like happiness.

In September, there would be noisy rituals with deer rifles, sighting in from rest at a target, minor adjustments with little tools, all this technology and reverence for the ancient dictates of comradeship, no drinking until later. On opening day, he would take my brother and me and we'd ride horseback into the evening, up through the rocky breaks, where the rattle-snakes were already in hiberation, through juniper groves, to the lava-flow rim behind our house, some fifteen hundred feet above the valley. I can still see the exact configurations of that dark rimrock against the evening sky; in my mind's eye, it is the edge of the real world. If the weather was fine, as it almost always was in mid-October, my father would sit with his back against a juniper tree, holding his high-velocity rifle and wait-ing out the night under stars. Rain or not, he'd be there. Now I imagine he was thinking thoughts that might come to some-one hoping he knows not only what he is doing but why. In those days, I thought he was sure. From the rim, he could see into the valley below, shrouded in darkness before REA elec-tricity. The sky off east, over the deserts toward Idaho, would begin to lighten; then he'd slip a shell into the firing chamber of his rifle.

At daybreak, deer season would begin in eastern Oregon. Mule deer, bedded in juniper thickets, would move to water at the tiny springs, then back above the rim to graze the sagebrush swales. My father could see them silhouetted, dark and silent against the dawning sky. He liked to have his buck down before the season was ten minutes old.

"We're done with rifles," he'd say. He preferred shotgunning. Or at least the pretty China ring-necked pheasants and the multitudes of quail, and the flocks of waterbirds we had in those days, abundant as stars. Each year when our oat and barley fields had all been harvested, he'd go to town, drink with the crew, then signal the beginning of fall by coming home with two or three cardboard boxes of scotch whiskey and half a dozen wood cases of shotgun shells. What I liked, in the morning up there on the opening day of deer season, on the rim looking down on Warner Valley as morning light fell across the fields and thickety willow groves and Lombardy poplars along ditches above our orchards, and the white house where we lived, was to never mind the shooting.

OUR OLD horseman's world existed inside ironbound yet vague traditions that were distinct from any enforceable law. The days and work were ordered by a mostly unspoken, if widely accepted, code that centered, at least as I understood it, around an utter refusal to admit defeat or frailty. Weakness was to be suffered in silence.

After horses were domesticated on the high steppes of central Asia some four thousand years ago, a couple different kinds of cultures evolved. One was made up of farming people who stayed home to tend crops; their villages evolved into cities and kingdoms and all that. The others were horse people who followed herds through the seasons, with never a true home; they became warriors, employed by the kingdoms, living a horseback-traveling version of the right life.

There were proper ways to live in Warner Valley, and the

chief among these involved caring for your horses. This was not because our rules borrowed much from kindness or compassion, but, rather, for reasons of utility. We cherished our horses if we had any *sense*. Without good horses, our world wouldn't function. It was high praise to say a man was "easy on his horses," and a man with sorry horses was regarded as useless, something less than a man. We were buckaroos, after all. Our traditions were stylish and Spanish, brought to southeastern Oregon out of California in the 1870s. Roping with home-braided rawhide riatas, we took "dallies," a set of quick wraps around the saddle horn, so we could cast off in time of trouble. We thought dallying was a pretty skill to watch.

Cowhands moved from buckaroo camp to buckaroo camp on chuck-wagon outfits like the ZX and the IL and my family's MC. In a few years, they'd be back where they'd started and pick up like they'd never left off. They saw a lot of country.

At daybreak on the high deserts of eastern Oregon, my father and some other men eased into a round willow-walled corral where sixty or so spooky geldings circled the rock-solid juniper center post. My father would turn serious and flip his rawhide riata effortlessly, drop the loop over the head of a roping horse, a quick stocking-footed bay, and ease down the taut rope toward the trembling animal. I have dim photographs my mother took of a soft-faced boy, his face shaded by a floppy hat and his shirttail out, leading a colt from the gate of such a corral. Moments from more than fifty years ago string together like a run of dreams.

The summer of 1945, when I was coming thirteen and feverish with yearnings, was the last summer I rode with the MC branding crew. A man named Vance Valorida, a good hand with horses, rode with us for a time, until he died.

Vance complained of headaches and then, unthinkably,

while we were branding calves near Lone Grave Butte, he rode away, saying he couldn't go on; in that world, a man stayed with it until everybody quit for the day, no matter what. When we got back, in late afternoon, to the wagon camp by an abandoned homestead shack, he wasn't there.

We saw a terrible wrong-way thing coming toward us from far off through the scrub sage, Vance Valorida's stocking-footed bay gelding pacing toward us with its head high and sidestepping, dragging the bridle reins, spooky-eyed and trembling. The cow boss for the MC, Ross Dollarhide, caught another horse and headed back toward where that bay gelding had come.

Vance Valorida was dead, his pants down around his boots. "Squatting there and fell over backwards. His eyes was wide open, staring at the sun. Hell of a way to die." Somebody figured it was good as any. The world gets away. What the hell, those men would say.

Come early September, I was awarded the high privilege of helping drive thirty or so saddle horses from the buckaroo remuda thirty-five miles over the Warner Mountains to Lakeview, for the Labor Day Rodeo (everybody who was capable of sitting a horse at least rode in the parades). The best part of that horse drive came when we cantered out of a canyon onto the asphalt streets downtown. Townspeople and kids—that was the part I liked, the kids—lined the sidewalks as we clattered along.

Those kids had to be jealous of a boy like me, on horseback with the MC buckaroos, men like John the Swede, who would spend most of his weekend in the bordellos out back of the rodeo grounds, and young bucks like Rossie Dollarhide and Casper Gunderson, who would, if there was any justice, be facing off in the saddle bronc finals come Monday afternoon.

After turning our herd into a corral at the stockyards, we unsaddled and grained our horses, then went uptown to the bars, where a boy like me was served a bottle of beer without any fuss if he was with men like the MC buckaroos, who would not tolerate townspeople telling them what to do. After that one sacred bottle, I was cut off and sent down the street to the Lakeview Hotel, where I'd sleep on a cot in the hallway outside my parents' room, listening to the shouting and laughter from down on the street, excited and secure.

We had, among my people, no official religion. Vance Valorida may have been buried by a preacher, but cowhands weren't much on doctrinaire ceremonies. Maybe one of those men lifted a drink to him. I can't imagine any morbidity connected to the gesture, just those men wiping their mouths, saying nothing.

Sounds pretty "western," men ducking introspection about what can happen. But I don't think that's what was going on. Those men weren't fools. They knew as well as anyone that our frailties can, without warning, be overwhelmed. But they were going at life on horseback and enjoying all the freedom they were ever likely to realize. They'd made their deal. They did their work, and that evening they were smiling at the Devil.

A thing I learned in boyhood—not that I made sense of it until decades later—was never to betray yourself by refusing to acknowledge what you want. The fortunate few can name their yearnings. For a while, I deceived myself into believing that I was destined to be a buckaroo, but I couldn't keep it going. I was the owner's kid. Buckaroos were wandering men, who'd quit just to see what was down the road. Their most powerful opinion was a disdain for settlers, townspeople, and farmers. I wonder what those men felt as they contemplated the spilled body of Vance Valorida. I revered them, still do, but we went our own ways.

AT THE AGE of fourteen, I was put to work in the hay field. Sweating and itching in the dry chaff, I was vastly bored, setting heavy rope nets out before the beaver slide for the hay-stacking crew. As soon as clouds over Bidwell Mountain formed into enormous hammerheads, I'd feel joy rising in me, traveling my body cell to cell as faraway lightning began to break against the darkness of some great storm.

Rain in the summertime was a serious hay-stacking disaster. Wet hay, if piled up, will rot, or heat and smolder, even ignite. So the day after a rain was always a day of waiting for the hay to dry. The crews went to town, some of them to start the drinking and never to return. My family dreaded summer rain: The hay went to hell; a day was lost. But I didn't think like a grown-up. I loved the transformed light and electrical odor the storms left in going. Men from the stacking crew would grin and talk about what awaited them in town, but there'd be no town for me. I was a kid, and the owner's son.

"You ought to slip your momma," one of those men told me, a man whose name I would like to recall but can't, lank and hard-handed, a southerner who'd come to Oregon during the Great Depression with less than half a stomach. He'd wrecked himself with drinking, he said, and the doctors had cut out mighty ulcers. "Can't eat much," he said, "but I'm hungry."

I remember unbelted trousers hanging from his lean hips as he washed his white body at the hay camp's washstand, his sweaty denim shirt thrown on the grassland stubble, the red scar from where his belly had been cut open. Each morning, he made himself a peanut butter sandwich, wrapping it carefully in wax paper. He would eat a bite or two every hour or so as the day went on.

"Big boy like you ought to come to town with us," he said

one afternoon when the thunder was rolling distantly. Wind and rain would reach us before long. We were taking a break in the shade of the beaver slide, sipping warm acidic water from a five-gallon galvanized can wrapped in damp burlap.

"You're old enough," he told me, showing his wrecked greenish teeth. "You come to town and we'll show you some of that holy old pussy." I knew only approximately what he was talking about. But "holy old pussy"? Those were not words I forgot.

The men headed to town in their half-wrecked automobiles, to whatever drew them so powerfully, and once the storm passed, I woke and crawled out of the blankets under my canvas tarp to stand beside that hay-camp tent on the shorn meadows in the light of a white circle of moon. The starry sky was utterly clear. Along the sloughs, where coyotes, raccoons, ring-necked pheasants, and magpies lived, the willows were shadowed and silent. I shook with vulnerability, wishing I could get into a hot shower at home and rub myself down with one of my mother's towels, but I was alone and awash in the sorrow of isolation, until I didn't care, walking around in my undershorts, arms outstretched and casting my shadow in the white light of the moon, awake and listening as the birds began calling, a kid waiting for sunrise.

ONCE EVERY YEAR, my father and mother took my younger brother, my sister, and me south to San Francisco on an overnight train from Klamath Falls. In the night, rocking along in my bed in a Pullman car, I'd gaze out to the lights floating past and feel as secure as I ever have been, because the essential world, as I understood it, was on that train with me. We'd wake to glories—sunlight on the choppy water and a chance to hang on the rail of the boat as we crossed the bay toward the towers of that never-never-land city, to the Ferry Building and a street-car ride up through the honking clamor of Market Street, to the cable car on Powell Street and then our hotel room overlooking Union Square, where flowers were always blossoming.

Most days, however, the world inevitably came to us. My parents got their news on evenings when my father cranked up the Delco power plant, turned on the electric lights, and listened to crackling voices on his Hallicrafter transoceanic radio. It was thus that we heard about Pearl Harbor. A young Irish woman who worked as my mother's live-in household help imagined we were being invaded, about to die, and wept inconsolably. But I knew better; already I had a thing about maps.

Having grown up happily unlettered, I was not much interested in things that went on in schoolrooms. But, most likely from watching over the seasons as my father drained and farmed the swamplands in Warner, I learned to love the idea of definable progress. I thought good work could be charted.

During the latter stages of World War II, there were maps of Europe and the Pacific theater of war pinned to the walls in my bedroom, and I watched closely as the Allies conquered Nazis and Japanese. In the fall of 1946, when I started playing football, I spent hours drafting plays, making order.

Most of us, in my generation, took a spin at trying to do what we thought we were supposed to. I eagerly accepted the radio rhetoric that attended the formation of the United Nations in my beloved San Francisco by the sea. I had inherited, I knew, a secure life inside a mappable dream of decency.

Soon after the war ended, my grandfather sent a herd of workhorses off to be killed for chicken feed and bought a fleet of John Deere tractors. The rhythms of life in Warner, though we didn't really notice at the time, began to go mechanical. I hung up my saddle and began a greasy apprenticeship studying the inclinations of internal combustion engines.

Men worked and played outdoors, and called the shots. Women washed dishes and raised the kids, and endlessly deferred to the yearnings of their men. It was an ancient system, which no doubt began in a division of labor that enhanced everyone's chances at survival, the women and children gathering while the men hunted and fought enemies, but it didn't work for my parents. Eventually, it drove them apart.

As Jo and Oscar aged into separate defeats and tranquillities, they got more and more crossways with each other. Or so I thought, for maybe they always had been; maybe I just didn't know them very well. Their troubles were far beyond the good old boys drinking and playing poker with their good old pals and leaving the women to wait at home with the children. In the beginning, their troubles involved political disputes and thoughts about injustice in the family, but their eventual distance was a result of partially unspoken deals struck when they were young, and a sense of mutual betrayal accumulating over years.

Their marriage, I have come to think, was essentially a partnership between secret radicals, and it broke down when they were clearly defeated in their efforts to talk with a degree of openness and justice in the world they inhabited.

They forgot how to talk to each other. That seems to have been why each felt betrayed by the other; that was why they ran, and saw each other only once that I know about in the last twenty years of their lives. According to my mother, they always made up their troubles in bed. Late in life, she wanted to talk about such things. But as you get older, she said, your times in bed don't matter so much. After hearing that my father was dead, she looked directly at me and said, "He was the only man I ever wanted to marry." She left it at that.

My mother and my father are dead, as are most of the people in that yellow-painted dining room in the Golden Hotel. I can't help mourning for times when I woke up in the morning and heard my parents talking, and thought they, and I, were bulletproof.

WE LIVE and evolve inside self-organizing systems made of electricity, grieving and sporting, always trying to catch onto ourselves as if we were trout in the dazzling stream.

Nostalgia for a golden past based on dreams is not entirely useless. Stories help us think of ourselves as party to goodness. They help teach us to think life is worth the effort. Telling myself these stories is one of my ways of trying to know who I am, and thus render my days valuable.

In my boyhood on the deserts, I imagined the open sagebrush contours of that huge territory laid out like a model made of clay on a table, shrunk to a comprehensible size. Lava-rock canyons, bushy mahogany along the crests of the hills where mule deer rested, wet-weather springs, the stink of skunk cabbage in early summer heat—for me, this is the imperishable world.

Driving down Warner Canyon, there's a turn where you catch sight of fields and Lombardy poplars along the garden ditches. Except for my thoughts about the fact that so many people and the birds are mostly gone, and that the highway now is paved, it would be possible to believe that not much has changed.

Warner Valley is a hidden, landlocked world. Waters flow down from snowy mountains to the west but don't find a way out to the sea. My people went into that country as settlers avidly seeking a homeland and barricaded themselves into their newfound enclave—a commonplace and creaturely thing, turning homesites, towns, and watersheds into psychically walled-off empires where they could maintain control and feel unthreatened. Think of gated subdivisions, Venice, or cliff-top Hopi villages.

Dedicated to survival, my people overgrazed the deserts, working the valley as if it were a machine and insisting that such techniques were, in fact, necessary to our survival. We hardened our hearts and earnestly believed in the practicality of selfishness.

Beginning with a quite justifiable suspicion of the historically exploitative world outside the valley, we invented a family culture that was emotionally frozen. Reinventing our moral code would've involved admitting failure, which was unthinkable. Change was the implacable enemy.

Isolation diminishes physical, intellectual, and emotional pools of communal resources. Biologists say species can't evolve successfully when their gene pools (their fund of evolutionary possibilities) become too small. Isolated species are described as inhabiting "island bioregions." Which is what we were doing in Warner, flirting with extinction.

My leave-taking was accidental. I went to college in 1949 and discovered Whitman and Hemingway. Once married, I loved stories my wife's father told of working as a movie-set dresser in Hollywood during the 1920s and 1930s (his final movie, before a heart attack drove him out of the business, was *Gone With the Wind*). I wanted to visit that great world but had no idea of how to get there except as a runaway, an idea that frightened me. I also found myself—thrilled by my discovery of stories that seemed to bear directly on my life, like "Big Two-Hearted River"—compelled to write.

Trying to prepare myself, I read book after book and became a classic autodidact, who didn't know what to do with what he knew because he didn't have much experience in the "great world." So I traveled. But I'm not a formally trained biologist, anthropologist, economist, or historian of either environments or societies. This book proceeds more like a dance than an argument. It's my hope that, after reflection, readers may be moved to examine their private understandings and the stories they've created from their experiences.

How to explain what I'm attempting? My topic is ordinary yearning to take physical and emotional care, and thus help ourselves along the road toward a ration of freedom and even happiness. Physical and psychic health, what's helpful and what's not.

It's hard to talk of values without sounding like a propagandist, pushing an ideology. But that's not my objective. Ideologies are part of the problem. Most of us have learned to be suspicious of "true believers," whether radical, liberal, or conservative—heads of ethnic groups and nations and religions, national presidents and CEOs of transnational corporations, ecologists and environmentalists—all the cultural warriors. We expect them to play according to rules they invented to justify manipulation of information, as propagandists. We've spent the recent century hacking through thickets of fascism, and when we hear the words *universally valid* in almost any context, the smell of despotism is never far behind.

Acts of the imagination tend to be adaptive and help us stay located and sane, functional. But cultures spin out no end of locating narratives. Bureaucracies operating in the grip of some ideology tend to deny complexity in order to control and compartmentalize responses, fitting them into a manageable order, denying freedoms. It would be more useful to acknowledge and work with our need to evolve constantly. Isolation, inside locations or beliefs, is always an imprisonment. Chuang-tze, I think, was right when he wrote, "Never consent to be one thing alone." Insanity, personally or for an entire society, can be defined as being isolated in fantasies. Lately, we're asked to believe in fables of economic growth, which combine into another defining story, this one about the wonders of a world-wide culture that is dedicated to commodifying experiences, legitimizing greed, and thus distancing us further from the intimacies we are genetically driven to seek.

No matter our gender, race, age, economic or social loca-tion, we normally strive to be included. And we are. We are irrevocably bound into our situation with strangers working at stoop labor in Chinese rice fields and barbers who set up shop on street corners in Calcutta and convicts counting the num-bered hours in lockdown, and we are never able to escape except into craziness or death. Charismatic creatures roaming the savannas of Africa and migrating monarch butterflies, housebroken dogs and red piss ants and rain-forest ferns growing in the valley of the Hoh River on the Olympic Penin-sula, redwood trees and brown dogs and bacteria seen only through the lens of a microscope, and as-yet-unnoticed and thus unnamed insect species also share our situation. We are able to exist only in our ecological niche and are utterly codependent.

LIFE EVOLVES through the survival of replicating entities. Our eyes, teeth, and the electric connections in our brains that compel us to seek food, sex, and safety evolved over hundreds of thousands of years. They are coded into our genes. What we are develops according to complex mandates inscribed in that coding.

Nothing happens twice, but repetitions work in stories as in a hall of mirrors. A death casts light on a birth. One child reflects another. Their significance, to us, involved as we are in incessant reevaluation of our situation, often derives from how they are alike or not. A woman in a stream with her fly rod is shadowed by her dog, which works the world in a different way.

The most formative part of any human environment, at least since we learned to talk, is that of other human minds. In *The Selfish Gene,* Richard Dawkins posits evolving replicators that organize our mental structures, and he names these patterns "memes." They exist as languages, codes with which to run computers, mathematics, and as ideas, theories, stories, metaphors, even names. Any objects we fashion, whether swords or poems, are made by using memes.

The evolution of memes, our brew of concepts, clearly operates at speeds many orders of magnitude faster than genetic evolution. Our ability to process and quantify information goes on multiplying at a geometric rate. Consequences run everywhere, in our minds, pocketbooks, bedrooms. And the evolution of memes is speeding up. The rate at which minds and machines can invent concepts has flown past the pace of genetic evolution like some great migrating bird, high overhead and truly mysterious to the flatlanders.

Our versions of reality are constructs our minds create out of "information." News we are capable of noticing comes to us through physical scrims (we can't, for instance, see ultra-violet light) and through reactions that are genetically coded into us (babies are normally interested in their mothers' milk). Information also comes to us filtered through scrims we can consider as "learned."

It's important to acknowledge that the learned parts of

what we know, while we never completely shake them off, can, to a large degree, be rethought and relearned. That is, we're self-conscious, self-aware, and capable of rethinking our desires and goals, our private and public agendas.

Multiplicity is a key to evolutionary success not just in gene pools but also in the interreactions among various gene pools. As is true in the case of biological organisms, human cultures develop more successfully when a wide range of choices or chances is in play.

Because of such mirroring patterns, it seems reasonable to speak of our cultures using the concepts and language of biological scientists—even though in coalitions we are often inventing and reinventing the systems we inhabit. We can *think* and, to a considerable degree, control what we want; to that degree, we are responsible for our economic and political circumstances.

Selfishness is inherent in living systems, each intent on survival. We are all selfish—humans, whales, redwood trees, and mayflies alike. We use things, and one another; there is no alternative.

Altruism is the sacrifice of immediate benefit for the future good of ourselves or our kin.

Feedback loops are chains of influence that encourage behavior both selfish and altruistic. Cheat me once, shame on you; cheat me twice, shame on me.

In *short feedback loops,* the social rewards or penalties for treating other people selfishly or generously are immediate and obvious. My neighbor kicks my dog, so I kick his; bad times ensue.

Or, say, I look after my neighbor's dogs while she's out of town; she invites me over for dinner when she gets home. With sea bass and good dogs and fine wine, everybody wins.

This is an example of a *reciprocal altruistic coalition* (also known, slightly less numbingly, as a *complex adaptive system*), or neighborliness. Functional societies are based on multitudes of such coalitions, which often are also embodied in customs and laws. Traffic moves at least semirationally on the streets of Mexico City because most of the drivers are willing to treat the rights of other drivers with respect. And because of laws. When such coalitions collapse, civility can vanish. Consider Rwanda, Afghanistan, East Timor, or many American classrooms.

Long feedback loops, being less immediate, are easier to ignore. Children, if we console them through the troubles of growing up, will perhaps remember and feel inclined to help us as we confront the difficulties of aging and dying. Trout streams in Montana and Chile can be preserved, so their glories might be witnessed by unborn generations, which won't even know of our efforts on their behalf. Where is the reward in that?

Generosity is freely driven altruism, which is to say that it involves no discernible feedback except for "increased self-regard." We feel better about ourselves. The arrow of our intentions, however inaccurate, is always aimed in that direction. There is no other direction.

Feedback mechanisms, driven by memory and imagination, are embodied in the narratives we tell ourselves as we work to make sense of our lives and purposes. Our most useful stories evolve and survive, continually rethought in relationship to the turning complexities of our world and situation.

Reinventing our stories is an endless, nonstop search for ourselves. We seek an escape from what we have been while trying to imagine what we might be—in this, I am entirely self-indulgent, as we are inclined to be.

Given our imaginative powers, why can't we invent a culture in which everybody would feel semisecure? Humans are not by nature trivial and tight-hearted. We know society must be reasonably just and fair if we're going to be able to order our lives within it. Earth is the only setting where we can be sane, the only situation our senses intuitively understand. Maintaining the integrity and coherence of civil and economic justice and protecting our environment are of equal importance.

Extreme long-loop altruism is what I mean to advocate: generosity toward strangers and ways of life we never expect to encounter as a method of preserving both biological and cultural multiplicity and possibility. Acting generously helps many of us feel increasingly purposeful and coherent. Could we think up and fashion a worldwide culture based on practicing extreme long-loop altruism at every opportunity?

AMERICAN defining stories have so often been travel narratives—*The Original Journals of the Lewis and Clark Expedition, Moby-Dick, Huckleberry Finn,* and *On the Road.* The educational comedy of hitting the trail in an effort to refresh ourselves in a fountain of strangeness has been an American enterprise since Columbus and Cortés and the fur trappers, buffalo hunters, gold-field prospectors, and homesteaders.

Many immigrants came to America as malcontents, searching for freedom. The search continues—hoboes riding the rails, hippies hanging a thumb, Willie Nelson and his singing cowboy beatnik buddies going down the lonesome highway, all seeking freedom to be whatever they can manage. Maybe humans are an essentially nomadic species, best equipped with tools that travel, whether guitars and laptop computers or cash and credit cards. Bruce Chatwin wrote, "One characteristic of the Men of the Golden Age: they are always remembered as migratory."

Traveling is freedom. Wandering helps us create location. The oldest stories are about making discoveries or acquiring powers, then hauling them home. But incessant travel can also be a manifestation of despair. That's what I think when studying ads for ecotravel to pristine but vanishing habitats. See the tigers and elephants before they go, for we are of the last generation.

This is meant to be a travel book about combating despair by learning, going to wander through the intricacies of Paris and Venice, or to see the red bulls and leaping pregnant cows painted on the walls in the cave at Lascaux. It's about trying to imagine Lorca dreaming of old Walt Whitman with butterflies in his beard before Lorca was shot down one morning by true believers in the Andalusian hills outside Granada, where he had lived as a child, and about wondering if at that moment Lorca was capable of thinking and seeing, and what the people who shot him thought they were doing. It's about politics, about yearning, and about redefining intentions, obligations, and responsibilities, rediscovering home and acknowledging basic allegiances.

Paradise is life spent in the presence of the most deeply beloved, even for creatures like us, always aware of ourselves as phenomena in a process that pays us no special deference, and which we cannot ultimately fathom. Can happiness be only a matter of solving one moment and the next one?

Not entirely, I think. Life without hope of bettering the world—even if passively, as in Buddhist practices—erodes as surely as any enfeebling disease our sense of what we are. Humans feel grounded by the need to improve and to give, if only to ourselves, by conceiving of some purpose. We can decide to carry those drives too far, into an agenda, and of this, we have to be careful; idealism is every fascist's excuse. Attempting to protect ourselves and our kind by trying to satisfy physical and psychic wants, we end up building jails. How, then, to escape?

Such terms as *good* and *evil* don't seem very useful. People are moved to do whatever they do by their sense of what is demonic, or sacred, ultimately by an overpowering and genetically driven urge to care for themselves and their kin.

Chaos looms, if we believe reports from war zones like the Balkans and the Congo, and what environmentalists tell us about the possibilities initiated by an extensive species die-out and by global warming. We can decide what we want to do about these troubles without, clearly, continual reference to our "limbic needs." We are not entirely programmed by drives coded into our genetic makeup and doomed to selfishness. We can turn our lives into gifts. Many have. We can live in accord with our desire to take care—if we want to. That's the simplest version of what I mean to say.

Part One

The Old Animal

Man is the only animal that blushes. Or needs to.

—MARK TWAIN

*D*UST LIFTED in slow streaks off the alkaline playa in the dry basin called Long Lake. Tiny orange and white flowers blossomed among boulders of black lava-flow basalt.

Ten thousand years ago, when the first humans came to the Great Basin highlands where I stood, Long Lake was part of a sweep of swamps and vast watery basins fed by melting glaciers. Waterbirds lifted to wheel and settle, refolding their wings. Their movements, to my dreaming, are a flowering of momentum—in this, much like music.

At the end of a rocky two-track road, Long Lake is lost among the ridges rising from the east side of Warner Valley into an enormous run of uninhabited lava-rock and sagebrush highlands. I grew up believing there was nothing in the vicinity of Long Lake but shimmering distances.

Then, sixty-five years old, I found that I'd spent my boyhood near an ancient holy place. Over hundreds of thousands of years, the lava-flow ridge at my back had fragmented into intricate, smooth-sided boulders, which were everywhere inscribed—drawn on by ancient humans attempting to manage their luck and their fate. The inscriptions were particularly thick in places next to fractures, breaks where souls and spirits could be thought to have emerged from an underworld, and through which they might be fortunate enough to reenter.

Thousands of designs and figures had been pecked into the basalt surfaces with stone or bone tools, ranging from entropic (behind the eye) patterns of the sort seen in trances—grids and dot complexes—to discernible figures metamorphosing from moss to fish to men and women. Some were colored with pigment; others were delineated by thin encrustations of yellow and greenish lichens. The oldest images reach back ten thousand years.

Anthropologists suggest they were created by shamans, priests who thought all things, including stones, possess an innate soul. Animist cultures are a global phenomenon that seems to have lasted thirty thousand years or so, and still endure among people along the Yukon River lowlands of Alaska, in enclaves like the Kalahari Desert of southwestern Africa, and in central Australia. These cultures hold that their shamans talk to animals, that while the shaman's body remains locked in a trance, the soul takes flight through fissures in the rock (actuality) and goes down into the underworld in order to encourage the emergence of hunting animals, or even out to the Milky Way for instruction from gods and ancestors who live there. At least that's what they've told anthropologists.

IT WAS NOT that I'd never seen such inscriptions. At various points around the edges of Warner, there are smooth-sided boulders inscribed with what I'd thought were simplistic snakes and sunrises; or maybe the jagged lines indicated days of travel. Those etchings were ordinarily considered the work of ancestors of the northern Paiute, who lived in Warner when the white settlers arrived. But the Paiute were relative late comers, occupying Warner for less than a thousand years. Earlier cultures had come and gone since those boulders were inscribed.

Peter Farb, in *Man's Rise to Civilization: The Cultural Ascent of the Indians of North America,* explains that the people of the northern Great Basin had fewer than a thousand of what anthropologists call "cultural items." While this seems unlikely— can a dream of heaven be called a cultural item?—Farb contrasts it to the fact that, in 1942, George Patton's armies landed in North Africa with 547,000 different categories of nonmilitary hardware. This statistic illustrates the vast distance between the Paiute mind-set and our own.

In *Shoshone,* Edward Dorn tells of visiting a Paiute couple who claimed to be more than a hundred years old. Until midlife, they had lived the traditional wandering life, but by Dorn's time, they were living in a tin-sided trailer house on the Duck Valley Indian Reservation along the Idaho-Nevada border. Savvy about the games of anthropology, they asked for cartons of Camel cigarettes before allowing him to take pictures of them. Then they told him something extraordinary: They'd never heard of white men until they were adults.

Is it possible to imagine with any accuracy the psychology of people from that preliterate culture? What did they yearn for, and how did they define joyfulness? Can we guess, and would we know if we got it right? Open seas lie between my intuitions about the world and those of Paiute people. Yet here were those people, living in that trailer and demanding tribute in cigarettes, who seemed to have crossed those seas so easily.

A Paiute family lived just up the hill from us in Warner, under a row of Lombardy poplars planted by homesteaders next to a garden ditch. The man of the family ran Caterpillar bulldozers for my father—his name was Don Pancho—and his wife cleaned and ironed for my mother. The children—Vernon, Pearl, and Henry—played with us kids, and Vernon was my best friend (he's been dead for decades). Summer and winter, they lived in a pair of canvas tent houses, one with a cookstove and the other for sleeping. Never allowed inside, we used to wonder about what they did and said in those tents as they persisted in surviving what I knew even then to be poverty. Now I wonder if they despised us in their secret hearts, and if not, why not?

Peoples who tell their stories aloud are rapidly vanishing everywhere on earth. Did anybody from our culture ever take the time to find out much about the lives of native people who wandered the streets of northern Nevada towns like Lovelock and Winnemucca when I was a young man? Or were the northern Paiute basically invisible to a European culture obsessed with getting rid of them so that settlement could proceed. What do we know about the people who inscribed their designs on those boulders? Not much really, except that in fundamental ways they were just like us.

FOR MILLENNIA, Long Lake was a gathering place. I like to think it was sacred and thus invaluable. But in the years I lived there, preoccupied by visions of an agricultural dream as we diked and drained the swamplands in Warner, lost in rhythms of endless work, nobody ever guessed there was much of anything to value in this country except for the fertile parts. As a boy, I collected obsidian arrowheads and stored them in shoe boxes, yet I believed wisdom was found only in books. Later, I tried to read Aristotle and Kant, came to see my own emptiness, and went half-crazy. I was lost, quite desperately wanting to understand how my life in Warner, the happy land of childhood, had in the long run brought me to feel so entirely contingent.

People whose ancestors had made peace with isolation were still living nearby, but I didn't think of contacting them. What could they know? What I might have done was recognize that those people were like me. Another generation of Paiutes was no doubt still telling its stories; I might have understood more about what it means to be myself if I'd made an attempt to listen to them. But I didn't even think of this possibility, and in that way, I missed another boat.

What might I have discovered? The little wind went on stirring the white dust. The inscriptions at Long Lake were only props for unimaginable ceremonies. What I could do was forget the wind and unpeopled distance and think of the ordinary desperation that accompanied shamans on their voyages, as evidence of the degree to which we are all alike.

> *Under the rubble of World War II is the rubble of World War I.*
> *And under that there is a layer of struggle-to-make-ends-meet*
> *and yet bucolic, warless village-and-shepherding life. And*
> *under that, intact, is a circle of dwellings structured*
> *out of tusks and reinforced mud. And under that, some*
> *bones—like accent marks distributed in the earth—*
> *including some earliest human skulls. And in them:*
> *tiny figures, each with tiny skulls of their own,*
> *and brains the size of garden snails' bodies that,*
> *like any brains, are larger than the universe that holds them.*

—ALBERT GOLDBARTH, "If"

> . . . minds were designed to maximize fitness *in the environment in which those minds evolved.*

> —ROBERT WRIGHT, *The Moral Animal*

ANTHROPOLOGICAL CASE STUDIES are always partly make-believe, fictions invented out of research, and are often infected with an unconscious belief in progress—from a condition called "primitive" to one called "civilized." So they are frequently vehicles for condescension, in which dominion over other peoples is regarded as inevitable, if not entirely justifiable. In such documents, *primitive* sometimes connotes being less than human, and people are discussed as if they were animals, or objects. But while interest in "simpler" or more "innocent" or "purer" societies is often driven by simple curiosity or implicit condescension, we ultimately value anthropological research as useful in our search for models we can use in our efforts to reform and manage our own cultures.

It is often claimed that humans reached the limits of evolutionary adaptation during the Paleolithic period. Sharman Apt Russell writes that "we were few in number, tribal, creative, dependant on nature, in awe, in touch, in our natural setting. We were at home." Then she asks, "Was it better emotionally? Were we better? Were we more alive, more human, more engaged?"

With her, I wonder: If "primitives" were leading more natural lives, were they necessarily happier? Besides, what does "natural" mean? According to Russell, "We don't even know the meaning of better." But codifications of "better" seem to be part of every political agenda. Do we think the lives of preliterate people simple? An utterly condescending notion. There are no simple lives. Who would want one?

In 1952, I was a junior at Oregon State University, already and quite humorlessly trying to figure out what sort of creature I was. One rainy winter night, I stood and directed a question at a visiting lecturer, a white-haired gentleman named George Gaylord Simpson, author of *The Meaning of Evolution*. "How much smarter are we," I called out, "than the cavemen?"

"We're not," Gaylord Simpson said.

"Not what?"

"Smarter than the cavemen." Then he turned to a question from someone else. I sat down.

Simpson turned back. "They lived twenty-five thousand years ago. That's not long enough for anything to have happened in terms of evolution." Or so I recall his remark. Ancient brains, he meant, were every bit as complex and capable as ours, and so-called primitive people like the Paiute couple on the Duck Valley Indian Reservation are quite capable of thinking anything an astronaut or rocket scientist can think. There are, for instance, no simple languages. Our brains, George Gaylord Simpson was telling me, are still Paleolithic.

Staring at Simpson from that audience, I was thunderstruck. What he said worked to reconfirm my belief in equality, a concept learned in the horseback West, where the rigors of the work served as a great leveler. But he'd shot an irreparable hole through my belief in progress. We were all in the same boat, he was saying, but we weren't making much speed toward increasing perfection.

Those notions didn't fit my profoundly forward-looking American ideology. The idea of progress had always been at the center in my intuitive sense of life, so I was jarred and even frightened by the news that we're stuck with what we have at the moment, that we'd better figure out how to be happy in the going.

IN PHOTOGRAPHS, we see the blue pebble in black space. In some twelve-second history of earth, we see the tectonic plates grinding away, forming great continents, and the billion-bodied reefs of microscopic life, soft falling rain, tallgrass prairies, great cities opening like flowers.

People have claimed that all life on earth is a single creature—or goddess. But it would be closer to say that life is an animal made of animals. In *Life as a Geological Force,* Peter Westbroek describes the molecule called a polysaccharide. "Despite the fact that even under an electron microscope it can hardly be seen, its workings are as complex as a television set or an automobile." About 3.5 billion years ago, Westbroek tells us, "bacteria were the earth's first inhabitants." For another 2 billion years, they were the sole inhabitants.

"Bacteria never work alone," Westbroek says, "they always collaborate." Collectively, bacteria have the catalytic potential to make use of all the chemical elements needed for life. They can be considered as one earth-embracing organism, drawing on a single gene pool, continuously reorganizing itself, adapting to the changing conditions of the biosphere. Changes in environments "that result from human intervention may be a threat to our existence, but to the bacteria it can be no more than a ripple on the surface." Westbroek concludes that "bacteria dominate the natural environment" and that "we are simply a flowering of the bacterial community." So much for ego. And, again, for my cherished notion of progress.

NORMAN MACLEAN, in *Young Men and Fire,* tells of firefighters burning to death in a sheet of uncontrollable flame flaring upwind along a steep ravine above the Missouri River in central Montana. They ran before it, trying to save themselves. In the convolutions of Maclean's narrative, we sense the movement of life through continual fire. Deep in the night, one sorrowing man feeds a peeled orange, section by section, to a man whose fingers have been charred to stubs, a man trapped by the waywardness of existence and burned, pretty soon now, to death. Maclean implies that we live in fire as well as water, that love and not justice is more often than not the best we can expect. We sense the fire working in our lives, everywhere, livid and actual. Our brains evolve inside systems electric in nature and are complex, quite literally, beyond imagining. At birth, a baby has 100 billion neurons in its brain, about as many nerve cells as there are stars in the Milky Way. Our thoughts move like patterns in smoke.

In *Bright Air, Brilliant Fire*, Dr. Gerald Edelman writes, "If I unfolded the cortex and laid it out on the table, it would be the size of a large table napkin. And about as thick. It would have ten billion neurons, at least—and a million billion connections. If you counted the connections, one per second, you'd finish counting them all thirty-two million years later." There are trillions of possible connections inside the brain—from this, our consciousness emerges.

"One is talking about the most complicated material object in the known universe." Edelman's claim indicates, to me at least, that there's a lot we will never understand about our minds. Gretel Erlich, puzzling about the electric mind after being struck by lightening twice, in *A Match to the Heart* asks, "What is a thought before it registers?"

Our thoughts, emerging from this electric complexity, are organized into categorical systems of naming—likely the only thing we'll ever pin down about the whole electric shebang.

Out of this complexity, from metaphors embodied in evolving and entirely electric structures, our brains invent or construct what we individually take to be "real."

HUMANS HAVE LIVED in society, nose to nose, person to person, one to another, for at least 100,000 years. The time line of development runs something like this:

- Genetic analysis suggests that our lineage split off from the one leading to African apes about 6 to 8 million years ago. Recent discoveries of hominid bones in Kenya and Ethiopia are more than 4 million years old.
- About 2 to 3 million years ago, African hominids began making stone tools.
- Anatomically, modern *Homo sapiens* (Cro-Magnons) began evolving not more than 200,000 years ago. A thousand generations. They existed in southern Africa about 100,000 years ago and in the next 60,000 or 70,000 years spread themselves over most of the inhabitable areas on earth.

The creature we are, from our beginnings to now, developed into itself as a species on the uplands in Africa—subtropical grassland savannas broken by groves of trees, a snowy peak like Mount Kilimanjaro on the horizon. Our animal was capable of climbing in trees in part because of complex hands with opposable thumbs. The first tool was manual dexterity, which can also be thought of as the root of our mental ability to manipulate complexity.

The animals who were our ancestors turned into creatures with the capacity to walk upright, and run, then lost their ability to live at ease in the heights of the forests. They traveled slowly, following grazing herds during their migrations, scavenging off the dead, hunting an occasional small mammal, eating insects, reaping plants such as grass seeds, nuts, vegetables, and fruits (equipped to see colors, humans enjoyed a great advantage when picking ripe fruit out of the leaves).

Though their lives were short (those aged forty were elders), and the African savannas a mortal playground where terrible carnivores constantly prowled, some of those ancient people lived in circumstances we, at least from this distance, understand as our emotional homeland, the paradisal garden: grasslands teeming with grazing animals, shade-bearing trees along the streams, places to hunt and hide, prospect and shelter, caves in which to live, and, out below, fields on which to seek the ripe fruits and kill the beasts and dance the dance. We are a creature evolved to survive, and be comfortable, in such a setting.

Making emotional sense of the enormous slow span of time involved in human evolution is sort of impossible—hundreds of thousands of years in which the planetary climate warmed and the great northern glaciers melted, but nothing very noticeable about the social lives of people changed. Dreaming in caves on moonless nights before the discovery of fire, our ancestors must have dreaded the great cats that stalked and killed in the night. Demons were actual. Solace was found in one another, and in the sweetness of the world (it has been conjectured that civilization evolved around sweets, sugars drawing us together as surely as fruit flies).

Imagining that long a time is like trying to think about a dream. It's sort of but not quite there, and haunting. Our creature burned the savannas in order to clear brush, so the grazing herds they hunted would come to crop the new grasses, and they learned to eat the flesh of animals that burned to death.

We are able to see three-dimensional space because of how our eyes are placed. Human nervous systems, as they evolved, developed a capacity to simulate three-dimensional scenarios in the eye of the mind; in terms of survival, this was an enormously useful tool. Our creature was able to invent versions of the future and juxtapose imagined enactments with actual ones.

Our fundamental capabilities emerged in that ancestral dreamscape. Humans learned to live in safe places, to camp among trees, protecting the next generation while looking out over the hunting-gathering fields below, to cultivate fires like a crop, and to cook. Fire meant warmth, light, and security in the night. While we often eat on the move, like sparrows, as we travel through the woods or the Saturday street market, the hearth or home fire has encouraged gathering and storytelling and has often been considered indispensable, carried from place to place and regarded as sacred.

Judging from the practices of hunting-gatherers who have survived into contemporary times—such as the bushmen of southwest Africa, pygmies in its equatorial forests, and Aborigines in Australia—it seems that men more often than not hunted while women, accompanied by their children, gathered. In this division of labor, humans controlled their lives, the male bringing protein-rich meat to the diet his mate had supplied with more plentiful nuts and fruits.

Our brains are built of protein, but gathering was of at least equal importance. Thousands of years' attention to the intricacies of plant reproduction led to plant domestication and eventually to farming and villages, to irrigation agriculture and food surpluses, and thus to divisions of labor and to ruling classes, and ultimately to city-states and nations and all the labyrinthine entrapments and glories of civilization.

> The bond of love is one which men, wretched creatures that they are, break when it is to their advantage to do so.

> —NICCOLÒ MACHIAVELLI, *The Prince*

HUMANS YEARN for peace, yet they are incessantly warlike, and they are capable of sentimental weeping, followed by stone-hearted slaughter. They try to care for their own kind and everything alive with hands that are often bloodied.

We labor to invent compelling, believable stories about our purposes. We want meaningful work, demand pleasure, worship that which we consider sacred, and despise the demonic. We want family and friends, both the comforts of community and the exhilaration of independence, and to inhabit a world that fits in terms of scale or dimension; safety, a ration of danger, and contact with intricacies, new land to roam, but also a home to which we can always return.

At first, I couldn't understand how Jung's "collective unconscious" might actually exist. I then made sense of it by deciding that any collective unconscious was formed from inclinations encoded in our mental capabilities. Humans tend to respond emotionally to snowy peaks against a clean sky, boa constrictors in the kitchen, a full white midmorning moon or indefinable odors in our beds. Behind all these reactions lie configurations built into the brain during our evolutionary history.

Our behavior seems endlessly various from individual to individual and culture to culture, more unpredictable than that manner of "lower" species such as bluebirds, cats, or chimpanzees. But many of our responses are not only routine but also common to nearly all mammals.

British psychologist John Bowlby spent his life studying common responses in animals and infants, concerning himself particularly with the effects of separation from the mother on the development of human personalities. Patterns of behavior found in people the world over seem to be instances of instinctive behavior.

In his magnum opus (the trilogy *Attachment, Separation,* and *Loss*), Bowlby writes, "Man's behavior is very variable, it is true, but not infinitely so; and, though cultural differences are great, certain commonalities can be discerned." For example, he states, "The young child's hunger for his mother's love and presence is as great as his hunger for food," and "her absence inevitably generates a powerful sense of loss and anger." The operative word in this is *inevitably.* Animal inclinations have evolved through thousands of generations and millions of years, their codes installed in the genetic structures that control actions. Creatures from beetles to humans strive like hell to stay alive.

In the 1960s, biologists began working with the mathematics of sacrifice among ants, and the courtship ritual among birds. Their thinking was pulled together in two groundbreaking books, E. O. Wilson's *Sociobiology* (1975) and Richard Dawkins's *The Selfish Gene* (1976). Both men were engaged in extending a theory of natural selection, which Wilson called a "new synthesis," their work suggesting that family loyalties, friendship, courtship habits, and political allegiances are dedicated to enhancing our chances of survival.

IN North American Cattle-Ranching Frontiers, Terry G. Jordan describes the Fulani, 7 million people who for hundreds of years have moved their herds over savannas that reach 2,600 miles across a landlocked basin centered on Lake Chad, from Senegal to far beyond the Niger River. These nomads, Jordan writes, "conjure up images from ancient Egyptian art of staff-wielding pedestrian cow-herders, suggesting an African continuity of cattle management methods reaching back twenty-six centuries . . . less a commercial venture . . . than a religion."

The Fulani venerate their cattle, linking "the myth of their tribal origin to the creation of cattle," and "measuring their wealth in cattle," holding animals in trust for future generations. These tame animals are trained to follow a herder, and they are known individually. The Fulani never kill a cow or eat meat. Their staple, milk protein, is produced five times more efficiently than meat, and it can be harvested from the same animal over and over, day after day.

In *Millennium,* David Maybury Lewis observed that a Nigerian subgroup of the Fulani, the Wodaabe, are preoccupied with courtships outside of marriage, which are sanctioned by a protocol: "What the eyes do not see did not happen."

The Wodaabe don't "measure their comfort or success in terms of material possessions. What they do value, almost above all else, is personal relations." They speak of themselves as being "like birds in the bush." Young men are luridly made up for a yearly dance contest in which they compete to be chosen the most charming and beautiful. "Men are constantly on the outlook for lovers, and women are often willing to leave the stability of their arranged marriages and go for love into the household of a man who has charmed them. But life goes on, even if they do. Their children are not uprooted, and orderly relations of Wodaabe society, which are built around marriages, are unaffected."

What to make of these accounts? Jordan describes their

deepest beliefs entirely in terms of bovine veneration (Wodaabe are called "Cattle Fulani"), and Lewis doesn't mention their herding activities at all. Can these be the same people? The only common denominator running through both depictions is each group's eagerness to pursue their lives unafraid of intimacy. This inclination is inscribed in all our genes. Confounding it is a royal route to making ourselves neurotic and miserable.

MY OWN CLOSEST companion for over two decades has been Annick Smith. A widow and the mother of four men, she lives on 163 acres backed up to commercial timberlands just above the Blackfoot River about twenty-five miles east of Missoula. Her husband died of a heart attack in 1974, aged forty-one, on the kitchen floor in the house where she still lives (where we live together much of the time), while she pounded on his chest and tried to breathe life back into him. Two boys, her six-year-old twins, were watching. Annick is willful and wise to the world, and a very quick study—she was executive producer for the award-winning film *Heartland,* a producer for *A River Runs Through It,* and had a short story included in *Best American Short Stories* the year that series was edited by Robert Stone. Her soul tempered by a terrible event, she knows what and whom she loves, and she's not soft-minded about saying why. Yet she's inevitably driven frantic by the debris and skid trails, the stumpage and vast heedlessness we encounter when walking out in the logged-off woods behind her house.

But after a half hour or so, we circle behind a cliff into open groves of huge yellow-bark ponderosa pine, from which Annick gazes down on her hand-hewn log house in the meadow.

The prospect before her is whole—family and home, smoke drifting from the fireplace chimney—and amid the last remnants of the ancient forests. A version of the primal garden, it calms her.

Creatures perform in ways that have been proven to ensure survival, if not always as individuals, most certainly as a species. Humans commonly experience the urge to protect lives outside their immediate kin or species, even all life and its habitats, the so-called biosphere. Caring for the place where we live is clearly a primal way of caring for our progeny.

This urge was named "biophilia" in a book of that title by E. O. Wilson. Stephen R. Kellert, in *The Biophilia Hypothesis,* explains it as "a human *need,* fired in the crucible of evolutionary development, for deep and intimate association with the natural environment, particularly its living biota." Wilson and Kellert reason that the inclinations encoded into our brains add up to an innate desire to "cherish and protect life." Much of what we do is a result of a need to affiliate. People help one another in bedrooms, on buses, and in hospitals, every day. Encoded to be cooperative, we respond as much to the urge to give our good away as we do to greed.

Predominately adversarial models of motivation are clear nonsense. In *The Liars' Club,* Mary Karr writes, "Kindness grows wild." Shakespeare understood. "I pant for life," Edmund says in *King Lear.* "Some good I mean to do,/Despite of mine own nature." Generosity, despite the self-serving nastiness we hear of constantly in the media, is commonplace.

Chaos theory demonstrates that certain structures that seem dangerously out of balance are, in fact, at turning points in their evolutions. Perhaps our own species—as humans grow more and more self-reflexive, able to talk about the creatures we are, or want to be—is at such a point. Maybe we'll be capable of reimagining ourselves into a diverse, worldwide society that defines itself as "cherishing." Too late, of course, for the extinct. Wouldn't it be, as Hemingway indicated, pretty to think so? A lot of what drives pleasure is a sense of having a purpose, of being useful to ourselves and our people and kind, to the pilgrim's progress of our progeny, to our band of companions, our communities, the entire dream.

> Lo-lee-ta: the tip of the tongue taking a trip of three steps down the palate to tap, at three, on the teeth. Lo. Lee. Ta.
>
> —VLADIMIR NABOKOV, *Lolita*

BEFORE SPOKEN LANGUAGE, humans must have used a system of gestural communication shared by most mammals. Displays of status and power—as in who has the switch in barroom fights, politics or warfare, bedrooms, and colonial economies—are activities of conquest, aggressive and combative responses to real or imagined threats. This dynamic informs almost every human relationship. As in nature, there are rules. Dogs in a pack, bears in the wild, cats in the kitchen, hens in a pecking order, economists in think tanks—each knows how to accept victory, to cringe when defeated, signal submission, and thus avoid another challenge. Partway animal, we know exactly, without being taught, how this system works. We are born to it. Looking away equals surrender, and meeting the gaze eye-to-eye is a challenge—a code grizzly bears in our national parks understand, as do the poker players in expensive games at the Mirage in Las Vegas, or the thugs in Clint Eastwood movies. Humans have the most elastic faces of any primate, and they are capable of elaborate facial gestures, which are themselves a complex language.

In *The Spell of the Sensuous,* David Abram reminds us that humans were always intimately aware of sounds made by other creatures, and by the wind and flowing water. Sounds like the honking of geese call up an imaginative response. Abram says that "particular sensations are evoked by the sounds themselves, and whereby the shape, rhythm, and texture of particular phrases conjure the expressive character of particular phenomena."

Hearing, as our species evolved, was enormously important, since survival often depended on interpreting sounds correctly. Sounds, too, can be thought of as a language, capable of stirring vivid emotion and conveying crucial information. The howl of wolf or cougar resounds in our minds like the haunting wail of steam trains in bluegrass music.

While no one really knows, it seems likely that music and dance, because the most intuitive of our play, are as old as body language and facial expression in the arts of communication. Aside from the discovery of flutes made of hollow bone in caves inhabited by the earliest humans, no physical remains of these arts have been found. Nevertheless, it's reasonable to imagine that early speech was mostly made up of imitative sounds and gestures that to some degree evolved while those people played music and danced. And that those sounds and gestures came to function as metaphors, and metaphoric systems like the songlines; and that the gurgling, sighing, barking world is still alive and speaking even in our own sophisticated time, in the things we are able to say and, therefore, think about.

It's also reasonable to think that precise and definable meaning began with spoken language. The luck of our species might have begun some 150,000 years ago with the run of evolutionary accidents during which the vocal tract evolved. Our pharynx is unique among mammals, located low in the throat, creating the large chamber above it in which sounds can be shaped and modified. Thus evolved the possibility of speech and spoken languages. The syntax of articulated memory, which can be passed from generation to generation, constitutes an enormous evolutionary advantage.

Somehow, our animal learned to talk. All but monstrously brain-damaged people understand some complex form of language. With that pharynx and quick, agile mouth, our kind could project a wide variety of noises. It's not possible to know which came first—did hands do the deft trick, lighting the fire before the mind learned to name the quick act?—but a consequence seems to have been consciousness. What I am is the result of currents running through an enormously complex weave of electrical circuits. According to Gerald Edelman, "Consciousness arises with the evolutionary onset of semantic capabilities, and it flowers with the accession of language and symbolic reference.

"As a syntax begins to be built and a sufficiently large lexicon is learned, the conceptual centers of the brain treat the symbols and their references and the imagery they evoke as an 'independent' world to be categorized. . . . Concepts of self and of a past and a future emerge. . . . The result is a model of the world. . . . High-order consciousness leads to the construction of an imaginative domain, one of feeling, emotion, thought, fantasy, self, and will."

The Aborigines of Australia developed a distinctive art, X-ray painting, based on imagining the interior of whatever creature was being depicted, the skeleton of the snake laid out alongside digestive organs within its undulations. It was a useful art, based on seeing to the heart of things.

To pass on accumulated information about their place and

advice on conduct, the Aborigines told a nearly endless sequence of tales about forebears who walked the land and sang it into being as they went, the act of naming understood as creating; whatever was caught in the song was known intimately, caught in the breath, likely to be beloved, breathed out like a gift. The paths walked by the forebears crisscross the continent and young men walk them every year before initiation by circumcision, a traumatic and painful ceremony. Before turning up for the ritual, they paint emblems of the songline stories they sing upon their bodies, and carve those emblems into soft-wood storyboards.

People walking the world, singing its glories into being, naming each creature, plant, animal, or insect—it is all a method of remembering, of memorizing creation. We are what we can say or sing.

Apache on the White River Reservation in eastern Arizona often name physical particularities of their territory—river crossings and rocky outcroppings—after incidents that happened there. Anthropologist Keith Basso writes of going there in the 1970s and being asked to make maps. "Not whiteman's maps, we've got plenty of them, but Apache maps with Apache places and names." The maps he made had such place names as Widows Pause for Breath and She Carries Her Brother on Her Back. The Apache maintain a mesh of significance that tells them who they are, where they reside in history, how to act if they wish to think of themselves as responsible. They are trying to be located both physically and emotionally, and thus find security.

Hunting-gathering cultures are often organized around ceremonies designed to encourage recollection. Women among the bush people in the Kalahari Desert carry their children over distances most of us would consider desolate and empty, telling the children the names of plants, when they bear fruit, which roots are good to eat, in which season, where water can be found, as well as the names of animals, when to hunt them, and where, naming the useful world, imaginatively re-creating it in language. Those women are teaching their children linked narrative structures, traveling and talking, maybe singing the stories and occasionally dancing down the path.

Any child who encounters incessant face-to-face talk from another person, their mother most likely, before the age of one is given a terrific advantage. Facing complexity, our brains grow. Naming, ofttimes through storytelling, enables us to understand the light that comes to us at various stations of life. As those mothers walk and talk, they are passing on to their children the secrets of the routes their people have always walked, and inciting them to be intelligent, so that they may endure. In the bustling kitchens, in taverns, and on park benches, whether hiking in rough country or bathing the children, we talk all the time. Our old animal understands a silent world to be semidead.

IN 1956, at a meeting of the Institute of Radio Engineers held at MIT, twenty-seven-year-old Noam Chomsky, a Junior Fellow at Harvard, presented a paper entitled "Three Models for the Description of Language." It was a defining moment. Daniel C. Dennett says in *Darwin's Dangerous Idea*, "Retrospective coronations are always a bit arbitrary . . . but Chomsky's talk to the IRE is as good an event as any to mark the birth of modern linguistics. . . . Not many great scientists get to found a whole new field, but there are a few. Charles Darwin was one; Noam Chomsky is yet another."

Two-year-olds, not yet capable of abstract thought, suddenly develop an ability to absorb and use languages, which is a phenomenal accomplishment. Language just comes, not only the words but also the syntax. In *Syntactical Structures* (1957), Chomsky put forward a theory of universal grammar based on innate predispositions. Categorizing structures are part of our brains, he wrote, and are much the same in all humans.

The idea of "deep structure" was not so much born as given new life. Thinkers at least since Kant, like Bowlby, had long been positing such a notion. But if humans are "hard-wired" to make sense of language in a specific manner, as Chomsky argued, wiring in our nervous systems might also cause us to perceive actuality in patterned ways.

Steven Pinker, director of the Center for Cognitive Neuroscience at MIT, makes the case in *The Language Instinct*. "Language could have arisen, and probably did arise . . . by a revamping of primate brain circuits." As Bowlby points out, the inclination of a baby to focus on its mother's breasts is common, built into every nervous system. Similarly, an ability to learn languages is likely encoded. Pinker writes that Chomsky "would have everything to gain by grounding his controversial theory about a language organ in the firm foundation of evolutionary theory." But this is an idea Chomsky has never sanctioned.

It's easy to understand why. If behavioral patterns are coded into our genes—there is no other mechanism—the news is clear: Our complex feelings are the result of wiring. And the notion that conduct is predetermined has been used to justify claims that various genetic strains are superior to others.

Feelings of superiority in cultures from the Comanche to the French have obviously sanctioned endless warfare, sexism, racism, and homophobia (not to speak of the creeping political correctness that is paralyzing dialogue everywhere). Citizens in generous, civic-minded towns all over America find themselves capable of ignoring famine among millions of refugees in northern Africa or the merciless exploitation of peoples on the other side of the globe. The disenfranchised—so this refusal implies—are some other kind of creature, and not quite or entirely human.

Gore Vidal, in his novel *Empire,* suggests that the ultimate weapon is the power to give people the dreams you want them to have. Chomsky wants to give us a dream of freedom, but he seems unwilling to acknowledge that liberty exists within a system of built-in physical constraints. What's important is the fact that those constraints can be transcended, as the vastly complex possibilities in a cortex reveal. Individuals are notoriously idiosyncratic. There is a good statistical case to be made for the notion that no thought has ever been exactly repeated.

LANGUAGE IS the tool humans use to transform experience into ideas. Speech was a new technology, like fire and sharpened stones, but enormously more fruitful, ordering experience and facilitating the working out of concepts. With the emergence of language, change accelerated.

We are partly an intentional creation. Ancient people found that education increased their likelihood of survival, and self-creating (individualism) began to be understood as a skill and a pleasure (as in gaming), as well as a survival mechanism. "Watch this," I say to my true love, hoping she'll make a try at admiring whatever goofiness I'm up to, thus reinforcing my sense of myself as a potentially marvelous pool shark or interpreter of literature.

How much are we able to name? Is it true that we are able to see only those entities that our minds are able to label and thus locate in the flux surrounding us? We are capable of objectifying and see ourselves as a "thing," an object with attributes, and this, too, is a survival tactic. But if what we take to be real is determined by a system of structures in our mind, a set of metaphors that acts as a sort of lens, what we *think* we know in ordinary life obviously can't be assumed an accurate image of what is. This includes our ideas of who we are.

Naming helps people witness themselves and reflect on what they've seen. It is the beginning of talking to ourselves, that most primal business, in which we invent and reinvent ourselves all day long, incessantly thinking and feeling, talking ourselves into being. People inhabit a dialogue with themselves: They speak, listen, think, then act out the implications of what they hear and go on with the talking, thus circling the issue of becoming individual and distinct.

This naming can be thought of as the invention of point of view—I'm in here; everything else is outside—which delivers humans into a serious double bind—mind/body problems and an irrevocable distance from knowing a "real" world outside. A survival mechanism, then, and potentially an existential entrapment.

LANGUAGE FLOWERS with meaning. Poetic writing derives its legitimacy from the fact that connections continually emerge from the interweavings. But languages are also complex evolving systems depicting categorical relationships. We see structure in experience partly through the organization of our languages, and meaningful patterns—such as syntax—are analytical tools that help us see repetitions and patterns. Discoveries accumulate and evolve. Naming and syntax become both technology and shelter.

Our brains also build communal imaginations. In cultures that organize language in terms of subject-verb-object syntax (most of the Europeans), thoughts about quail, elephants, salmon, forests, and people are organized just like thoughts about inanimate objects like rocks. A sentence about injecting a shell into the firing chamber is built just like a statement about nursing a child. Languages structure meaning, and those most used in the political world (like English and French) teach us to think manipulatively.

Humans are capable of understanding and solving intricate problems. But we are still vertebrates, variations on an ancient genetic line. Wolves and bears, cowboys, investment bankers, raccoons, we all attempt to care for ourselves. Nature drives us toward goals that aren't fundamentally distinct from the life force of a mole or a fungus. Our survival depends on our ability to respond to movements in the system of energy in which we exist. We cannot be another creature, nor can we shake loose of that old beast who evolved on the savannas, traveled in bands in perpetual intimacy with the dirt, trees and grasses, insects, other animals, family, and one another. Predator and prey, hunter and hunted, we are tied to the safety of home and to the killing fields.

Our stories center on ancient preoccupations, their essential natures determined by our everlasting anxieties. Our central narrative may be about the weak facing down the strong, fighting off killer cats in the night, and despotism, incoherence, and death. Tales of isolation in postmodern urban hinterlands echo fairy tales about children lost in the spooky woods.

By reminding us of who we have been, stories help us imagine who we want to be. Even static arts like architecture and pottery work off implied narratives—who made them and how they are useful and what they may be intended to mean.

Without stories, we're not much more than what Spinoza called "falling stones." Narrative may well be our fundamental survival strategy, from which all the complex rest of our schemes follow.

THROUGH MOST of my life, having grown up in the intellectual backlands of America, I disdained the idea of grand tours. Friends at the University of Montana would tell stories about traveling the northern coast of Spain in Volkswagen buses, and I would turn away to pour myself another drink. I'd seen the pictures, and that was more than enough. My true world was the West, where I knew the lingo. But the summer I turned fifty-nine, I was caught in a cycle of stupid aimlessness, and felt myself running down, so maybe it was time for a shot at reinvention.

Probably I would never have tried Europe if it hadn't been for Annick, who was born in France. Her Jewish parents, then strangers, left Hungary for Paris, met, bore this child, then had the wisdom and luck to move on to Chicago before World War II. Annick gave birth to her twin boys, Alex and Andrew, in England, lived in Spain, speaks passable French, and is endlessly more capable of living in textures of the moment than I will ever be. "Listen," Annick will say, and when I'm in my right mind, I try. So when she encouraged me to try Europe, I went. She was my safety net.

In early January of 1992, we were flying toward Paris and what I hoped would be a wake-up call. I wanted to stand at a bar where Hemingway had sipped gin while gazing from a wide, clean window into what James Joyce called the lemon-colored light of Paris, his bare forearms planted on the cool zinc. The part about gin came true pretty often.

Once we'd meandered a few hours along the narrow streets on the Left Bank, Paris evolved from exotic and strange into a playpen. We sat in the Brasserie Lipp and smoked between servings of six-dollar-apiece Belon oysters; while out walking, I stopped for another little cup of heavily sweetened espresso every twenty minutes; Gertrude Stein and Alice B. Toklas had lived just down the street from our hotel by the Luxembourg Gardens. I eyed the work of Vincent van Gogh in the Musée d'Orsay as if it had been painted by a lunatic neighbor; I myself went to bed drunk and woke up wired.

We drove to Venice and Florence and the south of Spain, taking in the cultural extravaganza: the old bullfight ring in Ronda, and the terrifying visions by Goya in the Prado, and the streets where the bulls run in Pamplona, and the casino coast of the French Atlantic. Heading back to Paris, we drove through geometrical commercial forests to Les Eyzies on the Vézère River in south-central France. Some twenty thousand years ago, bands of humans lived in semipermanent villages on sheltered ledges above the floodplain valley along the Vézère. We meant to see what we could of those prehistoric sites.

"PRIMITIVE" THOUGHT reveals itself in its weak ability to perceive the boundaries between things. Animist cultures approach reality by attempting to find connections, not by tracing causal ties, but by skipping over them. The operative linkage is not one of cause and effect; rather, it is one of meaning and purpose. People in animist cultures, as opposed to our mechanistic actuality, believe in what we call magic.

In *The Savage Mind*, Claude Lévi-Strauss argues that magical thought is no less rigorous and systematic than science, even if it is often less informed. But scientists are schooled to accept their inability to know, and they confess when they don't get it, whereas savage thinkers push on to establish categories and unearth significance from intuited or magical connections between dreams and cosmologies, ideas of destiny and fate, and variously witnessed manifestations of energy, whether exploding volcanoes or birds flying by. Breaks in the earth (as at Long Lake) are sometimes thought of as the source of all life. We've seen it ourselves, bean sprouts coming up, cracking the crust, or mommy and daddy coming out from under the covers on a Sunday morning.

Many societies imagine themselves as having come forth in such a manner. The Hopi locate their emergence in a blue-water spring in the canyon of the Little Colorado, and the Zuni place theirs at a small waterfall on the north side of the Grand Canyon. Here, according to legend, their ancestors came forth into the light of day, growing and withering on the earth, sprouting again, season after season after season.

In our off-season hotel in Les Eyzies, Annick and I ate badly and slept worse. But morning sunlight cut the mist as we wandered up to the Museum of Prehistory, tucked under the limestone cliff overhanging the town. The exhibits included items I'd seen in textbooks—most vividly, a figurine of a great-breasted woman holding a ram's horn. I assumed, peering through thick protective glass, that it was a copy. But when workmen came to test the alarm system, setting off a racketing electrical Klaxon, I knew the Venus before me was the genuine ancient article; otherwise, it would not have been guarded so expensively.

There were others much like it, except for the ram's horn, and I took them seriously, finding them unsettling, utterly alien. Nonexistent feet and wide hips, enormous buttocks and flowing bellies and great breasts, tapering upper body and shoulders, tiny heads—they resembled my mother as she grew old, heavy and bedridden. I saw her naked only once after she was incapacitated; I called a nurse, who would know what to do, and then left the room, telling myself that my mother's vastness was only human. But even as her child, I was frightened by her body, cascading with an amplitude I had not been taught to witness or admire. We compartmentalize our lives; we put the infirm and aged in storage to wait for death. My mother had done it to her mother; I was doing it to her after managing to live for decades as an adult without accumulating much experience with frailty so close to the bone. My response in that room where my mother was to die a few years later was an absolute failure of nerve and empathy, which haunts me to this writing.

A number of those iconographic ample-bodied feminine figurines have turned up over a belt of territory reaching from western France to the central Russian plain between the Ural and Carpathian mountains. They were made while glaciers hovered over northern Europe and Asia between 20,000 and 29,000 years ago. It seems likely they were the product of a single tradition, but we're left to wonder who made them, and why. Figures of flowing-breasted women struck from stones and leaping pregnant animals inscribed in caverns—it's easy to connect these images to a desire for regeneration and freedom. We think the artisans who created them maybe valued feminine opulence and fertility. Or maybe these figures simply fit the shape of a stream-worn stone, and crafting them was an idle thing to do, like playing the harmonica or whittling on quiet hours in autumn sunlight. But fatness has also been understood as a metaphor for wealth. In cultures where abundance is ordinary, it has often been fashionable to be lean—no need to store up when our riches are inexhaustible. Leanness becomes a statement about our powers to have and thus resist having, to give things away casually, as in the potlatch, or else demonstrate superior health.

Later that morning, Annick and I visited the cave known as Font-de-Guame, guided into absolute darkness by a woman with a flashlight, along narrow galleries winding into the earth, etched and painted and repainted with figures of animals, such as a line of painted bison (I imagined them heading along the walls toward the entrance and onto the sunny green and grassy riverside).

The most compelling images at Font-de-Guame, for Annick and me, were not my bison but a stag, a doe, and their evident devotion. Curving black antlers were painted on the wall, and a line of backbone sweeping up from them. The rest was incised, minimalist and sexual when seen in the right light, the black stag licking at the snout of a doe on her knees.

"Kissing," Annick said. What she saw on a wall of a cave painted 25,000 years ago was not conquest but kissing. We laughed in the manner of people trying to avoid a topic that isn't actually so funny. We were, after all, together, willing to care for each other.

There are many versions of the trip to the underworld, tours through the levels of darkness. The shamans at Long Lake, Ulysses, Aeneas, Dante—all were seeking knowledge by talking to men and women whose lives were finished, witnessing the workings of fate in the lives of the dead. What, specifically, announced itself at Font-de-Guame? A sense that a world outside—whether the cave, the head, or the brain—was sufficient and that we were part of it. Or maybe that life is best thought of as something to be kissed away. Munificent ways of going out into the world were important to someone who loved deer long before we loved each other.

FOUR YEARS LATER, we were back in the Dordogne. On another sunny winter's day, Annick and I drove our rented Peugeot up twisting roads across limestone ridges overlooking the Vézère River as it wound through the valley—landforms scaled to walk and right for hunting, with brilliant water always nearby. Fields were drying, farmers were plowing, and I kept wanting to feel what it had been like during a brief respite in the Ice Age, when great herds of horned animals grazed and migrated upriver. It is probably impossible to value the images in the caves along the Vézère without imagining the people who made them. Ice covered Britain and the Alps and Pyrenees; Europe was open tundra, where red deer, bison, wild cattle, and horses wandered. It is a stunning conjunction: The short, difficult lives of those people, and the startlingly evocative and sophisticated paintings in those caverns. My response mostly sprung from my hope to see this place as a lost Edenic never-never land, and from certain resemblances to Warner Valley, particularly Lombardy poplar lining the fields.

Among the other habitations we visited were the rock-shelf dwellings known as la Madeleine, and, a few kilometers upstream, Roque St. Christophe, perched on a ledge above the meadows, inaccessible and easily defended, with views and shelter, a home to humans for thousands of years. In 1864, five years after Darwin's *Origin of Species* was published, an ivory tusk from a mammoth was dug up at la Madeleine. Incised with an image of a mammoth, this was the first depiction of an extinct creature ever discovered. Up the river from Roque St. Christophe is the village of Moustier, the site of Neanderthal discoveries (Mousterian is the name anthropologists use to designate an era in the lives of those people). A young visitor to the lady collecting tickets—the French charge admission—walked across the fields below and a stonework bridge to a crossroads store and carried their lunches back in a brown paper sack. He hiked in continuity with thousands of years of humans walking paths across those grassy meadows.

Around these limestone cliffs above the river, there existed a palpable continuity of time, from people constructing fires against the night to a hungry tourist like me, engaged in his own abstract and yet pressing constructing. There is no point in dreaming of a return to the ways our species once lived—in fact, we have never truly left, since those rhythms are inscribed in us and will not evaporate in any living future.

What does "holy space" mean, exactly? Is it a situation where humans feel secure in the knowledge that they're where they belong in the passage of things? Here, we were surrounded by rock walls people had used to back up their hearth fires for millennia, the embers burning down in the night, clans and families warming and drying themselves while snow fell through the darkness and they dreamed of spring, when the tundra would flower and the great animals would return.

AT LASCAUX, after a perfect lunch of soup, gizzard salad, and duck, followed by a walk in the sun, Annick and I were given an hour inside the humidity-controlling doors at that famous cave (no longer open to the general public). The first surprise, after having entered into darkness that would've been utter but for our guide's flashlight, was the size of the great bulls painted in red ocher on the crystalline white walls.

Deep caves like Lascaux are very different from the rock shelters. There's no evidence anyone ever lived inside the cave of Lascaux, even though, before the entrance roof collapsed, that first calcite chamber was dimly lighted from outside.

The art at Lascaux and Font-de-Guame has remained vivid for over twenty thousand years because, while stylized, it is also individual and particular. Each cluster of work in the Dordogne, and in caverns such as Altamira on the northern Spanish coast, is specifically idiosyncratic. The kissing reindeer at Font-de-Guame seem calm and quiet, as if they might be dreaming of a green morning, while the red bulls in the rotunda at Lascaux are endlessly restless, reminding me of the Mexican steers my grandfather imported from Sonora in 1945. As we tried to ship them from the Klamath Marsh, hundreds escaped into the unfenced timberlands of the Cascade Range, where some roamed for years.

What does that restlessness imply about the artists who worked by the light of torches to create those bulls at Lascaux? Why do their animals mostly face into the earth, downslope into the interior darkness, where those from the underworld pass in secret dreams and fantasies? Farther in, beyond the red bulls, are reindeer, their antlers interwoven one over the other in thin intricate detail. The relationship of images leaves viewers with a sense of kinetic force counter-poised with delicacy. The art at Lascaux is hardly "primitive" in any sense; in fact, it is characterized by quick-handed virtu-osity. The red bulls, never retouched, are masterpieces exe-cuted by a master or school of masters.

The rotunda puts the viewer in mind of the cool darkness of the cathedral at Chartres, where on a bright day I gazed up at the vivid storytelling windows. Like those windows, the bulls' power resides not in some specific meaning but in the wholeness and reassurance they radiate, reminding me that I could make my peace here as well as anywhere. Deep inside the cave, illuminated by torches when they were painted, the horses and cows were sway-bellied and loomingly pregnant. In *The Falling Cow*, Annick saw leaping and joyousness. *The Great Black Cow*, in the nave, is to my eye as elegant and fine as any depiction I've ever seen, the equal of Oriental masterpieces, or Picasso's sketches.

In the apse, which seems a central ceremonial section of Lascaux, small figures—mainly horses—and signs are engraved one over another, again and again, repeatedly redrawn, perhaps winter after winter or generation after generation. It's reasonable to expect that this is where instruction took place—to whatever point, in whatever language—spiritual leaders reinscribing the figures through hundreds and maybe thousands of years. In *A Match to the Heart*, Gretel Erlich writes, "The synapse is holy. *Apse* comes from *apsis*, whose roots mean to loop, wheel, arch, orbit, fasten, or copulate, and the apse of a church is a place of honor."

Annick and I, as tourists, were not allowed to visit the quintessential image at Lascaux, hidden in the farthest darkness of a chamber beyond a ledge and down some eighteen rockfall feet: the image of a bison dragging entrails in what must be the agony and rage of death as it goes toward a four-fingered man with the head of a bird, who is falling rigidly backward, perhaps killed, or entranced, his penis erect, having lost both his spear and another shaft topped by a full image of a bird.

Were the artists at Lascaux hunters who supposed some magical connection to birds? Surely we want to think these images capture the essence of their beliefs. Perhaps the caves were ceremonial centers where initiates were imprinted with a sense of the importance of their duties and obligations, among which might have been the recitation of holy stories—without which, ensuing generations wouldn't know who they were and why. So much the better if these initiates were frightened shitless, since things learned during stress are often seared irrevocably into our memories.

Before the invention of writing, communal stories survived only by passing from the mind of one generation to that of the next one rising—containing all they knew, from when to fish and where and how to bless the hunt, including genealogies of tribal heroism and perhaps even a rationale for a fellow feeling with birds. Nowhere but in people's memories, or in art like that at Lascaux, could this essential knowledge be recorded. These were not simple people. So much was known that remembering became an endless task.

Homeric texts, derived from oral tradition, are thick with lists, repetitions, verbal formulas and such mnemonics as stock epithets and a driving repetitive meter. Telling tribal stories from a stockpile of verbal icons, these storytellers were perhaps like rap singers, riffing on lines and themes. Such repetitive forms of remembering and celebration can be acts of reverence, as in Whitman:

> *I knew a man, a common farmer, the father of five sons,*
> *And in them the fathers of sons, and in them the fathers*
>   *of sons.*

Or, in cautionary poems, acts of admonition, as in Sharon Olds, writing about her parents:

> *I want to go up to them and say Stop,*
> *don't do it—she's the wrong woman,*
> *he's the wrong man, you are going to do things*
> *you cannot imagine you would ever do,*
> *you are going to do bad things to children,*

you are going to suffer in ways you never heard of,
you are going to want to die.

Lists and repetitions can lead us into imagining synaesthesia—sights and smells and sounds coming to us in one sensory experience. For a moment, the living world breathes all its meanings into us, luring us into understanding yet again that we are contained in flowing complexities that won't hold still for naming.

INITIATION IN a painted cave was probably simple enough: Go deep into blinding darkness, sing and hear the old stories, light torches, see the startling images again, and be reborn into wisdom. Then return home, whether from the underworld or the Milky Way. Metaphorically, it's like bears emerging from hibernation. People saw the bears vanish into the earth, only to reemerge as winter gave way to spring, and imagined rebirth and resurrection, the basis for our most hopeful religious story.

Ceremonies that act out storytelling are part of the glue binding cultures together. During the last of the Ice Age, perhaps people at Lascaux and Font-de-Guame and Altamira were attempting to give life magically to animals they killed for food, hoping to energize the spirits of the deer and bulls and horses and ensure the return of the grazing herds in slow migration with the next roll of seasons. Or maybe the people who drew on those walls thought that caves were like the inside of a mind, and that the animals might live there, illuminated whenever they were thought of. Such people perhaps thought the animals would vanish forever if no one paid them any mind.

Humans had no choice but to live by consuming the world

so as to fuel their bodies, which can be thought of as a kind of burning. In Warner Valley, we hunted little quail in the tall sage beside the granaries, thousands of quail feeding there on spilled barley. We killed them with .410 shotguns and no thought of sport, firing number seven shot whenever we found them in the dusty cheat grass, then ripped out their breasts, tossed the remains to barn cats, cooked up, and ate.

Killing is everywhere, and incessant. Our yearning to live makes our voluntary involvement in this destruction deeply problematic. We demand our own life and yet deny it otherwise, each of us in some ways a hunter, interested in assuaging hungers real or imagined, physical or spiritual. Human societies perpetuate themselves through killing, so obviously we're capable of predatory violence. Man has been called "a hunting ape." But while such conduct is probably to some degree instinctual, it is mitigated by guilt—about having done violence to innocence. The result, even when the killing is done for food, is an emotional double bind, stretching the tension between undeniable personal and societal needs for sustenance and concepts of justice and fairness—trouble in mind that must have perplexed humans from the moment of self-consciousness. One consequence is melancholia (and given our foreknowledge of death, maybe "the melancholy ape" is a more apt description of humans).

In order to lessen the guilt caused by killing, humans create an emotional distance between themselves and the victim. It seems sensible to imagine that hunters saw themselves as players in a story of community, sanctified by a ritual in which animals sacrifice themselves. From Roberto Calasso's *The Ruin of Kash:* "Eating and killing. These are the two acts in which the arrow of time wounds with a wound beyond healing." Sacrifice can be thought of as a giving back, a reestablishment of equilibrium, earning the right to kill, thus to live. Cultures around the world practice blood sacrifices, which reiterate the fact that, like creatures killed for consumption, we, too, will be consumed by nature, which moreover should be regarded as holy.

At Lascaux, Annick and I stood up close to the artwork of a hunting culture struggling to survive as humans do, attempting to name animals, their culture, and themselves into eternal being. Hungry people might institutionalize dreams to preserve communal memories of a golden, dreamland age when the hunting was easy. No doubt they were like us, like any child, yearning to confide and to be reassured.

THE CULTURE responsible for the artwork at Lascaux, even in their time, was ancient. The recently discovered Paleolithic art in the Chauvet cavern in the valley of the Ardèche River, which flows, through a deep canyon from the central highlands to the Rhône in southern France, and the paintings and engravings found in a cave beneath the sea at Cosquer on the Mediterranean coast near Marseille (the entrance some 120 feet underwater, drowned when the seas rose after the glaciers of the last ice age melted) are seemingly of the same tradition, yet they have been dated some twenty thousand years older.

On a later trip, Annick and I snooped along the Ardèche Gorges, a great river-course canyon with gray-white cliffs, where you could step off and fall hundreds of feet to the water. We were hoping to get inside the Chauvet cavern. But our chances turned out to be less than zero. Instead, we ended up witnessing the far, dark side of cultural coherence, where the unthinkable persists in sweet green valleys.

We stayed in the tourist town of Vallon-Pont-d'Arc, a couple of kilometers upstream from a natural bridge across the river. In the bar of our hotel, we sat over gin and tonics as the owner told how his parents had led their family into hiding during the German evacuation at the end of World War II, hauling their most precious possessions up into the hills, to the cliffs, on a child's red wagon.

"We went to wilds," he said in hesitant English. "Those were dangerous times. Now I find we were camping just at the entrance to the painted caverns, which were collapsed for thousands of years. We didn't know it until we saw the setting of the caverns on television." His story, implying an improbable run of interconnections, and how glories hide just where we'd never suspect them, resonated like a magical scrap of meaningfulness.

On his advice, the next morning, on highlands a few kilometers across the river, we visited the tiny rock-work village of Les Crottes and saw how dangerous the Germans had been while evacuating in defeat. Here they had shot and killed the entire population—seventeen people.

Resting on a rock wall, I noted some of the names on the back of a restaurant receipt, a scribbled list that begins with "Unknown" and includes:

> Lucien Boyer   age 75
> Ernestine Boyer   age 68
> Georges Boyer   age 36
> Louis Brunel   age 47
> Josephine Brunel   age 44
> Adrian Mantacrier   age 45
> Madeleine Mantacrier   age 43
> Georges Mantacrier   age 17
> Noel Galizzi   age 44

Theresa Galizzi   age 43
Antoine Galizzi   age 17
Michael Galizzi   age 16
Jacques Galizzi   age 15

What do human beings think they're doing? Wild violets were in bloom around this scatter of stone buildings, which until recently had stood empty. Now, after fifty years of neglect, these dwellings were being refurbished and reinhabited. It's in our nature to keep coming back, touching the wound, trying to heal ourselves.

IN Keeping Together in Time, a history of military drill, William McNeill claims that people who danced and then hunted together on the African savannas were more likely to survive than loners. "Human beings desperately need to belong to communities that give guidance and meaning to their lives, and moving rhythmically while giving voice together is the surest, most speedy and efficacious way of creating and sustaining such communities that our species has ever hit upon." McNeill says "keeping together in time" arouses warm emotions of collective solidarity, as in sex, ideally a mutually rhythmic way of physical and emotional bonding. In many marriages, when words and logic fail during a quarrel, the court of last resort is the bedroom.

Communal rituals are almost always manipulations, which doesn't make them evil. Shamans and tricksters, politicians and kings are often good-hearted people, hoping to preserve a culture they love, believe in, and depend on, and they cannot bear to watch as it, like all cultures, fails and disintegrates. But insisting, we know, can go terribly wrong.

It's difficult to assess the archaic beginnings of our regional, ethnic, and national societies except in reference to contemporary cultures whose practices happen to be analogous—the Koyukon in Alaska or Australian Aborigines. But much of what we claim to know about people who attempted to influence "nature" through the practice of magic is simply guesswork, an attempt to tie things together with metaphor. In any event, however, it does seem that the leaders at Lascaux understood that a key to controlling a society lies in defining the ways information is presented. Claiming expertise in communicating with the spirit world, intimacy with the gods, some would become shamans. And hereditary chiefs evolved into kings, and descendants of their kind evolved into such rulers as the pharaohs, who were thought to be gods in their own right.

Words delivered rhythmically, accompanied by repetitive gestures, can arouse powerful, even sexual emotions. Standing on stone podiums in front of roaring thousands, Hitler can be seen as trying to name beliefs into actuality, and certainly he understood the uses of art and ritual. At the 1936 Nuremberg rally, great processions trooped in while searchlights flashed across the heavens above great banners; massed bands played music intended to inspire and arouse, as music does best among all the arts, and then the Führer strode into view.

When he spoke, Hitler uttered rhythmic nonsense imitative of sacred texts. "Now we are together, we are with him and he is with us, and now we are Germany." Theatrical staging, music and incantatory language, the simple gesture, the thousands of upraised arms, and the multitudes chanting *"Sieg heil"*—it was a ceremony designed to mesmerize, to promote a highly emotional and anti-intellectual feeling of unity in a system of significance. The point was, We are together; it's not meaningless.

In *Landscape and Memory,* Simon Schama writes of visiting

Giby, where in 1945 people accused of supporting the Polish Home Army were killed by the NKVD, Stalin's security police. The hill "had been given a fresh crown of yellow sand on which rested roughhewn slabs of polished granite. The stones were engraved with perhaps five hundred names. . . . But the real shock waited at the top of the mound. . . . The ground fell sharply away to reveal a landscape of unanticipated beauty. A bright fringe of young trees marked the horizon floor, but at their back, like giants holding the hands of children, stood the black-green phalanx of the primeval forest."

He continues: "We are accustomed to think of the Holocaust as having no landscape. . . . It is shocking to realize that Treblinka, too, belongs to brilliantly vivid countryside, the riverbed of the Bug and Vistula; rolling, gentle land, lined by avenues of poplar and aspen." This sounds much like the valley down the hill from Les Crottes, or the one in southeastern Oregon where I began to enjoy the green light of morning.

My reverence for the images of moving, searching animals at Lascaux is to some degree derived from my reverence for what I take to be a long-ago, simpler, more natural time in my own childhood. But however sweetly done, with all of an open, even joyous heart, naming is also a selfish, claiming act. We begin by defining and then move on toward containing, owning, excluding.

From Robert Hass's *Twentieth Century Pleasures*: "Nostalgia locates desire in the past where it suffers no active conflict and can be yearned toward pleasantly. History is the antidote to this."

AS EARLY as the first century A.D., the Roman historian Tacitus wrote of the "barbaric" Germanic people who lived in the forested lands of northern Europe as living in "timbered virtue," unconfined by masonry walls and the carpentered world of cities. Tacitus took such virtues to be our natural heritage, easily forfeited in an urban, overcivilized situation.

Even in our time, people living close to "nature" are often considered exemplars of the virtuous life, in more intimate contact with the ways of the world than anybody else. This is a theme we hear echoing in much revolutionary thinking—a yearning for purity, which people like to think of as a lost birthright. What's dangerous, as with the Nazis, is the consequent willingness to clean, weed, and kill in the interest of re-creating some Valhalla that never really existed outside the realm of idealistic theory and consequent mythmaking.

The French writer J. M. G. Le Clezio, in *The Mexican Dream: Or, the Interrupted Thought of Amerindian Civilizations,* holds that for the peoples he calls barbarians, "good and evil is instinctive, without hesitation or ambiguity. The barbarian is not immoral, he is beyond all morality, in that sort of original purity which is at the legendary sources of life." This is all nonsense, reeking of primitivism.

In *Gone Primitive,* Marianna Torgovnick writes, "The primitive becomes a place to project feelings about the present and draw blueprints for the future," and she says that we often consider " 'being physical' to be coextensive with 'being spiritual.' "

Primitivism dismisses the complexity of the past, and thus it is condescending to people it means to herald. Human lives were never simple, not to speak of "beyond all morality." We should see beyond fantasies about false simplicities to the fact that our kind will never be remotely "primitive." Instead, we ought to think through and then try to act out the obligations and possibilities inherent in the creatures we now are. A yearning to go "native" is mostly a desire to escape.

No one knows what the artists at Lascaux were thinking as they painted those animals. Maybe they were only entertaining themselves, creating decorations for the dance.

Years ago, in a sparsely furnished house in Port Alberni, a logging town in the forests of Vancouver Island, Annick and I visited a native artist named Ron Hamilton, who would not allow his work to be photographed, much less sold. (Based on the prices we saw on much less impressive work in galleries, he could have been wealthy in short order.) We asked him why, and he said, "It's only props, for the ceremonies."

His notion was that art becomes valuable only when it proves useful in the ceremonies we use to bring order to our adventures. This unselfish kind of thinking sustained craftsmen who worked anonymously on cathedrals, with no hope of seeing the great projects ever close to finished. Similarly, Ron Hamilton was intent on keeping to his priorities.

The paintings at Lascaux could conceivably be the remnants of some age-old bacchanal featuring drink and drugs and sex all around—imaginative and artistic creatures turning the travails of the world briefly upside down, the beginnings of comedy and carnival. I myself find release in breathing to the syncopations of Miles Davis while driving the reaches of the West at escape velocity. Though it might seem tame, it doesn't often fail me.

What I want to imagine of Lascaux is a people taking pleasure, moving like the animals our kind will always be, and singing, getting ready for the next dance, joking and cutting through all the received truths, tricksters each and every one.

Part Two

Agriculture

*T*HE ONLY JOB I ever quit at first sight involved hoeing beets. A junior at Oregon State, I was broke and thus happy to have a job at the Agricultural Experiment Station. Then my boss stopped his pickup truck beside an unending field of beets. "Those will be yours," he said. "There's the hoe. You're after the pigweed." A country boy, I knew pigweed at a glance.

Hefting the hoe while that good man dropped his pickup into gear, I then said, "Wait." It was as close as I got to hoeing beets. Ever since, I've never had a problem understanding that farming is not necessarily an improvement on hunting and gathering.

THROUGH 99 PERCENT of our race's tenure on earth, human beings were hunter-gatherers—every single man, woman, and child through all the eons in every possible place. Millennia passed until, when populations totaled roughly 10 million, people in sites all around the world, over a few thousand years (in the long view, simultaneously), developed agriculture, an accumulation of techniques that encouraged useful plants and animals in the vicinity of seasonal camping sites.

Evidence of harvesting native grass seeds has been found in archaeological digs along the Nile dating to 12,000 B.C.—grindstones, and flint blades with "sickle gloss," an indication of use in harvest. Similar discoveries suggest that within another four thousand years, as the Paleolithic period petered out, people on the north coast of Spain were also harvesting.

In fertile, naturally irrigated sites, people had noticed that they could scatter seeds of small grains and then the next year harvest a crop. As people harvested the yield in their traditional, unplanned way, they gathered seeds that hadn't shattered on the ground, and those which had matured at the same time, which they planted during the next cycle of seeding. The development of uniform crops began with such selective accidents. Developing techniques to manipulate the breeding of plants and animals was like learning to control fire, another shaping of nature to serve human needs. Most of this intricate work was likely done by women, who around the world handled the gathering while men focused on hunting.

In settled places, animals were increasingly domesticated. A grave in Israel, circa 11,000 B.C., held the body of an old woman and a puppy, though whether it was a captured wolf or a domesticated dog is unknown. Remains of the latter, dating to within two thousand years of that time, have shown up in sites as far apart as England and Utah. After dogs came sheep and goats and cattle (by 8000 B.C. in southwest Asia), cats (7000 B.C.), llama and alpaca (4000 B.C. on the Andean Altiplano), honeybees in the Near East and silkworms in China (2000 B.C.), goldfish (China, A.D. 1000), and canaries (A.D. 1500) on, of course, the Canary Islands.

At the same time, farmers were domesticating the 130 or so plants we reap to feed ourselves. Most important are nine species—maize, barley, sorghum/millet, sweet potato/yam, potato, soybean, and sugarcane. Like livestock and pets, they coevolved with humans, with human encouragement.

People bred horses for speed and endurance, for the Arabian Desert and the Shetland Islands; they cultivated maize exactly adapted to particular high valleys in Mexico, as well as rice for the lowlands of southern China, cattle for bog lands in England, grapes for specific hill slopes in Umbria or Burgundy. Five thousand varieties of potato are grown today, three thousand in the Andes alone. Some of the most useful genera of species known today resulted from this refining work—as much an art as painting or poetry or governance and warfare.

As people turned to tending crops and domesticating livestock, they increasingly began to forgo seasonal migration, settling in villages and claiming ownership of houses, fields, tools, and more property. By 7500 B.C., the Near Eastern village of Jarmo had about twenty-five dwellings; the inhabitants farmed barley, peas, and emmer, a primitive wheat, while herding their goats and sheep. Hunting provided only about 5 percent of their food. As a consequence of this long sequence of reinforcing effects, societies over much of the world were changing radically.

Hunting-gathering groups were, despite shamans, mostly egalitarian. But settled communities were increasingly specialized and usually came to be dominated by a ruling class. Food surpluses freed certain citizens to specialize and devote their lives to craftsmanship—pottery or weaving, for example—or to war, or to becoming full-time priests or kings. Power flowed to those who controlled food.

By about 7000 B.C., Jericho was a settlement covering ten

acres, with a defensive wall thirteen feet high and a half mile in length, and having at least one tower thirty-three feet in diameter and twenty-eight in height. By 5000 B.C., irrigation canals were in use along desert rivers in the Near East; by 3000 B.C., they existed in the high valleys in New Guinea. These extensive developments obviously imply labor parties, and organized politics—almost certainly despotism, bosses.

By 4000 B.C., Uruk had a population of fifty thousand, and pyramidal temples called ziggurats were being constructed by Mesopotamian cities in an effort to imitate mountains, since such cities were surrounded by river plains and had no high ground in sight. In *Architecture: The Natural and the Man-made,* Vincent Scully points out that temples that mirrored significant landforms like double-horned mountains were thought to be cosmically significant, such as those in Egypt and Angkor Wat, among the Maya and Aztec and Inca, and that at the North House at Taos pueblo. Societies defined themselves as part of nature, while their pharaohs and priests set themselves in closer proximity to the sky and the sun and the gods. Rising (as in mammalian male sexuality) is often construed as a route toward power. Platforms are places to look down from.

Ceremonial attempts to participate in the rhythms of nature and also to help or force nature to deliver rain or fertility and consequent good yields to farmers and hunters alike were by now commonplace. Sacrifices of plants, animals, and the occasional human were understood as feeding nature. Power and responsibilities accrue to rulers who lead their populations through communal ceremonies, ranging from church to dinner.

The location and growth of cities never resulted from merely a conjunction of trading routes and irrigated lands;

rather, these factors always depended upon commercial plans and politics. City-states in Mesopotamia were involved in constant warfare, whereas Egypt evolved as a peaceable kingdom under irrigation. Egyptian culture lasted thousands of years and no doubt seemed eternal. This complex sequence of societal changes is called the Neolithic Revolution. Agricultural techniques proliferated in the Near East, China, Southeast Asia, India, and along the coasts and in the highlands of Mexico and Peru—and they provided the basis for an explosive and profound eight-thousand-year reinvention of survival tactics.

By the time of Christ, the great majority of mankind lived off the products of agriculture. Farmers cut down forests and displaced hunter-gatherers, and the arithmetical increases in population began—from a few million to our present 6 billion—along with divisions of labor and class, cities, walls, warfare, and a concept of private property that would have been truly ridiculous for hunter-gatherers, who specialized in traveling light. The Neolithic Revolution left a long litany of effects, from which we continue to suffer and benefit. After all our "progress," we're still neolithic.

WHY DID this global shift toward settlement and domestication occur? In my mind's eye, I see those rows of beets on the Oregon State University farm and recall the weight of that hoe in my hand, then think of women on their knees in the valley of the Nile and in China and India and the American Southwest, grinding corn day after day until crippled, and I wonder at the cost.

Hunting-gathering people gave up a lot to settle down and start farming. In the 1960s, anthropologist Robert Lee lived among the !Kung tribesmen of the Kalahari, who enjoy plenty of calories and protein, and generally live as well as people in most non-Western societies. Their desert ecosystem provides the !Kung with a widely varied diet, easily gathered, and buffers them against the disaster of famine even during drought. !Kung adults average about two hours a day in their quest for food, or less time than it takes for a trip to the supermarket. Even in extremely marginal circumstances where farming is not possible, hunter-gatherers often have more available food than they can use. Uninterested in surpluses or capital goods, they regard the carcass of a large mammal or all the nuts from a grove as a nuisance to carry around. Nothing indicates that hunter-gatherers shifted to agriculture in order to save labor or increase leisure time, or that contemporary hunter-gatherers perceive an advantage in settling down. Lives dedicated to work on a daily basis must look pretty boring, since the !Kung already spend much of their time playing and telling stories, on a sort of lifetime vacation. In that, they resemble golf pros and small-town stockbrokers.

What drove the shift to agriculture? In *The Food Crisis in Prehistory: Overpopulation and the Origins of Agriculture*, Mark Nathan Cohen suggests it occurred because populations had surpasssed the carrying capacity of "wild" food supplies— together with the fact that densely populated areas tend to expand into the emptier surround.

There are other reasons, too. The arts of farming are, after all, complex and thus attractive as arts. The impulse to maintain a refuge can manifest itself in an urge to plant crops and flowers and even an orchard and to run water in an oasis garden, where no harm can ever come, or to create an Eden such as those constructed by the autocratic emperors and pharaohs who came to power in the Near East—the Hanging Gardens of Babylon, for instance, or the Alhambra a couple thousand years later in Granada. Such hideouts are not different in kind from the elaborate garden a wife tends behind her ranch house in the sagebrush distances of Nevada, or the barley fields we farmed as meticulously as possible in Warner Valley. People persist in wanting a place where they can live in harmony. Domesticating wilderness and making peaceful, orderly places lead us to feel we're saying no to the forces of entropy. But, as with any act of imagination, even the practice of gardening is also to some degree a conquest, and also, therefore, satisfaction of a wholly different sort.

HUMANS CAME to be what they are while thinking magically, using mental models in which cause and effect was often thought of as emanating from spiritual forces embodied in the land and in other animals. Superstitions, whether black cats or not stepping on a crack, are remnants of that thinking. You might just fall into an underworld. I knock on wood, praying for luck. People I know in Montana insist on the importance of life close to mountains. Few are immune; most of us have our secret magic.

In agriculture, even in its fundamental stages, humans had to think objectively. Manipulating crops and water, digging canals, building headgates and water-driven mills for grinding grains, winnowing and reaping, they continually saw causes and effects linked in direct, if complex physical, ways. They were approaching that radical notion of scientific thinking in which the reasons why things happen are understood in terms of the observable. In the long run, magical thinking didn't turn out to be as useful as strong arms and sweat and functional implements when it came to getting the farm work done.

Making sense of cause and effect was the key to the lock of

materialism. Seeing the world in terms of complex chains of physical consequence would become another tool, alongside talk, fire, digging sticks, and sharpened flint. A fundamental change in our sense of how entities—soil and weather, society, maybe even spirits—played off one another, it also encouraged people to regard other people, as well as creatures and places, as objects to be used and manipulated, without any sense of obligation or remorse. They put emotional distance between themselves and the weak and politically or economically disenfranchised, and kicked the goats and dogs, cows, cats, and all other species out of the metaphoric house. One long-lived result has been the progressive withering of our ability to care much about anybody but ourselves, which has led in turn to a harvest of anomie.

ANOTHER RESULT of the Neolithic Revolution was the development of intricate systems of private ownership. As people settled in houses in cities or on farmsteads to practice trades, they wanted to own those places and their tools.

No doubt humans claimed hunting and gathering grounds from time immemorial, as well as implements such as grinders and spears and paint pots, but settlement meant they could hoard more things to call their own. Preconceptions about what was common property and what was private began to change profoundly.

Is property actually ours? We know that we can't be truly secure except inside the only thing we can ever own for sure and good, our own somewhat-together self. But property, in contemporary systems of ownership, is split into a multitude of kingdoms, each closer to one or another of two basic camps: things that are ours, to be used as we see fit, and the commons, which belong to everyone, to be guarded responsibly. Private property often gives citizens at least the illusion of security against the collective power of the community or state, and even against nature or death. A sense of ownership claims that this part of things is mine and here I stand, so scatter my ashes over my lava-flow rimrocks.

Property is both liberating and imprisoning, establishing boundaries, helping us define who we are and what we stand for, which things and places really count. In this respect, you are what you own—because when we discuss property, we're actually talking about emotions and ideas. Things don't define what we are, but feelings and ideas connected to those things often do.

My pleasure comes not so much from my automobile with its CD deck playing Bach cantatas, or from the cigarettes I wish I no longer smoked, but from the continually renewed sense of autonomy this ownership provides me. Yet communal properties, similarly made of places and things and feelings about them, are ours in exactly the same way, and they bestow the same burdens, pleasures, and responsibility as any other property. What we have in common—from public timberlands and hunting ranges to clean air and our political institutions and downtown boulevards—are also liberating and imprisoning sources of pride and obligation to be cared for like children or aged parents or our portfolios at Merrill Lynch.

One can make this generalization about men: they are ungrateful, fickle, liars, and deceivers, they shun danger and are greedy for profit; while you treat them well, they are yours.

—NICCOLÒ MACHIAVELLI, *The Prince*

IN THE RUINS of ancient Near Eastern trading centers, archaeologists find thousands of marks on clay tablets. Writing seems to have evolved from commercial record keeping. The transformation of speech into marks was a method of pinning down negotiations and keeping track, and the eventual source of enormous power. We can talk only to those near enough to hear, if they understand our language, but in writing, we can reach people thousands of miles away and hundreds of years in the future.

It can be argued that the single most powerful onetime invention in world history is the Greek alphabet—an elegant and universal system of notation that can account for, in twenty-four letters, all the sounds we can vibrate through our vocal cords and shape with our mouths.

Around 1500 B.C., Hebrew thinkers established the original Semitic *aleph-beth,* using one character for each of their consonants; vowels were added by readers according to context. This was utterly simple—the total number of characters necessary to produce written script could be taught to a child. The seagoing Phoenicians passed the notion to the Greeks, who further simplified it.

Alpha and *omega.* It made writing and reading, for the first time in history, intellectually, if not always practically, available to anyone of common intelligence. The Greek alphabet was in use by 700 B.C. It makes me happy to hear, true or not, that the earliest extant line written in Greek, on the Dipylon vase, translates as "Who now of all dancers sports most playfully?"

The Greek alphabet, a wholly abstract method to represent speech in writing, had to be discovered only once. Its invention meant marks on the page no longer needed to resemble the subject at hand—no stick figures or hieroglyphics, however complex or linked with other representative designs. With the alphabet, possible combinations were inexhaustible. This method of recording speech has much of the precision and accuracy of numerical accounting.

A principal difference between European and Chinese civilizations is the degree of difficulty involved in use of their respective writing systems—the Greek relatively easy to learn, the Chinese requiring the work of a lifetime. (At present, there are some eight thousand Chinese ideograms in use.) As knowledge of reading and writing became widespread, the general populace's ability to think abstractly and independently was enhanced and essentially democratized. Not only could universal epics like the *Iliad* be fixed on the page, their existence no longer depending on memories, but individuals were also encouraged to write historical or imaginative stories in personal voices as distinct from one another as the language of Sappho, Aeschylus, and Thucydides.

But the Greek alphabet has not been an unmixed blessing. According to David Abram, in *The Spell of the Sensuous*:

> With the advent of the *aleph-beth,* a new distance opens between human culture and the rest of nature. . . . The written character no longer refers us to any sensible phenomenon out in the world, or even to the name of such a phenomenon (as with the rebus), but solely to a gesture to be made by the human mouth. A direct association is established between the pictorial sign and the vocal gesture, for the first time completely bypassing the thing pictured. The other animals, the plants, and the natural elements—sun, moon, stars, waves—are beginning to lose their natural voices. In Genesis, animals do not say their names to Adam, rather they are *given* their names by this first man. Language, for the

Hebrews, was becoming a purely *human* gift, a human power.

Like agriculture, the Greek alphabet accelerated the remaking of self-definition, and it was another discovery that gave us power, even as it led us off into increasingly labyrinthine enclaves of our own devising.

OUR HISTORY is the story of people enlarging their claim on agricultural and other means of production so as to eat better and raise strong, quick, intelligent children. Humans evolved as a wandering, seeking animal, driven by a haphazard world to move on over the hill into the next valley, perhaps beyond the seas to another homeland. Settling and clearing fields, sowing crops, irrigating, suffering invasion or the injustices of an increasingly static class system, moving on again, our kind of creature developed a complex of culturally—and genetically—driven inclinations both to stay home *and* go out adventuring.

Violence, among hunter-gatherers, was no doubt ordinary. There's evidence in burial sites around the world of death by projectile wounding. Accumulating power, whether in tribal Burma or in boardrooms, is exhilarating, addictive, and ultimately, corrupting. People fought over hunting rights and fields, conquering their neighbors, acquiring colonies. Walled villages were built. After horses were domesticated about 4000 B.C., the stirrup was invented and warriors traveled on horseback, and chariots and complex bows were developed by 3000 B.C. Hunger for power, combined with mobility, drove warhorse societies from the Assyrians to the Comanche. Courage in subduing the world was a supreme virtue. Warrior codes are everywhere much the same, from prehistory to Realpolitik, involving pride, revenge, and a clear-eyed ability to confront the sorrows of mortality without morbidity or excessive melancholy.

In *The Iliad, or The Poem of Force,* Simone Weil writes, "The true hero, the true subject, the center of the *Iliad,* is force. Force employed by man, force that enslaves man, force before which man's flesh shrinks away." For those "who perceive force, today as yesterday, at the very center of human history, the *Iliad* is the purest and the loveliest of mirrors." She then writes, "To define force—it is that *x* that turns anybody who is subject to it into a *thing*. The hero becomes a *thing* dragged behind a chariot in the dust." But Weil doesn't discuss the possibility of leaving war and coming home, even though the other seminal Greek epic, the *Odyssey,* is about ceremonies of welcome and civility, the healing arts of bringing warriors back into society.

Combat is isolating, its warriors sacrificed for the good of society. Achilles knew he was destined to die defending Greek honor. His life was a gift, given to his people. They, in turn, blessed him much as hunters bless the kill. Warriors defend society, and they are rewarded with honors and wealth—a trade-off central to the Greeks' warrior code: You perish in combat; our quieter lives continue.

The *Iliad* moved me fiercely when I was young. When Weil writes that the *Iliad* has "no room for anything except courage and love," she might have been writing about the culture I grew up in on the Oregon deserts.

One summer day when I was ten and my brother Pat was seven, we armed ourselves with butcher knives from our mother's kitchen and went along the irrigation ditch behind our house, engaging in one of our sports, chopping young branches off the poplar trees, drawing those heavy blades back and dropping the tender shoots with a single satisfying blow. Then there was my brother's hand and the blade descending, and the blood, his left thumb almost chopped off, splintered white bone in the flesh. The thumb was saved, leaving a scar Pat has borne throughout his life—but the truth of that summer morning is still, for me, in the heavy blade descending, and the blood—that quick happenstance locked to a memory of yellow jackets and bumblebees humming just steps away in the plum grove. The world held still and flashed for an instant; then my brother was howling. What I see in that incandescent flare speaks like an angel, an annunciation as impenetrable as the face of God. We had been enjoying a shared moment, chopping away, children involved in their capabilities; then suddenly it had gone too far. The pleasures of reshaping the world had led to betrayal and blood. And families, hired hands, livestock, waterbirds in great flights on a summer morning—they also became *things* dragged in the dust behind the chariot of our ambition to own the world.

The rage of Achilles, after the uproar, is a berserk fury focused on revenge. He is capable of any atrocity, none of which heals a damned thing; thus his rage betrays both self and society. But there's also a hero of the *Iliad* who is most important as a domestic man: Hector, whose worth is revealed by his regard for creatures; he embodies the loss we suffer when we destroy life. So the *Iliad* is not entirely a warrior's story. The final line in the translation I first read was "Thus they celebrated the funeral games of Hector, Breaker of Horses." I was thrilled. Maybe my boyhood spent in emulation of horse-breaking men had not been a waste of time.

IN LATER CENTURIES, the Greeks acknowledged that humans seem driven to establish hegemony over other humans. By institutionalizing law and democracy, they hoped to control the chaos that commonly results from that urge.

Thucydides' *The History of the Peloponnesian War* is suspect as reportage, though it serves us well as a cautionary tale whose message resonates throughout democratic constitutions. Pericles, in his funeral oration for the Athenian dead in the second year of their war against Sparta, claimed, "Our way of life made us great." He then defined "the form of government under which our greatness grew, the national habits out of which it sprang. Our constitution is called a democracy because power is in the hands not of a minority but of the whole people equal before the law. We conduct our public life as free men. Our city is open to the world."

But the Athenians were also building an empire and afflicted by the corruption of power. During their war, a plague brought down on Athens a moral catastrophe "so overwhelming that men became indifferent to every rule of religion or law. Rich and poor are equally dead. Why should a man not take a little pleasure?" Facing sickness and random death, citizens embraced heedlessness. The culmination of this process, as Thucydides recorded it, came during the sixteenth year of the war (416 B.C.) when Athenians decided to add the Aegean island of Melos to their holdings. The citizens of Melos asked to remain neutral, but the Athenians gave them no choice and refused to debate rights and wrongs. "The strong do what they have the power to do, and the weak accept what they have to accept."

The result was merciless. The Athenians besieged the island and eventually killed the men, sold the women and children into slavery, and then sent colonists to repopulate the empty towns and farmsteads. Neither democracy nor their faith in the rule of law could steer the Athenians from this savagery. In Euripides' *Trojan Women,* written in response to this heartlessness even as it proceeded, Athena mocks the Athenians: "Treaders down of Cities . . . yourselves so soon to die." The war played out in devastation.

The centuries of Roman history—another progression from social civility to imperialist cruelty and inattention to the common welfare—yield much the same moral point, as do so many other stories from around the world.

Waves of nomadic people intent on takeover and pillage began materializing out of central Asia in the fourth and fifth centuries A.D. Huns drove the Germanic tribes—Vandals and Visigoths, Burgundians and others—before them like animals, and they sacked Rome in 410 A.D. A century later, the Avars drove the Lombards into Italy and Slavic tribes into the rough southeastern European highlands. Arabs conquered the Iberian Peninsula, crossed the Pyrenees into France, and were turned back only by defeat in the Loire Valley in 732. Magyars came to settle on the sweet plains of Hungary. Vikings in longboats terrorized the seacoast settlements of Europe from England to Sicily. Mongol horsemen burned Asian cities, tearing down stoneworks and using the streets for grazing, as if determined to bring down all the pretensions of civilization before settling in themselves to rule after the Turkish capture of Constantinople in 1453.

Histories of the world can be understood as an endlessly repeating series of cautionary tales, suggesting it might be a good idea to rethink the cyclical story of conquest, empire, and decadence, and to stop acting it out, which message took on particular urgency with the invention of nuclear weapons.

OF 100,000 HUMAN GENES, we share all but about 1,500 with chimpanzees. Both species have big brains, walk on two legs, and spend years raising infants. Adult males of both species attack, maim, and kill one another over territorial disputes. Male chimpanzees continually jockey for power and prestige, and they prove their sexual dominance by violence and rape, often battering females into submission. The rewards of violent aggression are sex, popularity, pride, and power, just like in a high school movie. But this does not mean that we're irrevocably bound to act like chimpanzees. We can talk to computers and sing along with Elvis. We can be the kind of creature, ethically and morally, we want to be.

War, Barbara Ehrenreich writes in *Blood Rites: Origins and History of the Passions of War,* is an idea with a life of its own, constantly mutating and evolving. It's possible to write a history of war as a concept. The idea is a meme. War can become a location, a place to live. We can't simply rethink and thus alter our inclinations, but we can recognize that war is a malignant idea with a life of its own, which feeds on other malignancies, such as ideas of revenge. Like diseases, these preoccupations can be cured.

In *Achilles in Vietnam,* Jonathan Shay points out that warriors often "withdraw emotionally and mentally from everything beyond their small circle of combat-proven comrades." A result, when the veterans return home, is often self-imposed isolation, withdrawal from community, which can be defined as any group with which we can openly share joy and grief. The warrior, loyal to a lost troop of old comrades but without any sense of mission beyond battlefield survival and conquest, becomes an unemployed adventurer, endlessly awaiting another assignment, always ready to demolish, sometimes furious but mired in the past and thus creatively impotent, stranded and unable to begin building a future. Such citizens, we've seen, are occasionally willing to embrace secular conquest idolatries—for instance, the recent upsurge of skinhead fascists around the world—which promise to give life meaning. "When mistrust spreads widely and deeply," Shay writes, "democratic civic discourse becomes impossible." One cure, Shay argues, is learning to welcome our warriors back into civic communities. The Greeks seem to have understood in the long run. Along with the *Iliad*, they also revered that great saga of homecoming and welcome, the *Odyssey*. Enough with Achilles and his anger.

An Arctic shaman is supposed to have said that the trouble with life is that we eat nothing but souls. The urge to stake a claim is, to some degree, built into our genes (it drives me to write this book). But the guilt which accompanies killing can work like cold water poured into the soul. Passion and rage don't grant us the right to call the shots on anything.

> Some people happen to find themselves together, taking shelter from the rain under an arcade, or crowding beneath an awning of the bazaar, or stopping to listen to the band in the square, meetings, seductions, copulations, orgies are consummated among them without a word exchanged, without a finger touching anything, almost without an eye raised.
>
> —ITALO CALVINO, *Invisible Cities*

FOR A MAN from the windy towns of the American West, it is both surprising and fulfilling to encounter the communal life at the medieval heart of small European cities like Florence and Lucca, Nimes and Arles and Avignon—stony cobbles in the squares worn by centuries of use, thickets of intimacy in the cafés. My first experience of walled community was Aix-en-Provence, and I wandered the crowded, crooked streets on an evening promenade, examining carrots and cashmere topcoats and sculpted pastries in vividly illuminated shops. The notion of walking out every evening for talking and browsing, smoking and drinking, gossiping and flirting—an hour or so of sociability—was new to me. After eight o'clock, the shops closed, the streets emptied, and we retired to a meal of delicious shellfish I'd never heard of, some of them orange, others purple. I was thankful to have discovered such diversions before dying.

In the outback American West, we'd gone at sociability quite differently. Various people got together at one church or another; most women occasionally traveled to town for ceremonial sprees; men customarily gathered in taverns. Ranching families like ours gathered for grade-school Christmas programs (younger children each delivering a memorized poem, the older ones cavorting in one-act plays), and there were Harvest Moon Dances in midsummer (fiddle music and hot whiskey from the bottle and eventual bloody fistfights in the dusty parking lot, illuminated by the headlights of pickup trucks while the music played on in the empty dance hall). We didn't have much truck with outsiders. We lived in an economic colony (as walled in its own way as any medieval city) and defended ourselves with scorn for anything from beyond the valley. At the same time, just about anything local was okay. We both censured and took care of our own.

But the *boulevardiers* ease I saw in Aix would mostly have been impossible out west, if for no other reason than the vast distances, and to a considerable degree unthinkable; after all, the forebears of many westerners had crossed oceans to escape the confines of European status. Our valley was largely populated by Irish from County Cork, and my own family lived at one generation's remove from poverty. We valued our right to govern ourselves and do as we pleased, and we disdained what we saw as the ant farm of cities, which most of us felt we were lucky never to have known. Still, I was beguiled by Aix-en-

Provence. Having done without on-the-street pleasure and intimacy for most of my life, I now rued this deprivation.

AFTER A SUNNY morning on the grounds of the emperor Hadrian's great playhouse villa east of Rome in the foothills of Tivoli—gardens and fountains, libraries and theaters, all in elegant scattered collapse—Annick and I drove south past Naples. We were inland on the autostrada, missing the sights as we drifted into twilight over the Agri Valley and descended a twisting road over precipitous mountains falling to the town of Maratea, perched above the sea in darkness.

Here, in the late 1960s, our friend the poet Richard Hugo spent a winter over his poems in rooms rented from the post-mistress, gazing out at the rain. Annick and I had no purposes in Maratea beyond honoring Dick, who, though dead a dozen years, seemed to be with us. I could still hear him reading from his collection *Good Luck in Cracked Italian*: ". . . the local dialect has no word for hope."

Dick was a man who had suffered and survived grave emotional wounds, and he believed in the efficacy of failure and defeat; that difficulty with life makes people more humane; and that our capacity for compassion and empathy is central in the ball game of life. In all this, he was no doubt correct. He also claimed that southern Italy—where people had survived defeat after defeat, army after army for thousands of years—was perfect country for a man who thought as he did. After serving as a bombardier in Italy during World War II, he went back twice. That one winter, trying to make contact with an interior life he could stand, Dick wrote, in "Pizzeria S. Biago":

When you hobble, tattered through the square
they say: Come in. We keep the maimed alive.

On the square that night, while Annick negotiated for a place we could sleep, I studied the twisting streets and curving walls, the men shooting pool in a bare room as women shopped for the evening meal, the automobiles parked helterskelter in the glinting lights, the dark tangles of forested brush on the slopes just above us, trying to imagine Dick Hugo drinking alone in the café and sorrowing over what he regarded as his homelessness.

The next morning, Annick and I headed north on back roads and found ourselves following a funeral procession of old men and women shuffling uphill through narrow, curving streets in an ancient village, carrying roses. We could only wait. The pavement was littered with petals. Maybe Dick had been right—this was the perfect country in which to relearn the slow, tough arts of quietly defending what we love. The agricultural backlands beyond were softly beautiful, roads being upgraded for tourists. Citizens in a funeral procession, sorrowing for a lost companion, soon would constitute local color.

We dropped out of the coastal mountains onto a seaside plain, to the classical temples at Paestum, a town built by Greek traders around 500 B.C. Vincent Scully writes, "The Temple of Hera at Paestum is the most thoroughly overwhelming image of divinity in temple form that remains to us. . . . The type is never compromised, precisely so that each thing can be read as distinct. Now the old imitation of the forms of the earth is given up." The classical stonework Grecian temples stood alone and utterly apart from nature. Ancient Paestum was a trading city, smaller than the place where I live in Montana, but its public buildings have endured more than two thousand years and are equal in significance to any public buildings anywhere.

To dramatize the difference between cultures that work to maintain their connections to nature and those, like that of the Greeks, that insist on standing apart, Scully contrasts the

North House at Taos pueblo, which echoes the sacred mountain behind it, to the Temple of Hera, which projects the willfulness of its builders. Still, I think of the clamor of children running the avenues in between those great stone temples, and of bright flags in the sea breezes. In World War II, the temples at Paestum were part of a tented hospital, and I wonder if Dick Hugo ever got there.

That night, we put up in an elegant hotel on the seacoast heights in Ravello, overlooking lemon groves terraced into the steep slopes along the Amalfi Coast, where Wagner and Truman Capote once stayed. Gore Vidal lived nearby, in a villa reputed to be even more elegant. From the balustrade, we could look down two thousand feet directly into the sea.

Often, visiting other people's sacred places, we try out their values, at least in the imagination, trying to rethink ours. Annick and I walked the bricked-over square on the uphill side of the Tuscan city of Arezzo and around the Piazza del Campo in Siena (both sites of ritualized horse races) and, farther afield, along the narrow cliff-top passage where the snake dances are held in the Hopi village of Walpi—I'm trying to show that in widely disparate communities, separated by continents and oceans, folks have hooked up with the hum of chance through rituals like horse racing, snake handling, or falling on their knees.

We seem hard-wired to find certain places, images, odors and sounds and touches—those associated with the renewal of life—more reassuring than others. I feel at home in crossroads taverns in the American West, looking out onto a semibarren platter of sagebrush country much like that east of the valley where I was raised. While I mostly loathe institutional religion, I enjoy Gothic cathedrals. Columns in Egyptian temples represented the papyrus reeds of an oasis, and Greek temples were modeled on sacred groves; Gothic windows to me resemble branches reaching to deity, which is represented by the fractured light falling through them. The Hopi cathedrals at Walpi, on the other hand, their kivas, are underground.

In hilltop towns like Orvieto and Todi and San Gimignano it's easy to imagine how the churches could stand for the world, whole and provident and safe, overlooking the hunting ground, just as the enormous châteaux built by French nobility in the Loire Valley, dream castles like Chenonceau, Chaumont, and Chambord, defined by their elaborate gardens, were places where disorder and harm could be stopped at the gates.

NEAR THE Rialto Bridge in Venice, we watched imperious locals negotiate the chicanery involved in changing money. But nobody was much tricked. We're always intent on the business of survival, and much of the time we enjoy it.

The Venetian Lagoon was formed since the last ice age, by currents from the rivers Po, Adige, Brenta, and Piave, and by tides of the Adriatic Sea. Outside the river channels, its depth averages twenty inches. Clay and sand deposits created salt flats, which are home to plants capable of surviving on brackish water, glasswort and sea lavender and aster; they filter out salt, retain freshwater in their plump foliage, and bloom in late summer, touching the Lagoon with patches of pink and blue.

During the sixth century, as Roman rules of organization and law were slowly collapsing, citizens in the Roman administrative district called Venetia were forced to the uninhabited islands in the Lagoon by tribes like Lombards from the north, who were themselves being driven west by "barbarians" from Asia. Here began the creation of this historically secretive, textured city.

Venice can be thought of as a palimpsest: built, rebuilt, torn down, the materials used again, the place written on, the writing overwritten and erased and overwritten again. People moved to the islands to escape a chaotic existence amid incessant warring on the mainland and too much sadness, with nothing to lose but further misrule and loss. This going to the islands was extraordinarily difficult, an undertaking that spent the energies of generations. Hauling their belongings in boats, they lived in shanty villages on the mud flats, where they walked mud floors and mud streets. While it's easy to consider their refuge wilderness, it wasn't. They knew this place well, its marsh harriers and reed bunting and black-tailed godwit and curlew, its secret channels and tides, which no one else could easily follow. Maybe some of those soon-to-be Venetians felt like winged creatures capable of vanishing off into the horizon, an ability they perhaps loved.

When you visit, go to the northern rock wall, the Fondamente Nuove, and catch a ferry to the island of Torcello. Here, you will revisit those beginnings. John Ruskin, the nineteenth-century English writer, after arriving at the elegant Grand Hotel Danieli in 1849 to begin sketching and measuring the city stone by stone for his three-volume *The Stones of Venice* (1853), was to call Torcello the mother and Venice the daughter. Coming off the ferry there late on a January afternoon, Annick and I found a seemingly abandoned, brushy lowland place with a few houses at the edge of the fields; a walkway beside a narrow canal led to a grassy compound with Locanda Cipriani, the first-rate and expensive branch of the famous Cipriani restaurant on the Grand Canal, a seventh-century baptistry, and the Cathedral of Santa Maria Assunta, considered the oldest example of Venetian architecture. The date of its foundation is A.D. 639.

As the first cold hints of evening fell over the Lagoon, we entered the cathedral and confronted Byzantine mosaics: Christ enthroned between the archangels Gabriel and Michael, his right hand raised in blessing, angels holding the Lamb of God above him; a twelfth-century procession of the twelve apostles; and a Virgin and Child dating from the same century. These stern images demanded that I inhabit emotions they didn't cause me to feel. Hard-edged and formal, they were news from a world that I had never inhabited, so they remained, for me, a set of vivid abstractions. Make of us, they said, what you can. But they were news from someone else's reconciliation with death, designed to honor a deity who seemed mostly oppressive and thus emotionally useless to me.

So most of my time was spent at the other end of the cathedral, studying a twelfth-century mosaic depicting the Last Judgment. I went outside to smoke, then returned to this vision, which brought me to emotions more useful than dread. Everything depicted there hung in the waves of Eve's flowing golden hair, a cascade of significance reaching downward from Christ's crucifixion to human dead yielded up from the enveloping earth and the digestions of animals and sea creatures, the elect and the damned, their souls attended to and placed in balance.

This, I felt, is how things actually are, interconnected by a fragile living tissue. Eve's hair was a metaphor that I could grasp. The creators of these mosaics at either end of that cathedral must have believed, simultaneously, in two ways of seeing: In one, we're part of everything; in the other, we are judged.

On Torcello, they built a city that lasted seven or eight hundred years, until the ship channels silted in and the swamps turned malarial. By the twelfth century, the stones from Torcello were being moved across the Lagoon to the islands called the Rivo Alto (Rialto), where they were used to build Venice, work that took centuries, requiring the perfection of techniques that are of great interest to people like me, who at least once found meaning in the task of remaking the physical world. Timbers were rafted south on the rivers Piave and Brenta from the mountains of Cadore, then sharpened and driven into the layer of compacted sand and clay which form the floor of the Lagoon to support buildings mostly built of wood and plaster. Venice today is inhabited by the descendants of people determined to build on this muddy foundation. Over centuries of survival, they—as D. H. Lawrence said of the pioneers who came to America seeking all its ease and natural generosities, only to encounter its indifferent difficulties—hardened themselves. Their society lost its natural human softness.

Venetians never took sides. Theirs were the finest ships in Europe. They made enormous sums of money hauling the Crusaders back and forth across the Mediterranean. In 1202, the Venetians persuaded the leaders of the Fourth Crusade to forget the Holy Land and instead participate in the sacking of Constantinople, the richest city in Europe and the center of Christian civilization for nine centuries. Called the Crusade Against Christians, the invasion was typified by murder, rape, and looting. The racial and religious hatreds born during the sack of Constantinople reverberate still in the Balkans.

Astonishing wealth and some of the most revered art preserved through the chaotic centuries after the fall of Rome then flowed to Venice, whose act of invasion transformed it into a prime European power. Inside St. Mark's Basilica stand four life-sized bronze horses taken from Greece to Trajan's Column in Rome, from there to Constantinople and thence to Venice—Napoléon removed them to Paris for a sojourn lasting until 1815—but now those horses and their rich history, in which the story of our civilization echoes both pridefully and sadly, must be considered Venetian.

A little less than a century after the sack of Constantinople, Marco Polo returned from decades in China; Venice controlled the eastern Mediterranean, and now the Venetians were traders to the world; silks and spices and jewels funneled to them through the fabled Orient. For three hundred years, Venice was Europe's chief marketplace, its citizens demonstrating a mercantile coldness of the heart; people and their yearnings were items to be traded and exploited. Becoming what they feared at their beginning—a society that valued rapaciousness above all—they were cynical and endlessly intriguing, cruel, as was necessary in service of a greed they seemed to regard as natural. Venice became enormously powerful, and the most hated state in Europe; as the centuries passed, it imagined itself invulnerable, acting as if there was nothing to fear.

Venice's decades of disaster began with the Turkish capture of Constantinople in 1453. Then other nations began to encroach on their sea-trading monopolies, and in 1509, defeated on the mainland, the Venetians were forced back to the islands. These reversals were understood as "signs of God's displeasure," which response likely reflected a ration of societal self-loathing. In 1512, "to placate the anger of our Lord" and put an end to an "overt display of sensuality," the doges enacted decrees limiting the wearing of jewels and clothing intended to be sexually inviting.

In 1516, in another attempt at purification, the Venetians pressed Jewish citizenry into a walled-off section called the Ghetto Nuovo, thus inventing that unfortunate archetype, because some Jews had been lending money for profit. According to Richard Sennett, in *Flesh and Stone: The Body and the City in Western Civilization,* many Venetians thought all Jews were involved in usury, which they understood as a social disease akin to prostitution. By thus separating themselves, the Venetians attempted another move, this time spiritual rather than physical, to a place where they would not be contaminated. This would not prove possible. Their hegemony of the eastern Mediterranean no longer controlled the markets of Europe, so Venice turned to the tourist business, hauling an endless stream of pilgrims to the Holy Land after selling them provisions. The old city became a courtesan. The mercantilist warriors stayed home and grew soft. Venetians gave in to diversion, whether decorating their bodies or their great houses. Art became the city's business as well as a shield, a version of purity, a defense behind which they could pretend to be emotionally invulnerable.

Carpaccio (ca. 1460–1525) depicted Venice with precision and attention to the textures revealed by different light as it fell on citizens at their various tasks and on the stonework that surrounded them; his work demands to be taken as testament to what was actual. Painters of the next generations—Giorgione, Titian, Tintoretto, Veronese—were given to swirling, sumptuous visions of events in places like heaven and not like Venice, and then life turned mimic to art, and public buildings were dolled up in an intricate, enameled manner, much of it layered on with less of an eye to beauty than to reconfirming the importance and power of the owner.

The old seagoing city became a festival. The carnival (the fleshly feast) is a universal and probably essential form of conduct. In *Rabelais and His World,* Mikhail Bakhtin writes that "carnival celebrated temporary liberation from the prevailing truth and from the established order; it marked the suspension of all hierarchical rank, privileges, norms, and prohibitions. Carnival was the true feast of time, the feast of becoming, change, and renewal. It was hostile to all that was immortalized and completed." Carnival was also "a consecration of inequality. On the contrary, all were considered equal during carnival. People were, so to speak, reborn for new, purely human relations."

We put on masks and take a run at being someone else. Permissiveness is all. We laugh and eat and drink and fornicate, too, if the chance comes along. Carnival in its classical form, as it has been practiced throughout history, is an emotionally cleansing frolic, a getaway dedicated to celebrating otherness, bringing down the high or elegant or mighty through mockery and satire, a bloodless form of uprising. But incessant carnival didn't have that effect in Venice.

Venetians believed that civility would never conquer life's discontentments, and there ensued centuries of heedless and heartless fooling around. Bulls were tied in the piazzas, to be killed by dogs, and citizens used their shaved heads to batter clawing white cats to death before audiences; bloodiness can be the only point of this. Misrule ruled. In 1797, Napoléon sold the city to the Austrians even before conquering it.

What remains on the islands is an intricate maze of stonework and glass factories and shops, of endless decoration, some foolish, some magnificent. Venice is one of the world's great mirrors, a facade made of remnants, new building stones perfectly discolored so as to fit with the ancient, a playground doomed to be rediscovered by generation after generation of writers, from Byron to Henry James to Ruskin to Thomas Mann to Hemingway to James Wright, stage for their own dramatic callings and a perfect set for film festivals. Our yearning is reflected in Venice, the brute facts of what moves us to profanity and prayer as we go on attempting to reimagine ourselves.

It was a Venice . . . of cold, lashing rain from a low black sky, of wicked wind raging through narrow passes, of general arrest and interruption, with the people engaged in all the water-life huddled, stranded and wageless, bored and cynical, under archways and bridges.

—HENRY JAMES, *The Wings of the Dove*

So you never know as you move through these labyrinths whether you are pursuing a goal or running from yourself, whether you are the hunter or his prey.

—JOSEPH BRODSKY, *Watermark*

IN CHILL January rains, Annick and I walked stone-floored trails between dark buildings, over bridges, and along the concrete border beside the Lagoon, into a working-class quarter where the midwestern American poet James Wright lived a few months toward the end of his life. In a poem titled "A Winter Daybreak Above Venice," he wrote:

> *I can*
> *Scarcely believe it, and yet I*
> *have to, this is*
> *The only life I have*

We could only speculate about Wright's reasons for going to Venice, but it's possible he was seeking one more vision of burgeoning life. In Missoula during the late 1970s, Wright had come to stay several days with Dick Hugo; they'd been at graduate school together at the University of Washington, studying with Theodore Roethke, and were longtime drinking companions. But by then, Hugo was on the wagon, given to devouring huge platters of ice cream while watching old black-and-white crime movies on television, and Wright was constantly drunk, frantic and pacing and talking, always talking, as Dick sprawled on his couch, watching the screen. That's how it was the few hours I spent with them, and Hugo told me that's how it was the whole time. Wright was supposed to end his visit with a reading at the university. "He can't do it," Dick said; "he can't sober up."

But Wright insisted. He stood before the crowd, wavering as if wounded, and recited poem after poem, many of them from other languages and traditions, only a couple his own, from memory. It was a performance against which I could judge my own worth. What I wanted from Venice was another such model and enlightening experience, which might have been what James Wright wanted in the end in a city he knew to be double-hearted. After centuries of cruelty and avarice, the Venetians may have seemed to him capable of forgiving any transgression. Dick Hugo claimed working-class Italians were particularly decent. "They've had enough with the endless defeat," he would say, laughing.

On another cold afternoon, we strolled through the mostly empty piazza at the center of the Ghetto. Annick is Jewish—by bronze plaques listing the names of those people shipped off to be murdered by the Nazis late in World War II, she stood and wept. I, imagining frantic, inconsolable leave-takings, feeling fragile and furious, rapacious, heartbroken, cruel, ready to weep or strike out, ducked my head, and yearned for a walk, an escape, a drink. Later, in Harry's Bar with the sable-wrapped rich, a couple of Bellinis made with peach juice cost us about the same as a good lunch for two, including wine, in the blue-collar quarter where Wright had lived.

VENICE MUST BE Italo Calvino's foremost "invisible city," life threaded with secrets horrible and fortifying. Both the city and Calvino's work can be understood as primers on how we inhabit narratives nested within narratives, how coherencies and significances fall in multiplying configurations and echo through the chapters of our lives. Sometimes it's difficult to keep track; worn-out, and lost in market squares and cathedrals of story piled atop story, we yearn to relax with a cup of tea or an icy Bombay gin martini, straight up. Give us a little emotional lift and we'd be willing to participate some more. We'd be willing to read on. *Invisible Cities* is like that, narratives that sit alongside the ones we ourselves encounter on the streets of New York as we try to read the dreams of the beggar and the rich woman and the aged uniformed man who guards her door in terms of our dreams of what we are and want to be, while knowing that we, too, like them, are make-believe, made of stories.

Kublai Khan, to Marco Polo: "Confess what you are smuggling: moods, states of grace, elegies." Reading the world as a hunter, whether for meat or wild fruits or photographs or experience, involves attentiveness. Such reading, as David Abram writes in *The Spell of the Sensuous,* is at best synaesthetic, involving a blending of senses. Stories work in us, John Gardner said, like specific, continuous dreams. Our lives circle them like shorebirds in the wind. The dreams elicited by stories, by our reading, by listening to ourselves as we read and listen, are transformational if the language incites us to re-create what we know in a new light, moving us to reimagine our master plot in versions surprising enough to be considered magical, alive, and evolving, stories or thoughts flowing like water in trickles and waves.

Trying to recall my time in Venice, those views across the Lagoon to banking fog and walkways ending at ancient stonewall constructs, with all its densities and resonating voices, thronging purposes and complexities I'll never comprehend, I feel beguiled and resisted. For centuries, for visitors like me, Venice has meant whatever we have most wanted it to mean. As I understand it, the city is absolutely a construct, while unalterably connected to mud and water and the doings of rapacious waterbirds and feral cats in the cemeteries. It is famous for celebrations and duplicitousness and cold cruelty, torture before execution, but also thick with families who know the history of their blood relations for centuries. In Venice, I imagined underground corridors even while sure there was only mud down there, the sand and clay permeated with salt water and an infinity of broken cups and other sunken artifacts.

> Clay is the word and clay is the flesh.
> —PATRICK KAVANAGH, "The Great Hunger"

> We were driven like cattle, and flew away like birds.
> —EASTERN OREGON RANCHLAND IMMIGRANT MATRIARCH

IN HIS great novel of early-twentieth-century farmstead life in Iceland, *Independent People,* Halldor Laxness tells of a man and his daughter looking out over the sea.

> "Isn't there anything on the other side, then?" she asked finally.
> "The foreign countries are on the other side," replied her father, proud of being able to explain such a vista. "The countries they talk about in books," he went on, "the kingdoms."

Millions of peasants, from Ireland to China, over thousands of years and hundreds of generations, colonized every inhabitable area on the globe, plowing and dreaming of heavens. Agriculturalists built irrigation systems and cleared forests for fields. They took over entirely in Europe, crowding the hunter-gathering people onto marginal lands, onto salt marshes, into the Pyrenees and Alps and the northern forests, where winter dropped on the world like a hammer. Farmers can be thought of as moving northwest across the fertile lands of Europe at a rate of about a mile a year, transforming ecosystems and setting up a mosaic of fields and feudal kingdoms, peasant farmers defended by a warrior nobility in their castles.

By the Middle Ages, 80 percent of the people lived on the land, part of an enormous disenfranchised and static peasantry. Life was an extended family and village, ordered by the cycle of the harvest. Peasant homes were built of mud and thatch, the floors (if any) rough planks over beaten earth. There was a door but no windows, one table, sacks of straw for bedding, a fireplace for heat, light, and cooking. These hovels were crowded with hungry children and, in winter, maybe a fattening hog. Meals were mostly meatless, and the house stank of bare feet and unwashed clothing. There were plagues of killer diseases, and in any event, peasant lives were not long; most of them didn't reach the age of fifty. Always, in the fields of the master, unending labor awaited. Hatred of the powerful ran everywhere, commonplace as water.

But eventually, shipbuilders built better vessels. Prince Henry of Portugal (1394–1460), known as the Navigator, sponsored the development of navigational instruments, mapmaking, shipbuilding, and voyages of exploration down the west coast of Africa—a rationalist program of "planned discovery." In 1441, a Portuguese ship brought gold and slaves up from the sub-Saharan kingdoms of Ghana, Mali, Songhai, and Benin. In 1488, a Portuguese named Bartolomeu Dias led an expedition around the Cape of Good Hope, discovering the sea route to India and the Orient. Spices and herbs from Southeast Asia and such East Indian islands as the Moluccas could be brought to Europe in quantities and at prices shippers like the Hindus and Muslims, and the Venetian and Genoese Christians who traded with them, could never hope to match. In 1493, the *Niña* returned from the distances of the Atlantic. Columbus said he had reached the islands of Japan, and that it was reasonable to think of reaching the East by sailing west. It was possible for even the peasantry to dream of leaving their servitude behind.

ON A LATE spring morning in southern France, Annick and I crossed the Rhône at Beaucaire, where I made a traffic mistake and had to recircle the old market quay beside the river. Annick had been reading to me about the summerlong medieval fair that had taken place along that riverside for centuries, and I was happy, threading through crowds of people carrying flowers or bags of beans on their bicycle seats.

Abundance is an ancient song murmuring in Whitman's lists and advertised on television and on every other page in glossy magazines. I was imagining raggedy boys and girls running the riverfront, stinking crowds and casks of salt and great clusters of bright radishes—all in contrast to our age of mechanical replication and manufactured order. In Europe, as the High Middle Ages became the Renaissance, people began acting out what Fernand Braudel called "a psychology of joy" in *A History of Civilization.* "Rarely in history did people feel so powerfully that they were living in fortunate times."

Stories from China and America blew in the wind. Peasants envisioned liberty and a chance of relief from brutish labor and the constant threat of starvation. According to John Hale, in *The Civilization of Europe in the Renaissance,* their hopeful-ness was a result of feeling they stood together not only as Christians but as citizens of a culture that was accumulating power over happenstance and even destiny. Their sense of con-trol over nature was a result of discoveries and inventions, such as a steel plowshare that cut a deeper furrow, horseshoes, a sys-tem of collar harness for horses imported from China, grain mills driven by the wind, and, of course, Chinese gunpowder. Europeans were cooking up a world made of technologies and mental constructs.

Flowers and bacon were sold in stalls on street corners in cities like Barcelona and London and Paris. Perpetual markets sold yarn and shoes, furs and wine. There was a corn market in Toulouse as early as 1203. The Beccarie in Venice, where meats were sold, stood next to the Rialto Bridge over the Grand Canal, right across from great banking houses. The collection of market buildings in Les Halles—halls selling seafood, leather, wine, and flowers—was known as the "belly of Paris." Flour, butter, well ropes, secondhand clothing, and furniture were sold from stalls wedged among the pillars. Usury was practiced, and pockets picked. White-faced mimes, magicians, and clowns did tricks. The squares of Venice were crowded with 100,000 visitors.

Carnivals, in late medieval times, were spoken of as the "Land of Cockaigne" (*cockaigne* means "little cake"), and they turned things upside down and grotesque. With music, jug-glers, tumblers, fortune-tellers, tooth-pullers, and tightrope walkers, among many other acts, these were the early days of vaudeville.

"Break the bone," Rabelais says in *Gargantua and Panta-gruel,* "and suck out the substantific marrow." He wrote carni-val narratives, undermining the pomp of the powerful. Bring down the false, the high and the mighty, fools who don't even realize they're missing the point of life, festivity of all its ten thousand forms.

Many peasants left their ancestral homelands to escape poverty; others left their fields to taste frivolity and see things they had never imagined. People went off to find where freedom lived and never looked back. But the world was already populated, the mines already being mined, the fertile lands mostly being farmed. Colonization and enslavement of the natives were the usual remedies. By the beginning of World War I, Europeans ruled about 85 percent of the earth.

IN THE EARLY 1600s, my people began leaving Britain for America's eastern seacoast. My great-great-grandfather Kittredge left Massachusetts for Michigan, and my great-grandfather left Michigan for the gold-camp West. In 1849, he returned to Michigan and married, then went west a second time in a wagon train. He mined, raised children, taught school, never settled, and spent his life on a migration in circles, driven as if by instinct, and suicidal at the end. He died in an unpainted shack on alkaline land near Silver Lake, Oregon. The supposedly wild lands and great cities of America were partly populated by relentlessly searching, uprooted people like him. And, as Annick forcefully points out, by immigrants like her own parents, who came from the Jewish culture of Hungary to Paris in the 1920s and moved on to Chicago before 1940, escaping oppression all the way, a very different, intensely family-centered people.

By the late nineteenth century, of the 1.5 billion humans on earth, around 80 million were on the move. Thirty-five million Europeans went to the Americas. Ten million went to Asia.

Fourteen million people shifted from homeland to homeland in Southeast Asia and eastern China. Two million Irish, escaping famine, went to the United States along with one and a half million Germans and 765,000 English. By 1990, 13 million people of Mexican/Indian origin were living in the United States. Between 1960 and 1980, about 67,000, mostly Jews, came to the United States from Israel. The last time I was in Oregon, many of the motels were owned and managed by immigrants from Pakistan.

This restlessness, despite tragic dislocations, is not deplorable. We in the United States have long defined ourselves as a melting pot, and we are increasingly multicultural. We can hope that intermixing cultures will eventually prove fatal to despotisms built on notions of racial and ethnic purity.

> Everything has been painted in Europe, everything has been sung in Europe. But not in America.
>
> —PABLO NERUDA

ON A LATE afternoon in the early summer of 1993, in the green hills above East Glacier Park, Montana, looking over the Great Plains from the foothills of the shining mountains at the edge of the Blackfoot Reservation, a crowd of us rode off to see the sights in a convoy of old top-down red Mercedes tour buses. We curved along two-track roads, in and out of aspen in white-barked groves. Calm sunlight played through the thunderclouds. A breeze swept waves across the deep grasses; we were passive and willing to be diverted.

Seminaked young horsemen hired off the Blackfoot Reservation materialized, silent and challenging in that first instant, as if they had always been waiting, their own paint matching that of their horses. It's difficult to express the degree to which I was transported, moved, taken—jarred out of my habitual irony—as they galloped away. However phony, the reenactment shocked me into witnessing a dream of the New World. I was willing, for a transported moment, to adore horseback glories.

JOHN COLTER'S snowy several-hundred-mile walk across the West is a defining American legend. The autumn and winter of 1807–1808, traveling through country no known white man had seen, Colter went from Fort Lisa, at the junction of the Big Horn River and the Yellowstone, down to Jackson Hole and the far side of the Tetons, then back through the steaming spectacles of what would become Yellowstone Park.

At 7,731 feet above sea level, nighttime temperatures on the banks of Lake Yellowstone in winter run to thirty and forty below zero, and snows are a dozen feet deep; but hot sulfur springs boil up, and the grass is still green beside them, snowbanks high above one's head. Bison drift through cold mist near a river where the trumpeter swans glide on glassy, steaming ponds.

Colter had been with Meriwether Lewis and William Clark when they climbed the long grade to Lemhi Pass on the Continental Divide, longing to see the headwaters of the Columbia, an easy route to the Pacific. Instead, they saw blue mountains, range after range, shadowing away west to the sky.

On an October afternoon in 1982, cruising highway passes at close to ten thousand feet through the San Juan Mountains in southwestern Colorado, a friend and I were hooting about how Colter would've walked over the pass. Imagining a raggedy man in greasy buckskins peering down from a cliff onto the vanities of upscale Telluride, then picturing him on ski-town streets like some skid-row refugee, we, in fact, were laughing at ourselves.

Studying a daylight moon over the Tetons, John Colter might have felt he was as close to the center of things as anyone ever had been, and privileged to be there. Colter represents that adventurous part of us which is at home everywhere, or so I like to think. I want to think he was running on wisdom and not just simpleminded courage, that he accepted his isolation as a version of what we always carry within us. I also hope I'll approach the final quarter hour before death with the assurance of this man walking off into the snowy unknown.

AROUND 100 B.C., people in the high valley of Mexico abandoned their farms and hamlets and moved to the great city of Teotihuacán (its population was eventually well in excess of 100,000), and built—in alignment with natural features—two of the largest pyramids in Mesoamerica. Those beginnings were likely repressive, since monumental building is usually evidence of conscripted labor. And there is evidence of human sacrifice.

But something soon changed at Teotihuacán. No more vast monuments were built; instead, they built apartment blocks where people could live in material comfort and security, without evidence of obeisance to a ruling class. Teotihuacán lasted 850 years. To endure so long, their elite—and no doubt there was one (there always is)—had to have made at least a convincing show of moral legitimacy and concern for collective values.

In this, Teotihuacán was unlike other great prehistoric urban gatherings, except for perhaps the Harappan culture in very ancient India. In *Teotihuacan: An Experiment in Living*, Esther Pasztory suggests that Teotihuacán embodies "a social ideal in which everyone participates and is 'lost' as an individual within a cosmic whole." Was this a good thing, or bad? It depends, of course, on the degree to which the individual was "lost." This interpretation, by a scholar who spent decades trying to fathom what happened there, resonates around the idea that Teotihuacán may have developed a culture centered on treating each citizen humanely, and that's heartening. Maybe ancient people in the valley of Mexico thought they were facing down darkness by living generously. Maybe they lived that way on purpose. Maybe they developed folkways and laws which demanded generosity. Or not. Nobody knows. Teotihuacán perished for unknown reasons around 750 A.D., and its culture seems to have been forgotten by the time of the Aztecs. Nothing remained but the mysterious, spooky ruins.

But in 1519, when the Spaniard Diego de Ordaz, accompanying Cortés, climbed Popocatepetl and gazed down onto a great lake where great white cities seemed to float more than a mile from shore, connected to one another and to gardens by causeways, he may have been seeing a reflection of Teotihuacán. Bernal Díaz del Castillo reported, "We were seeing things that had never been spoken of or seen, or even dreamed about."

In "The Destruction of Tenochtitlán," writing about the city on the lake, William Carlos Williams describes the gifts Montezuma sent the Spaniards: "A gold necklace of seven pieces, set with many gems like small rubies, a hundred and eighty-three emeralds and ten fine pearls, and hung with twenty-seven little bells of gold." The list goes on. "Four fishes, two ducks and some other birds of molten gold. Several fans of gold and silver mixed together, others of feathers only." When the two leaders finally met "Montezuma spoke: 'They have told you that I possess houses with walls of gold and many other things and that I am a god or make myself one. The houses you see are stone and lime and earth,'—then opening his robe: 'You see that I am composed of flesh and bone like yourselves and that I am mortal and palpable to the touch.' "

We give gifts; we can share the earth. But those gifts did not return in kind. Yearning for gold, which for the Spanish equaled power and destiny, Cortés attacked and reduced the natives to slavery, initiating a catastrophe.

Williams writes that the city's organization "evidenced an intellectual vigor full of resource and delicacy," a place "half land and half water," where "the streets were navigated by canoes" and you could buy "the skins of some birds of prey with their feathers, head, beak, and claws" and "nasturtium, leeks, artichokes, wine. There was an herb street, there were shops where they shaved and washed the head." Yet Williams says, "At the very breath of conquest it vanished."

Williams also describes another otherness, a white city where blood sacrifice was vehemently part of life. "Here it was that the tribe's deep feeling for a reality that stems back into the permanence of remote origins had its firm hold. It was the earthward thrust of their logic; blood and earth; the realization of their primal and continuous identity with the ground itself." This was not, surely, on William Carlos Williams's part, an endorsement of blood ceremony. In their directness, in what we imagine as innocence and willingness, Williams seems to be implying, the citizens of Tenochtitlán were exploring a possibility that no longer makes sense—to preserve the world through sacrifice ("making sacred").

But it's easy to be wrong here, and maybe Williams was. Perhaps the Aztec were simply hypnotized by the bloodiness and excitement. Maybe what happened was no more profound than bull fighting or bear baiting—sport as warfare—or, in this case, as religious enactment. Or perhaps it was no more than a demonstration of power.

In "The Passing Wisdom of Birds," Barry Lopez calls Tenochtitlán "The Aztec Byzantium." Throughout the city, Lopez says, "wild birds nested." Cortés burned them out. "The image of Cortés setting fire to the aviaries in Mexico City that June day in 1521 is an image I cannot rid myself of. It stands, in my mind, for a fundamental lapse of wisdom in the European conquest of America, an underlying trouble in which political conquest, greed, revenge, and national pride outweigh what is innocent, beautiful, serene, and defenseless—the birds."

"But Cortés's act can be transcended," Lopez continues. "It is possible to fix in the mind that heedless violence, the hysterical cries of the birds, the stench of death, to look it square in the face and say that there is more to us than this.

"Again, I think of the animals, because of the myriad ways in which they have helped us since we first regarded each other differently. They offered us early models of rectitude and determination in adversity, which we put into stories. The grace of a moving animal kindles still in us a sense of the Other.

"It is the birds' independence from predictable patterns of human design that draws us to them. In the birds' separate but related universe we are able to sense hope for ourselves."

EDUARDO GALEANO'S ignored masterpiece of reportage, *Memory of Fire,* is a retelling of conquest and settlement history in the Americas. In "1711: Paramaribo," Galeano writes that "the Dutch cut the Achilles tendon of a slave escaping for the first time, and one who makes a second try gets the right leg amputated; yet there is no way to stop the spreading plague of freedom in Surinam."

Galeano tells of blacks hung from iron hooks stuck through their ribs, of female slaves who escaped with quantities of rice, corn, bean, wheat, and squash seeds in their "enormous hairdos." Once they reach safety in the jungle, "the women shake their head and thus fertilize the free land."

Millions of natives and slaves died from work in unventilated underground shafts in the silver mines owned by the Spanish crown at Potosí, Bolivia, which, at 13,780 feet above sea level, tied with Lhasa as the world's highest city. By 1611, Potosí's population of 150,000 (including 6,000 black slaves) made it the largest city in the Americas, a great Christian city, rivaled in size only by London, Paris, and Seville. John Hemmings writes in the *Conquest of the Incas* that "Potosí had all the trappings of a Klondike or Las Vegas: fourteen dance halls, thirty-six gambling houses, seven or eight hundred professional gamblers, a theater, a hundred and twenty prostitutes, and dozens of baroque churches."

The mines at Potosí, the largest source of silver in the world, were worked by pre-Columbian methods. Excavating and maintaining each underground gallery was equal to constructing a cathedral. One-seventh of the male population on the Altiplano were conscripted, one year at a time, three weeks on and three weeks off. This provided about 13,500 laborers, more than half the workforce.

In 1670, according to Eduardo Galeano, Count Lemos, the viceroy of Peru, wrote to his king, "There is no people in the world so exhausted. I unburden my conscience to inform Your Majesty with due clarity: It is not silver that is brought to Spain, but the blood and sweat of Indians."

"The viceroy has seen the mountain that eats men," Galeano writes. "From the villages the men are brought in strung together with iron collars, and the more the mountain swallows, the more its hunger grows." Miners climbed down hundreds of ladders into darkness and narrow, asphyxiating tunnels, only to climb back out with sacks of ore on their backs. Count Lemos banned the practice of leaving miners underground for a week at a time, and in villages out on the mostly unroaded Altiplano the Aymara and Quechua cultures survived. At present, there are about 1 million Aymara speakers, and 3 million who, as the Inca did, speak Quechua.

In the Peruvian city of Puno, on the shores of Lake Titicaca, at 12,648 feet in elevation, and with ten times that number in population, Annick and I sat in white plastic chairs, sipping local beer and watching *folklorico* dancers in elaborate traditional garb (and some others besides, such as the young fellow in a green Spiderman costume sitting nearby on the curb, hungover and holding his head). The festivities were winding down after weeks of events starting around noon and running late into the night. Brass bands with dozens of very serious men playing great dented tubas followed the dancers as they moved through the thin afternoon sunlight and then through thronging crowds of peasants seasoned with a few tourists. Fighting off dysentery and altitude sickness, my head aching and body chilled, I found this fiesta excessively distant, and I mostly wanted to crawl into bed and dream some familiar dream.

Next evening, the bus to La Paz broke down after we'd spent the day on a boat crossing Lake Titicaca. As we waited for taxicabs to come rescue us, I looked out the window at a vast new settlement at the edge of the Altiplano. Alto La Paz is the fastest growing city in South America, with thousands coming each month to join the 600,000 people already living there. Women born in traditional villages carried plastic jugs of drinking water and enormous bundles of fabric—wares they'd been hawking to tourists—while walking home on miles of dusty tracks between dark adobe houses.

What if I'd had the wit and courage to get down from the bus and set off along those streets, begging water and food and a place to sleep? Would that have been simply foolish, or would I be wiser now, more comfortable with myself? Or robbed and left for dead? Or, more likely, would some kind soul have notified the police, who, after examining my passport, would have glumly hauled the disoriented foreigner to downtown La Paz and the room he had reserved in the elegant Hotel Plaza?

There, a couple of nights later, having shopped along the steep streets all afternoon, buying hats and fabrics to take home as presents, Annick and I stood looking out our windows at the lights of that city of a million as they tumbled down the canyon from the Altiplano. Then, secure in La Paz's modern conveniences, we watched on a big color TV set the live telecast of carnival dancers from Oruru, a cold and grim Bolivian silver-mining city some 150 miles to the south. These I could see, unlike those who'd danced directly before me in Puno; my filters were back in place; I could respond with my rational mind, and not with semifrightened and thus offended feelings. Men with cameras slipped among the dancers as they wove along cobbled streets that shone bright as daylight in the arc lamps set up for television. Drunks, indigenous and European alike, stumbled in the Bolivian night across the screen.

The February dances evolved in ceremonies on the Altiplano for hundreds of years. The carnival begins on the morning of the Saturday before Ash Wednesday, when over fifty dance companies of up to three hundred dancers stage an *entrada* along a five-kilometer route through Oruru. In the lead is a motorcade festooned with coins, embroidery, jewels, silverware, and banknotes—all to recall treasures offered to the sun on Inti Ramya, an Incan feast day, and the wealth of *el tio*, the uncle who lives in the mines. The dancers are followed by a procession called La Diablada, led by a condor, dancing bears, and apes. Lucifer and Satan, in red robes with serpents around their arms, and the archangel Michael, prance ahead of female demons in red wigs who represent China Supay, Lucifer's consort. Then come companies of masked dancers and brass bands. The *morenos*, or blacks, perform the Morenada in tribute to the African slaves who were led in chains to the mines at Potosí, wearing masks with protruding eyes and tongues, signs of approaching death due to altitude sickness and the terrible fatigue.

In these festivities, satire is obvious. But another purpose is religious: making peace with the devil for carrying treasure from his underworld, while also honoring the Quechua goddess of the earth, the Pachamama, who manifests herself through the mountains, wind, clouds, water, moon, sun, and sacred places; a beneficent deity, the generative source of life. According to Quechua belief, humans were created from land and are fraternally tied to all other beings who share the earth. Private ownership of land is a sin, since the earth is not to be exploited or commodified. Caring for the land is a prime way of respecting ourselves, and, since it can't be replaced, our duty. The Pachamama is sacred, the land is sacred, and we, her children, are sacred.

This ceremonial mix of wisdom and frivolity is, in my way of reckoning, a brilliant response. Regarding tribespeople who live out their lives on the Altiplano of Bolivia and Peru as "primitive" because of their powerlessness in the First World is an act of mindless arrogance.

In his study of Native American cultures in the American Southwest, *Pueblo: Mountain, Village, Dance*, the architectural historian Vincent Scully details ceremonial events still taking place each season in the plazas at Taos and Santo Domingo, San Felipe, at Zuñi pueblo, and in Hopi villages such as Walpi, and among the Mescalero Apache. The architecture of the pueblos forms the stage. Most pueblos contain kivas—ceremonial centers that symbolize the place where ancestors emerged from the earth—and are organized around plazas, which serve as dancing grounds. Hunting dances reflect the courting of the deer and buffalo, and corn dances honor fertility, while curing dances and snake dances, rain dances and snow dances court the benevolence of nature. The dancers respect no differences between nature and man. Snake and clouds, mountains and humans—all are living, all the same. The pueblo societies are humorous, sophisticated, and ironic. Their ceremonies feature clown figures—mudheads—whose responsibility is the belittling of participant and witness alike. Would it be a good idea to populate our legislatures with satirists in masks, whose job centers on saying unsayable things, with wit? Perhaps we could learn a great deal about the true value of power from ceremonies conducted by the powerless.

What I never saw: the mines at Potosí, where you can still climb down to the deep and dangerous levels inside Cerro Rico, the pink conical mountain that looms over the city, and visit independent miners in the narrow shafts where they work and inhale fumes. Their inevitable silicosis becomes incurable after fifteen years, at an averge age of thirty-five.

After the television was shut down that night on the seventh floor of the Hotel Plaza in La Paz, I was confounded by the grace and willingness shown by those dancers, and I spent a dark hour thinking my life had been squandered on trivialities. One part of the cure involved the breathing of my true love beside me.

MERIWETHER LEWIS and William Clark, instructed by Jefferson, were the first significant writers about the North American West. They attempted, as they traveled and wrote in their journals, to detail the possibilities of life in the vast unknown territories, and thus began defining a national purpose in that run of open country. They saw fertile bottomlands and multitudes of thriving creatures, and a yeoman nation for the taking, if the oncoming settlers were tough enough.

A series of artists journeyed up the Missouri in the nineteenth century, intent on portraying this dream. George Catlin and Karl Bodmer and John James Audubon saw what was taken to be an emptiness and found it inhabited by people who were at home with birds and animals, in numbers that exist nowhere on earth these days, except in the deepest jungles and, for another decade or so, in enclaves like the arctic marshlands near the mouth of the Yukon.

In a great Catlin vision of the prairies near the upper Missouri in 1832, fleeing buffalo and pursuing Indians intersect with pony soldiers riding two abreast, trailing across a simple and symbolic grassland rendered in a startling and, to me, unreal shade of green. But on an April morning, as Annick and I drove from Oklahoma City to the Gilcrease Museum in Tulsa, grass-covered mounds along the freeway were that exact shade. I'd thought Catlin's green was intended to be emblematic, rather than real. But he'd gotten it precisely right. I was happy, because I wanted to trust Catlin. His work reeks of pleasure within a land thick with creatures. The heaven of the Great Plains was real enough, even though often tragic, as with a blinded buffalo Catlin shows being dragged down by slaughtering wolves.

By 1832, Catlin saw that the prairies were not inexhaustible; he knew he was witnessing a final act, and he wrote:

> Nature has nowhere presented more beautiful and lovely scenes than those of the vast prairies of the West; and of man and beast no nobler specimens than those now inhabit them—the *Indian* and the *buffalo*—joint and original tenants of the soil, and fugitives together from the approach of civilized man; they have fled to the great plains of the West, and there, under an equal doom, they have taken up their *last abode,* where their races will expire, and their bones will bleach together.

Catlin then proposed

> a magnificent park, where the world could see for ages to come, the native American in his classic attire, galloping on his wild horse, with sinewy bow, and shield and lance, amid the fleeting herds of elks and buffaloes. What a beautiful and thrilling specimen for America to preserve and hold up to the view of her refined citizens and the world, in future ages! A *nation's park* containing man and beast, in all the world and freshness of their nature's beauty.

We might dismiss him as a racist, except for the utter particularity with which he drew and painted and thus valued the uniqueness of the Plains people. Complexities of great worth were vanishing, and he wanted to stop the going.

A year after Catlin, the German painter Karl Bodmer traveled upriver on the Missouri. He, too, encountered people given to elaborate self-decoration, which connected their tribal culture to vibrant glories, a savanna dreamscape of animals. In his watercolor of sights witnessed on July 14, 1833, below the mouth of the Milk River (*Landscape with Herd of Buffalo on the Upper Missouri*), both sky and hills are swirling and the buffalo seem eternal as they drink along the edges of the mud flats. In brush, a white wolf watches, life preparing to feed on life.

Ten years after Bodmer, John James Audubon was on the upper Missouri, an aging man weathering his grief. His beloved thronging world was dying. Worn out by decades of travel, Audubon found his heart broken. He had never flinched from shotgunning birds if they might serve as models for his work, but this time he had had enough. On August 5, 1843, Audubon wrote, "This cannot last. . . . Before many years the Buffalo, like the Great Auk, will have disappeared; surely this should not be permitted." Back home on the north end of Manhattan with his wife, Audubon became an old fellow, one who loved to plant hen's eggs under sofa cushions in the parlor. He delighted in ringing the dinner bell at off hours, just to see if anyone would come.

Military barbarians like the idiotic George Armstrong Custer, who got everything wrong just about every time, acted out our need to subjugate and bring reality to heel. In 1877, Chief Joseph and his Nez Perce, during their historic retreat, came upon tourists in Yellowstone Park.

Buffalo Bill Cody was a lifelong slaughtering and showboating child. In 1913, he made a film about the 1890 Ghost Dance massacre, at Wounded Knee, on the Pine Ridge Reservation in South Dakota, an attempt at reclaiming an innocence both boyish and rapacious. Maybe Cody thought the film was just another way to make a dollar, but I like to imagine that a man who killed so many buffalo imagined his homeland was a mother who would always take him back, no matter what—pretending, even to himself, that he was fundamentally incapable of final transgression. Frederick Turner, in *Beyond Geography,* says Buffalo Bill "developed a great fear of dying in the arena before hundreds of anonymous faces." Cody must have been sick of witnesses. In 1917, he was buried on a mountainside overlooking Denver, "a great city humming where once there had been nothing but a wild New World." Cody had made himself into an icon, the myth of conquest incarnate. Over seventeen hundred dime novels were written about him before he died. His life was public property—or more likely, an act of commerce.

ERNEST HEMINGWAY'S life is another cautionary tale, about frantic disappointment after great popular success, and the psychic poisons associated with trying to live with celebrity. Glory in early life leads people to think they own the ineffable. It's a tough act to keep going. Life became a contest, and Hemingway found his days uninhabitably difficult. Love does not often last without tending, and fame itself is pretty much useless.

Hemingway, after his death by self-inflicted gunshot in his house on a hill outside Ketchum, Idaho, in 1961, troubled me enormously. The suicide of a man whose work I revered made for piss-poor sleeping. Hemingway's love of fishing streams and oceans had not saved him. The solace I found in fishing— not so much from the hooking and killing and frying up as from the beauty of the creatures as they lived—wouldn't necessarily save me, either. There I was, aging toward the uneasy edges of the long run.

Things had already gone wrong for Hemingway by 1934, when he was thirty-three, living in the big house in Key West, paid for by Pauline's Uncle Gus, just as Gus had paid for the hunting safari in Africa. Hemingway began asking friends to call him "Papa," and his talk oozed of blood-sport bravado; he was also eager to look on while someone else killed bulls, obsessed with slaughter and the cynicism of the knowing. What he saw must have been deeply frightening.

Two years later, Hemingway wrote "The Snows of Kilimanjaro" and "The Short Happy Life of Francis Macomber," both of which can be understood as lamentations for lost honor and his well-lighted days on trout streams in Michigan, northern Spain, and Wyoming. Hemingway's late troubles may turn on the fact that he forgot the pleasures of exact listening and seeing. In the early Nick Adams stories, he celebrated the value of being utterly *in the moment,* aware that without immersion our lives turn secondhand and emotionally distant. Maybe he forgot, or maybe that immersion was irrecoverable. Maybe after 1934 the quicksilver (trout) behind appearances had mostly slipped away. What brought Hemingway to shotgun himself? I tried to imagine his thoughts as he held a cold weapon and looked out his window to a sagebrush hillside much like the one outside my window. I came to believe he was a fool for giving in to what I understood as despair over his own faithlessness. This was at a time when I thought I could write the book on faithlessness. As I see it now, I was trying to excuse myself by judging him.

How to avoid some metaphoric shotgunning of the self? F. Scott Fitzgerald, in *The Great Gatsby,* said "for a transitory enchanted moment man must have held his breath in the presence of this continent, compelled into aesthetic contemplation he neither understood nor desired, face to face for the last time in history with something commensurate to his capacity for wonder." Locate something commensurate, then give your life to it. I think that's the right idea.

William Faulkner, like Dickens, was obsessed by the idea of having been turned back from the door to the metaphoric manor house. But his stories about injustice and consequent rage ultimately cut through to an understanding that our values derive from connection with the rearing symbolic bear (call it freedom) in our wilderness.

Resonances reach way beyond the Deep South. Gabriel García Márquez's *One Hundred Years of Solitude* is another celebration of wildness and comes directly from Faulkner, as García Márquez acknowledged. Wallace Stegner said the American West would never have a literature until we had a "western" Faulkner. But we did; it was Faulkner.

In *The Bear,* Faulkner's novella about a man, Sam Fathers, who turns his back on killing, he characterized this refusal as a central act in the American drama of learning to acknowledge responsibility. Faulkner was delivering news that we're only recently coming to appreciate. Killing all the bears would be a start at killing ourselves.

Enduringly useful, Faulkner defines models of society that help people far removed from Yoknapatawpha County to see and name themselves; his stories are about redemptive repudiation of the fundamental longing to possess and enjoy the never-never-land continent in a quite sexual sense, and about rage at the injustice of being excluded from the great commons.

Hemingway, Fitzgerald, and Faulkner are iconographic New World figures from the Jazz Age, which goes on and on; we call it postmodernism. In their work, we see our relationship to the natural situation, thus to ourselves, becoming irrevocably fractured.

Norman Maclean tells how his family used trout fishing to both adore and define the world: "In my family there was no clear line between religion and fly fishing." Maclean ends on what he calls tragedy, his family's inability to define their relationship to the flowing world. His father loved Norman's brother, Paul, because his fishing seemed to connect him to the workings of deity, but he did not respect him so much when Paul "learned to think like a fish" and ended up going too wild.

Maclean's father thought Paul should be at least as readable as a run of articulate fly-fishing water; his mother knew better. Maclean writes that after Paul died, she retired alone to her bedroom, isolated in her grief. Most likely, she wanted her son back, never mind the religious theorizing.

AS FIRST SEEN by Europeans, the Americas appeared somewhat extraterrestrial. Octavio Paz says that we "ought to rather speak of the *invention* of America than of its discovery. America never was, and *it is only if it is utopia,* history on its way to a golden age." America was and is and will be a weave of redreaming. "America is the dream of Europe, now free of European history, free of the burden of tradition."

Carolyn Merchant, one of our preeminent feminist environmental historians, writes of America in terms of an "agricultural origins story," about our fall from innocence and grace, and the chance of regeneration and restoration of health. "The recovery plot is the long, slow process of returning humans to the Garden of Eden through labor in the earth." She says "the long-term goal has been to turn the earth itself into a vast cultivated garden . . . the transformation of undeveloped nature into a state of civility and order."

Merchant states, "In America the recovery narrative pro-

pelled settlement and 'improvement' of the American continent by Europeans." Ours is a story about travelers redefining
themselves by settling in and cultivating a homeland garden.
But it's also ordinary to think of America as a last, once-upon-
a-recent-time unplowed island that has been transmogrified
by European settlers so needy that they were forced to heedlessness. Yearning for an example of innocence, we want to think
of America, before settlement, as untrammeled by man. This is
ridiculous. Huge expanses in America were managed like a
native garden by indigenous peoples. But Europeans needed to
call it wilderness, unclaimed, so as to claim it. America was their
safety valve, too, where the poor and disenfranchised could
escape, in which they might suffer isolation but could triumph
through perseverance. Always, the reimagining.

For Europeans, unmarked Americas were a mirror in
which they hoped to observe the working out of ideas, a final
untouched place where possibility might live unfettered, as
well as a hideout for runaway impulses, where people might
recover, where dreams could be repossessed. America might be
innocence for the taking, it was thought, the perfectable homeland. Surely as any river, we exist in movement.

It's no accident our stories so often turn on hitting the road,
riding into the sunset, lighting out for the territories, going to
sea, leaving loved ones by setting off to find a new self, while at
the same time shouldering the sadness of never getting back,
aging all the while toward death. We run to the mountains and
the sea, to sports and whiskey and work while fleeing our insistent hometown selves.

My mother's parents were as good to me as anyone ever has
been. When I was six years old and recovering from polio in
their house on Jefferson Street in Klamath Falls, across from
the Catholic Academy, they read *Robinson Crusoe* aloud to me.

These were not people who kept books in the house; and this story, too complex for a child, led them into endless explanations. What was it they were trying to give me?

Maybe they understood this story as the adventure of a man who was stranded and survived, an escape fantasy. My grandfather ran from home in Wisconsin at the age of fourteen to the reckless and hard-hearted mining town of Butte, where they put him at a forge, resharpening tools—picks and crowbars—used in the deep-shaft mines, training to be a blacksmith, his work for the rest of his life. "I was lucky," he said; "I was too young for the mines."

Did my grandparents intuit that Crusoe's story would instruct me about the survival value of America's imperatively self-reliant individualism, from Emerson to Huck Finn to *On the Road?* Could be. First- and second-generation émigrés had shown they were willing to change lives without looking back very much, even at the cost of emotional isolation. It wasn't that my grandfather was an adventurer; at thirty, he settled and married. But as a child, trapped on his father's farm with brothers and sisters he never, to my knowledge, spoke of or saw again, he'd felt he had no other choice but to escape. However fearful or sorrowful, he'd made his move.

But homeboys like me sat tight as chickens on a roost. My grandfather hated my cautiousness. "Christ Almighty," he once said, when I was about ten and we were batching for an evening, "can't you even cook for yourself?" What was wrong with me?

Part Three

Commodification

M Y FATHER was known for his fairness as well as his drinking and skills at the poker table. "Playing with Oscar," one of his friends told me, "you were with one of the boys who made up the game." For him, most of the time, life was easiest to think about if considered a sport, with clear rules. Its inherent unfairness was best ignored.

Families like ours—not only men like my father but also women like my mother, who spent years in Republican politics, and my aunt Viola, who rode on horseback to work with the cowhands many mornings of her life—considered themselves an aristocracy. I still see people like them in the Salt Lake City airport, distant land-rich millionaires in dusty Levi's among skiers with peacock feathers in the bands of their cowboy hats. (The other aristocracy I see in that airport are men and women wearing silver and gold Champion of the World rodeo buckles. Whatever you think of rodeos, those were courageously earned.) A ranch like ours was a fiefdom, a plantation pretending to function as a community. In eastern Oregon, the people who owned the land called all the shots.

Men representing the rangeland livestock business went to the United States Senate and promoted legislation designed to pump federal money into the West. They worked to authorize great dams and irrigation projects, to finagle clear-cut logging and cheap grazing fees for sheep and cattle on Forest Service and Bureau of Land Management properties; they voted to subsidize the economic lives of their people, and argued that their main interest was in preserving a lifestyle.

Theirs were the families that had won at the game of accumulation in the great West; and since their forebears had survived through terrible winters and summertime desolations on salt-grass ranches, they thought they'd earned those rights and powers. Now their time is ending, and they hate it, as any sensible person would, as my own people did.

The folk in my family seemed fearful of intimacy, and of any hint of discussing their lives in private, much less in public. As a result, many of them were doomed never to understand themselves. In the West, high individualism is taken to be an end in itself and considered absolutely invaluable. It is understood that the people who came west were adventurous and imaginative sorts and moved to conduct themselves as they saw fit, without apology. Westerners so often act as if pride is worth more than any softhearted thing. They like to regard themselves as emotionally invulnerable. (Who wouldn't?) But most of us have better sense. Results, in the West, have involved a drift toward isolation and pickup-truck wandering and sad yearnings to own a beloved childhood or lost lover, if only in recollection while listening to country-and-western music on a jukebox. It's a drama I spent a lot of time acting out in my country days.

Xenophobia—fear of strangers, or at least deep-seated mistrust—is endemic. My family took care of their own but had no time for sympathy or handouts. They despised the weak—for instance, anyone who talked too much. Certain that their ambitions were profound, they took great risks to realize them, without complaint. Bad luck or judgment was taken to be part of the game; however, failures of nerve, like uncontrolled drinking, were understood to be deadly.

It's easy to fault men like my father for lacking humanity. He had no use for the unemployed, but the men who worked for him stayed; he loaned them money, bought them whiskey, hired them back after the drunk was run, though he never allowed for an instant that they were his equals. He loved two fine women but believed women had no place in politics and should never have been given the vote. "They're not fit for it," he would say, smiling, yet not altogether joking. As he saw it, women played a different, more compassionate game, living by the rules of wife and mother—chiefly, generosity and compassion. Those were necessary rules in the house, but disastrous in business and politics, where only power—never love—always trumped.

This, like any argument intent on preserving prerogatives, is so easy to disdain that we're in danger of forgetting the virtues that also came west with those people at a time when theirs was the radical energy loose in the land. They brought intelligence and force of will to the task of realizing independence, and they believed absolutely in the nonnegotiable value of individualism, understanding freedom as the source of possibility. Those are hard notions to fault. They yearned for an inviolable homeland, as we all do. Some of them, for a while, thought they'd found it.

Men like my grandfather and father believed the world was made to be used, and could be owned, that property, including the family, was a source of identity. But those beliefs betrayed them. While continuing to think of themselves as horsemen, they became settlers, farmers, and card-carrying party-line members of an economic establishment. They joked about the uselessness of city lives but appeared on horseback only for ceremonial occasions like the Lakeview Rodeo, ordinarily riding around in Cadillacs, on paved roads, instead.

LISTENING TO workingmen in the West, I learned to think justice was a nonsensical idea. No matter how good or how true you might stay, you would get yours. This, I think, was a brokenhearted acceptance of defeat, which they used as a shield. Lots of us out there worked hard at the art of forgetting; it was a route toward excusing irresponsibility.

As I was raised, nothing was abstractly political. We worried about business, the cost of things, and income derived from selling fat cattle. We were furious about taxes of any sort and sinking cow prices, and we fought over water rights.

On the other hand, *everything* was political. The divisions that counted were between propertied and not, between rich and poor. In Warner, there was a clear division between my people, who were all, as a matter of course, Republicans, and the majority of other ranchers, who were Irish Catholics from County Cork, some of whom maybe voted the Democratic ticket. But the politics that counted were local. Our newspaper was the county weekly. We got our national news from the radio and eventually a single channel of television, and it seemed like reportage from another planet.

If you wanted to be involved in public life, you could start by running for a local school board and then step up to a run for county commissioner, and if you won that office, you got to oversee expenditure of local taxes, a practical responsibility. My father ran for the Oregon state senate, encouraged by both my

mother and the powerful friends—many of them politicians—
he ran with in the Shrine, men who came to Warner in the
fall for the bird hunting. They thought he would be a natural, exactly the sort of man who ought to be running public business. Men like him had been ruling the West for a
century, some, in absentia, from Washington, D.C. Some
still are.

But my father thought he was reaching above himself, and
that doing so was damned foolish. I think he felt fated to lose,
believing that he came from too deep in the sticks. Government, he thought, was best left to lawyers, who'd mastered the
intricacies of adversarial negotiation. When he lost, he was
relieved.

"It would have been going to jail." His allegiances, however
he disguised them, were centered in the end on independence.
For that, I honor him.

Wherever there were tyrants, their habit of providing simply
for themselves, of looking solely to their personal comfort
and family aggrandizement, made safety the main aim of their
policy, and prevented anything great proceeding from them.

—THUCYDIDES, *History of the Peloponnesian War*

Wealth is evidently not the good we are seeking; for it is
merely useful and for the sake of something else.

—ARISTOTLE, *Nichomachean Ethics*

Question asked of a manager in the Japanese whaling industry: "How many whales would you like to harvest?"

Answer (as close as I can recall, although I didn't make it
up): "The best way to amortize our investment, obviously,
would be to harvest them all."

HUNTING AND GATHERING is essentially a taking. So is everything else we do to feed ourselves. Business involves hegemonies, uses, and subsequent disenfranchisements. Commodification is as old as prostitution.

Around A.D. 1300, European cities began constructing huge mechanical clocks on towers. The result was a profound change in ordinary citizens' awareness of time; their days and work were increasingly ordered. Time was no longer flexible, expanding or contracting like an accordion as emotions ran hot or cold, but ticked along like a relentless metronome, passing in measurable quantities. Inefficient use of time began to be considered a serious failure.

Clocks were followed by reliable calendars and maps; the adoption of Arabic numerals and plus and minus signs; the use of mathematical variables and the Arabic idea of zero; and the development of a system of notation for music, and of perspective in painting, of spaces and punctuation and capitalization in written texts, and of double-entry bookkeeping. Mathematics and science are procedures and tools used to understand, measure, and manipulate physical causes and their effects, and their use gave the users enormous accumulating power. As a consequence, the mechanical reality described by Descartes and Isaac Newton—forces in motion, moving in quantifiable, categorized, and predictable ways—began to be understood as the only valid metaphor for actuality.

By simple extension, free-market capitalism was conceptualized as a system of forces in motion. Europeans taught themselves to believe anything that cannot be priced is without worth. Values like compassion and empathy, unquantifiable and therefore impossible to commodify, began to seem archaic, maybe unreal. In this system, stones and ironwork are objects, measurable and to be acted upon. We, at least the privileged among us, are not. But slaves necessarily had to be defined as objects so their owners could use them as they saw fit, with no reason for remorse. Indigenous people and the poor have usually fallen somewhere in between.

There were alternatives. In early medieval times, Saint Francis led thousands to dedicate their lives to care of the sick and poor, embracing and sharing the vast poverty. But such good works and sympathy did not, literally, add up.

European civilization could have infused the values of commerce with the humane vision of Saint Francis, but instead, it chose to think of ownership and trade as mechanistic relationships, and of work as yet another measurable economic object.

Capitalist ideology begins with the notion that acquisitiveness—bettering the self by acquiring possessions—is our main motivation to produce goods and services. We are likely to be better fed, more secure, and happier, according to this theory, in direct relation to our success as accumulating individuals. This is partly true, obviously, but it ignores the joy many find in working on behalf of fellow citizens or some particular environment. Cultures cannot afford programmatic selfishness. History has taught that lesson a good many times.

Economic theories do not so much describe phenomena as outline systems. Capitalist, socialist, or Communist ideas are defining stories told in service of a particular version of the world. Economic ideologies, at least in their so-called pure forms—mutual ownership of wealth, or everybody-for-themselves venture capitalism—have turned out to be universally impractical and unworkable; each limits liberty in ways that foment class-based despotism and injustice. Cultures will not put up with even partly pure systems for more than a couple of generations, as life is too fluid and complex to fit inside the theories. As international financier Georg Soros wrote,

"Economic theory is an axiomatic system: as long as the basic assumptions hold, the conclusions follow. But when we examine the assumptions closely, we find that they do not apply to the real world."

In *The Wealth of Nations*, Adam Smith wrote of an "obvious and simple system of natural liberty," in which "every man, as long as he does not violate the laws of justice, is left perfectly free to pursue his own interest in his own way." That is indeed an admirable ideal, but "pure" capitalism (unrestricted speculation) breeds disregard for caretaking and fairness, and it seldom serves the wider interests of society. Also, as Smith wrote, justice requires the "protection" of both property and "every member of society from the oppression of every other member of it." It seems reasonable to suppose that he was talking not only about oppressive individuals but also about oppressive citizens operating together as a corporation.

The wealthiest 20 percent of the population living in developed countries presently controls 86 percent of the world's gross domestic product, while the poorest 20 percent controls 1 percent. Of course, to many minds, this is not such a terrible thing. Many successful people prefer life in enclaves, where they are insulated against cultural perplexity, but where they are also in a psychic jail.

The predominant source of cultural unity in the last several centuries has been nationalism, and city-states and nations have been bases from which to strike in the interest of accumulating wealth and power. We incorporate despotisms. This was true in Venice, and under the rule of medieval popes, and it remains true today. The will to power takes many forms, but in the working out, it is quite predictable. Any social system is in essence repressive. Someone has to run things, and power, as has been so famously said, corrupts.

Bureaucracies are inherently self-perpetuating and ensure their continuity by courting the powerful. But they are not particularly responsive to the needs of the disenfranchised. The rich get richer as society becomes increasingly exclusionary, elitist, and nondemocractic. Only by resisting injustice can a society—whatever its economic and public organization— keep from turning ever more coercive.

Colonialist nations such as England, France, Spain, Holland, Belgium, Russia, and the United States, intent on reaping wealth the world over, chartered syndicates to occupy and develop commerce and trade. British settlement of North America was facilitated by the commercial efforts of the Virginia Company (1606) and the New England Company (1628), and the first fortune won in the United States was that of John Jacob Astor through the American Fur Company (1808). Later economic development was facilitated by canal corporations subsidized by various state governments and by railroad corporations subsidized by the federal government with 130 million acres of timberland ultimately logged by Weyerhauser, Potlatch, and Boise Cascade. Until the Civil War, corporations were tools used by nations in serving their needs. Their charters could be, and occasionally were, revoked. Only secondarily were they considered machines to create personal wealth.

But that relationship began to change with the discovery of oil and the innovations that drove the electrical, petrochemical, and automotive industries. Westinghouse (1866), Standard Oil (1870), Atlantic Richfield (1870), Carnegie Steel (1873), Scott Paper (1879), Exxon (1882), Mobil (1882), American Telephone & Telegraph (1885), Johnson and Johnson (1887), Dow Chemical (1893), Amoco (1889), General Electric (1892), International Paper (1898), Bristol-Myers (1900), Weyerhauser (1900), U.S. Steel (1901), Texaco (1902), Du Pont (1902), Ford Motor Company (1903), General Motors (1908), Union Carbide (1917), Allied Chemical (1920)—all these are names that resonate in American life. Corporations have long been thought essential to the nation's economic prosperity. And maybe they are, as it is presently understood. But they are also profoundly anti-democracratic.

In the 1940s, in *Inside USA*, John Gunther wrote that it was key to America's future that the power of corporations be reconciled with service to the public good. After the Great Depression, power increasingly shifted from the nation to these economic entities; since World War II, the corporate tail has been wagging the national dog.

The de facto United States government is now a consortium of state and federal officials and agencies, some elected but many not, an oligarchy of Fortune 500 companies and media and entertainment syndicates, research universities, law firms, and the military establishment. This consortium controls capital, oversees manufacturing, builds our cities, sets prices, shapes our landscape and our lives.

Corporations tend to serve one another's needs, in that each is committed to open markets and opposed to supervision or restraint by humanist or environmental interests; they exist in order to accumulate wealth through power. (And sometimes power is the primary objective.) They have again and again proven willing to corrupt governments; they cooperate with nations to create and exploit markets, but they are quite open to playing one nation against another—"Give us a tax break or we'll move to China." Then, despite the tax break, they move their production facilities to Indonesia or Mexico, where labor comes cheaper. It's a matter of economics, stupid. Meanwhile, they don't suffer the expense of protecting their interests with standing armies (a service provided free of charge by host nations).

Many corporations are economically more powerful than nations. General Motors's sales equal the gross national product of Denmark; Ford's are roughly the equivalent of the South Africa GNP; Toyota's sales equal Norway's GNP; Wal-Mart turns about as many dollars as the economy of Argentina; Microsoft's equal the GNP of Spain; and those of American Express equal the GNP of New Zealand. According to *Fortune,* the world's five hundred largest corporations had assets worth $34 trillion in 1997, brought in $452 billion of profits on $11.3 trillion of revenues, and employed 36.8 million people. The three hundred largest corporations control more than 25 percent of the planet's productive assets, and sales of the largest two hundred constitute about 25 percent of all economic activity. A consortium could have an economic reach far beyond that of any nation, including the United States. And, increasingly, they seem intent on teaming up.

Citizens other than stockholders have little voice in selecting corporate officers, as corporations operate as much as possible in secret. Because they own most of the major media around the world, their activities are consistently underreported. Corporate power went unmentioned by the major U.S. presidential candidates during the 1996 election. This obscurity makes it easier for corporations to pursue a wide range of activities, without concern for citizens anywhere, except for their stockholders. Definitions of responsibility focused almost entirely on profits have often, obviously, led to the destruction of environments along with the exploitation of the so-called underclasses, in the Third World and everywhere else.

Managers in this international network of production and distribution and money-managing institutions are not braindead. They know as much about morality as any citizen, but they are "liberated" from responsibility by an ideology that doesn't require answers to questions about environmental sustainability or justice. The entities they run are self-interest communities, required by law to be as profitable as possible. Since material progress is defined as humankind's practical goal, the creation of wealth is considered a civic duty; bottom lines are sometimes taken to be reports on social health and vitality.

As cultures become increasingly interwoven, with social chaos erupting on all sides, the need for a worldwide system of economic control and oversight has become urgent to First World nations and corporations. The notion of globalization is a front for this agenda. While linking communities around the world so as to share powers and insights is a quite legitimate humanist project, major nations and transnational corporations have transmogrified the idea into a device useful in their efforts to gather power and subsequent wealth for themselves.

At Bretton Woods in 1944, the World Bank and the International Monetary Fund were created—to fund development projects around the world and, second, to ensure the stability of worldwide lending. In 1967, a General Agreement on Tariffs and Trade (GATT) was approved by a consortium of nations, and in 1995, GATT was transformed into the World Trade Organization, in which corporate traders were excused from national oversight and thus encouraged to deal freely around the world. This, of course, was more of a codification of existing conditions than a reorganization.

It's inarguable that long-term humanitarian interests everywhere on earth would be served by spreading the wealth around. Only if Third World economies are responsibly involved in a worldwide system of trade—it's argued by corporate CEOs and their economists, and by chiefs of state—can they become capable, prosperous players in the international, market-driven game. Sounds great. Trouble is, it doesn't work, except maybe in some very long run. Instead, the wealthy are increasingly insulated from the rest of society, getting richer and less inclined toward social responsibility.

The World Bank has a history of promoting the interests of the corporate entities which became the managers of economies in Africa, Asia, and South America after such colonialist European nations as France, Holland, Germany, Belgium, and England were forced out. The result has been another version of colonialism. After some $300 billion in loans to "developing" nations, the economic distance between the First World and the Third World is greater than ever. In 1999, one-fifth of the world's population living in high-income countries controlled 86 percent of the world's gross domestic product, 82 percent of the world's export markets, 68 percent of foreign investment, and 74 percent of telecommunications.

The World Bank paid for huge dams, but they failed to provide Third World citizens with cheap irrigation water or electric power, though their construction did force millions of poor people to relocate, which even a World Bank anthropologist admitted is "next to killing them." Societal and environmental costs have been overwhelming. The World Bank loaned India billions to build coal-fired power plants not equipped for desulfurization, and the nitrous gases, carbon dioxide, and sulfur released into the atmosphere constitute what the Environmental Defense Fund calls "the biggest single source of new greenhouse gas emissions on Earth." In *Masters of Illusion: The World Bank and the Poverty of Nations,* Catherine Caulfield reports the bank's disdain for field knowledge and tendency to favor "strong" despotic governments able to act out unpopular programs. Funds often end up with corporations rather than with Third World nations or their citizens. The ordinary line of transmission runs from "Washington to Pennsylvania, where they manufacture the turbines, or Frankfurt, where they produce the dredging equipment."

The International Monetary Fund works to manage economies in order to create a stable floor under world trade, attaching conditions to their loans in order to prevent debtor nations from defaulting. In essence, these conditions constitute austerity programs, forcing nations to cut spending on health, education, and welfare, as well as subsidies for agriculture, energy, and transportation; to devalue local currencies; to raise interest rates in order to attract foreign investment; and to privatize state properties and lower barriers on foreign ownership of land and industries. These measures obviously weaken the position of locals in their dealings with the institutions they must borrow from. And they undermine any possibility of social development. As Amartya Sen, winner of the Nobel Prize for Economic Science for 1998, points out in *Freedom as Development,* nations with an illiterate and unhealthy populace almost always fail politically and economically. Then, as we've seen, chaos up and down the streets and in the fields and marketplaces often ensues—just what the World Bank and the IMF say they've been working so hard to prevent.

Good work, in most bureaucratic circles, corporate or governmental, is understood to be an activity much like warfare, problem solving driven by authoritarian rhetoric. Yet millions of poor people are increasingly disenfranchised, their lives more and more denuded. Officers at the World Bank, the International Monetary Fund, and the World Trade Organization—with support from the World Business Council for Sustainable Development, the World Industry Council for the Environment, the International Organization for Standardization, and the International Chamber of Commerce—determine to a considerable degree who prospers, which ecosystems and cultures flourish, and which perish.

Most of us have never heard the names of the CEOs and bureaucratic managers whose decisions have led to the extinction of so many creatures, indigenous cultures, and languages. Nor is it likely, if we continue with this antidemocractic distribution of powers, that citizens anywhere will ever be allowed a vote on these matters. The list of problems this process has created, and which its architects are now trying to sweep under various rugs, is nearly endless—nuclear waste, destruction of the ozone layer, loss of rain forests and fisheries, acid rain, overgrazing and desertification, and working and living conditions amounting to human rights violations. This record is unforgivable—the wealthy trashing the world while feathering their own nests. For the rest us to continue allowing it is to be brain-dead.

Corporations are consortiums claiming the rights of individuals. In the Supreme Court decision *Santa Clara County vs. Southern Pacific Railroad,* handed down in 1886, justices ruled that a private corporation was a "natural person" and entitled to protection under the Bill of Rights. Justice William O. Douglas declared it a decision that "could not be supported by history, logic, or reason." Corporations are not individuals; rather, they are entities designed to manage economic assets for profit. Unlike people, they owe no natural allegiances, not to bioregions, ethnic groups, indigenous peoples, or nations. They do not weep or sorrow, or fall in love. Acknowledging moral obligations only when their irresponsibility affects economic performance, they range the world like predators. We are their prey, and will be until we start defending ourselves.

How? For openers, put an end to the fiction that *corporations* are entitled to the rights of *people,* and enact campaign-finance reforms that will not allow them to subvert our politics. People get to vote, and money does not, under any circumstance, share that privilege. Eliminate direct corporate subsidies and recover through fees and taxes indirect costs such as those resulting from the poisoning of soils with pesticide use or storage of radioactive materials. Charge for the depletion of irreplaceable public resources like aquifers and worldwide petroleum reserves. And, most important, break up monopolies. Those are a few of the things we could do.

There's little doubt we're evolving into a world society. If it's not going to be both repressive and ultimately incapable of sustaining life, this society will consist of a thick and complex mix of evolving local cultures coexisting inside a wide variety of healthy ecosystems. Humans cannot escape their situation on earth in any foreseeable future. Mutual support is our only hope. Corporations will no doubt take part in that future, but we must insist they participate as full partners, devoting themselves to promoting justice and to putting a stop to starvation and environmental ruin, and help pay for first-rate health care and education around the world. Meanwhile, we don't have to buy the tasteless rock-hard tomatoes produced by agribusiness. We can grow better ones in our own backyards.

Most fundamentally, we must insist that the business of business is not moneymaking but servicing people and cultures and the ecologies upon which they depend. Otherwise, as I heard a man say in Butte, "Don't take Mr. Einstein to see where this road goes."

> I attach too little value to things I possess, just because I possess them and overvalue anything that is strange, absent, and not mine.
>
> —MONTAIGNE

> The dynamic of deprivation is at the heart of expanding consumption: purchase brought momentary satisfaction, followed by dissatisfaction and renewed longing.
>
> —JACKSON LEARS, *Fables of Abundance*

CERTAIN BIRDS in Japan are considered to be Buddhists, a notion perhaps originating with legends holding that the first beings were self-luminous, subsisted on joy, and flew freely in the skies until greed entered their minds.

Visiting in the Alaskan fishing town of Sitka, standing on a porch in front of a house perched over the sea in the sun of a June afternoon, waves sloshing below us, I heard a mountaineer say, "We've become consumers of experience."

In Montana, I see a sign saying TAVERN and go inside with an idea of what to expect. Traveling in France, at a hotel displaying three stars, I enter knowing what sort of room I'll find.

As anyone knows, however, advertisers are given to duplicity and prey on weakness; this institutionalized lying is designed to create desire where it did not exist by promising solace. I buy books, maps, and music, thinking I can purchase my way past an occasional descent into malaise; but it doesn't work in any enduring sense.

Teaching at the University of Montana, I would ask students to drive the strip through Missoula, studying billboards and listening to commercial radio. Their job was to count the number of times they thought they'd been lied to and tell me what it meant to them. Most hated the assignment, and I couldn't blame them. What comfort is found in the idea that we're incessantly tricked by powerful entities?

Visiting Key West, Annick and I wandered the main tourist-trap drag along Duval Street, which was thick with T-shirt shops and people wearing shirts with printed messages front and back, and buying more. David Quammen, talking about his journeys while researching island bioregions for his brilliant study *The Song of the Dodo,* had told us of getting off a riverboat in the backlands jungle of New Guinea: "The first thing I saw was a boy wearing nothing but a Wonder Bread T-shirt." Messages on T-shirts travel because of yearnings. People on New Guinea or in Key West want some link to the greater world, and wearing a famous advertisement may help them ignore their defeats. They want to hook up with power, to imagine being Michael Jordan and just do it.

Advertising creates desire by connecting products—new shirts defined as a first step toward a new personality, as with Gatsby—to imagined or real needs. Ads remind us that we are incomplete, then tell us we'd be whole if only we had a BMW or a face-lift or a bottle of microbrewery beer. Advertising gives us an entryway into dreams, and we become virtual tourists in a version of the world most of us can't actually inhabit—life in a story of opulence, starring ourselves.

Defining ourselves through the acquisition of "things" is inherently an endless process. We can never get enough of that wonderful stuff, whatever it is, new shoes or promiscuous kisses. Spending money becomes an erotic act—like sex, an act of self-completion—a transformative act if you want to become a new someone else, not so fragile or vulnerable. But as new shoes wear out, even the finest wines generate an occasional hangover. Maybe, if I want to assure an attractive new identity, I should try skins—a sable coat, say, as a disguise. In college, I began smoking cigarettes, and I listened to *Jazz at the Philharmonic*, yearning to be cool.

To an enormous extent, world economies are based on created desire. A fundamental tool advertisers use is a two-hearted sort of joke. All right, the joke goes, let's admit by throwing up our hands that the system is absolutely fucked. Thus, semihumorously, we embrace our powerlessness. Participating in that joke, whether as buyer or seller, helps us escape our moral culpability for the commonplace chicken-shit irresponsibility we encounter at about every economic level these days. Protest is sold as style. Disdain for commodification is commodified in the "Kerouacking of America." Hate oppression? Why not express your allegiances by cross-dressing, by pretending, by wearing logger boots and bib overalls in imitation of working-class people who have no choice in their duds?

We tend to think of actors and basketball stars as machinery, which can be customized, advertised, and sold. Ads for athletic shoes center on flying above the crowd. Athletes who star in them are understood to be heroes. What if those heroes spoke out about the degraded circumstances in which Third World citizens labor to produce the shoes? If those hugely rich runners and leapers appeared in television commercials, talking about impugning that exploitative system, would they be admired for their honesty or be written off as crazy, a laughingstock, and would someone take away their endorsements? Would that spell the end of their heroism?

We live in what's called "an image revolution." Arguments are made by showing pictures, since literacy rates are falling and nonverbal citizens are said to have trouble with abstract thinking, much less reading. Advertising treats us all as consumers capable of knowing only immediate and envisioned desires, which the agencies invent and drum into us with image-centered promotions. And it works. Its images crosscut in an ironic smart-assed game, as hip as any art. We're even asked to vote for the best new ads during the Super Bowl broadcast. And besides entertaining us, they swing in the cultural air and must therefore be meaningful, so we ought to pay attention. Isn't that the message? Advertising encourages us to inhabit a virtual world in which items on sale are important as components in the process of individual and social self-definition. Most of us invariably submit to manipulation, naming ourselves through repetitive acts. I don't order gin; I order Bombay. Society becomes increasingly mechanical, and it's easy to get into the habit of identifying ourselves through a kinship to automobiles or soup cans or brands of whiskey. *This fella loves his Willie Nelson and his Dodge Ram and his George Dickle.*

Jabber and fleeting images sell us things we mostly don't need, thus serving the purposes of the empowered sellers. We laugh and wonder whether to go to a movie, have a few drinks, or go shopping, whatever. Through our acts, we acquiesce, at once powerless, used, and complicit. We know these things, yet seldom do we deviate or protest. I don't know what else to do, so I buy in.

Terrible things can result. People demand the right to transform social reality into dreamscapes of their own invention. Too much lying and too radical a retreat from actuality and you can lose track of the difference between what you really think and what you're told, and then you're easy prey to ideologies of estrangement and purity, such as Nazism.

George Steiner, in an essay entitled "The Hollow Miracle," writes of "the collapse of the German language into Nazi jargon . . . called upon to enforce innumerable falsehoods, to persuade the Germans that the war was just and everywhere victorious. As defeat began closing in on the thousand-year Reich, the lies thickened into a constant snowdrift . . . into a frantic blizzard."

Languages can decay and die. Once the language that people use to tell themselves the story of who they are is debased, all sense of self is likewise debased. People become less than they were. Having allowed themselves to be swallowed by the lying, they often turn cynical, and their sweetness dissolves.

Unless we trust one another, our social possibilities melt. Nez Perce used to say that lying becomes more and more dangerous as the liar becomes the lie. The trickster sells himself his own bill of goods.

As consumers, we often think as babies, with no responsibilities except to our own insecurities and desires. I buy an elegant cashmere sweater in Florence and for a few moments am puffed up with respect for the person who owns it. Can I afford first-rate scotch, or what?

> . . . the absolute absence of a burden causes man to be lighter than air, to soar into the heights, take leave of earth and from his earthly being, and become only half real, his movements as free as they are insignificant.
>
> —MILAN KUNDERA, *The Unbearable Lightness of Being*

> The City is thus a sheepfold imposed over a Garden.
>
> —BRUCE CHATWIN, *The Songlines*

IN *Delirious New York,* R. E. M. Koolhaas says the first act in the creation of high-rise cities, which took place in Manhattan, was the decision to build on a rectilinear grid. The next was the invention of the Otis elevator, which lifted people and goods to heights no one would attempt by stairway on any regular basis, to living and work spaces stacked atop the grid in skyscrapers hung on steel skeletons. A "man-made Wild West, *a frontier in the sky,*" Koolhaas called it.

"Each block can now turn into a self-contained enclave of the irresistably Synthetic."

One result was urban isolation. "No longer does the city consist of a more or less homogenous texture—a mosaic of complementary fragments—but each block is now *alone* like an island, fundamentally on its own. . . . Manhattan turns into a dry archipelago of blocks."

Using bridges and watercraft, the Venetians wove islands into an emotional whole. In Manhattan, signs of irregularity and nature mostly vanished into a real estate merchant's dream of ever-increasing stacked space. Creatures, except for cockroaches, rats, and thronging pigeons and the peregrine falcons nesting on man-made cliffs above the traffic, were eliminated. The result might have been a stern, relentless efficiency. But it wasn't, thank God. The planners couldn't root out playfulness.

People want gaming. In Manhattan, some of the well-to-do might find it in business, manipulating properties, investing in futures. But they also want frivolities and cotton candy, cigars and brandies, furtive touches under the table and quicksilver promiscuities. After 1890, when night fell, the city turned on the electric lights to create daytime after dark. People wanted roller coasters and light shows and automobiles and aircraft, speed and flight. Electricity had cut them loose from gravity. They had animals in zoos—to witness, if not hunt; the rich had trophy houses on the seashore of Rhode Island or among the golf courses on Long Island, or lodges up in Maine or the Adirondacks. Whereas the poor were clustered in tenements and flophouses, where for seven cents they could sleep in canvas hammocks; two bits got a bed, a locker, and a screen. These individuals thronged to saloons and brothels and clubbed in gangs and preyed on one another in coldhearted ways, driven to it, people said, by need.

Also by boredom. There are two emotional states, according to an observation I've heard attributed to Henry James: excitement and lack of excitement; and excitement, James said, is unfortunately the most interesting. Bertrand Russell wrote that modern preoccupations tend to run "against instinct," and that as a result, people are often "listless and trivial, in constant search of excitement."

The poor, without many options, crowded into the stacked grid, seemed to go crazy sometimes. But no doubt things had always been sort of this way. Think of dark medieval cities in winter, streets like muddy paths and stone-walled rooms, the relentless cold. No wonder so many people drank near to the fire in taverns and seemed dangerous or, as we say, alienated. How they must have prayed for escape, excitement, voyages.

The ruling class in America, no matter how they blinked, could see injustice writ large. This was not how the Promised Land was supposed to be. No. America was supposed to be a new, democratic place, where there was enough good luck to go around. So, what to do?

By the end of the Civil War, the first railroad reached Coney Island, where the hot dog was invented (in 1871) and the roller coaster introduced. Bathhouses were built. The Brooklyn Bridge was opened in 1883. By 1890, "Electric Bathing" was advertised. There were Tunnels of Love, and a park called Steeplechase, which had mechanical horses. There were mechanical earthquakes. In 1903, Luna Park opened a make-believe spaceship that ferried customers to a magic moonscape city with white towers, minarets, and domes. Babylonian Hanging Gardens were built on the rooftops. The entire enterprise was enclosed in glass walls.

The last of these playgrounds was called Dreamland. Boys in Mephistopheles costumes were coached in the arts of acting by Marie Dressler before going out to sell popcorn and peanuts. The list of attractions, as described by R. E. M. Koolhaas, is staggering:

- a two-story steel pier reaching half a mile into the Atlantic
- a shoot-the-shoots into a lagoon
- the largest ballroom in the world
- Lilliputia, the Midget City, half the scale of the "real" world, where three hundred midgets were offered a permanent home in a setting where anarchy was encouraged
- the Blue Dome of Creation (a boat ride through pre-history)
- the End of the World According to the Dream of Dante
- a simulated flight over Manhattan before the invention of aircraft
- the canals of Venice, including a miniature Doge's Palace
- coasting through a replica of Switzerland on the Red Sleigh
- a Japanese teahouse
- the Leap-Frog Railway (bullet trains racing head-on toward each other)
- the Beacon Tower, 375 feet in height, illuminated by ten thousand electric lights, and visible for thirty miles (separately, a searchlight designed to lure ships off course, into possible wrecks, was proposed)
- and, finally, ironically, the Fighting Flames show.

Koolhaas says the builders "alienated a part of the earth's surface further from nature than architecture has ever succeeded in doing before, and turned it into a magic carpet, a conspiracy against the realities of the external world." These cooked-up antidotes to Manhattan were designed to be experienced by those without the means to escape or the wit to love what they had. But in 1911, Dreamland burned entirely. Elephants were aflame, and lions roamed loose on the streets.

Does this story mean something? Zoos and carnival rides are not signs of catastrophic imaginative or moral failure and do not inevitably foreshadow disaster. There's no reason to feel guilty because the evolving world is occasionally not enough and we resort to mechanical diversions. Planning escape into and out of make-believe has been incessant since shamans flew out of their bodies off amid the stars to visit the dead. Parks cut through by streams rising from pipes, sheep grazing safely, with no mountain lions or grizzlies—these transmogrifications of nature ought not to be punishable by fire.

But commodified dream castles where uneasy and somewhat disoriented people can feel free to slip away down some rabbit hole, thus evading the world's insistent responsibilities, can become addictive. Americans are reputed to spend an average of fifty hours a week in the vicinity of an operating televison set (and lately, often simultaneously, one supposes, hooking up through their computers).

In *Magic Lands,* John M. Findlay describes utopian social experiments at Disneyland, the Stanford Industrial Park, the Seattle World's Fair, and various Sun Cities. As Disneyland was being developed, management said they were creating a "new industry with happiness as its principal product." Disneyland represented, Findlay says, "a counterpoint to the malaise of city life." Customers were able to "drop their defenses" and fall into the illusion that they'd found a place where stress did not exist. Seeking to control the moods and thus the behavior of visitors, the managers designed experiences to lull the public into suspending "their disbelief in matters not only of fantasy but also of advertising and commerce."

Parts of the American West are evolving into theme parks with cowboys and Indians, miners and whores. You can see it in upscale museums on the west side of Houston and cheap fixed-up mining camps in the Sierra Nevada and the Black Hills, in gateway towns outside national parks and in antique stores on empty main streets in tiny, dying Oklahoma towns. Citizens doll up the idiosyncratic reality of their histories, hoping to find that their towns have become a tourist destination. Not that they *like* tourists, but for profit . . . people talk of authentic lives while watching other people they call "native" dance out a version of their culture designed to sell goods, often imitation cultural items. Tourism—witnessing for sale— is the world's largest business after agriculture. We try to find—or lose—ourselves.

Hobby ranches line the freeways on the north side of Scottsdale, and along the southern approaches to Antelope Valley in the Mojave—acres grazed down to dirt by bored horses. Many citizens in the American West hate the notion that their homeland is being turned into a theme—or nature— park. Ski resorts and gambling casinos, wild rivers and wilderness are used as gaming areas. Trying to identify ourselves as authentic, we go rafting or ride horseback, hunt, fish, get into organic gardening or cutting horses or evenings at the stock-car races. We speed on freeways or drive off-road vehicles in the backlands for sport, or turn to chess, surfing, or pool hustling. We sacrifice to own acreage. We drink and we drive.

One of the most politically significant population recontourings in the twentieth century is the migration of the rural poor, in countries like Indonesia, Algeria, India, Mexico, and even the United States, who, hoping to do better, move into an enormous city, which becomes even more enormous. And the well-to-do cut and run, escaping the sadness of witnessing such poverty, by moving to enclaves where they live amid gardens and lawns in a faux-nature dream of estates and elegance.

Architectural Digest devoted an issue to lavish photographs of Liz Claiborne's Tranquility Ranch in the Swan Valley of Montana, Robert Redford's Sundance Institute, and a run of multimillion-dollar houses in Santa Fe and Aspen, Telluride and Jackson, including a decorator "line shack" in Montana, where someone privileged could play cowhand for the weekend. All were partly concocted out of a yearning for authenticity, but each is like a dressed stage in a theater, ultimately designed to serve not reality but artifice.

Tourism can take the place of adventure. Childhood conditioning switches on chemical systems that help determine adult behavior. Early stress dooms some of us to live hooked on adrenaline, yearning to reconstitute what is called "natural life" in a refuge where accidents like death by falling off mountains can still happen. Visitors in Jackson Hole can climb the Tetons if they dare, or in Glacier Park encounter elk bugling in alpine meadows below the Chinese Wall. Others go visit the monarch butterflies in their high-mountain wintering grounds in central Mexico, or varieties of finch in the Galápagos. Through encounters with living creatures that bite, writhe, and snort, they attempt to escape mechanical time for more than the few seconds required by the roller-coaster ride off alpine peaks at Disneyland. Parks both urban and rural are meant to shield people from confusion and disorder. Ceremonial games like golf, rodeo, chess, and real estate, as well as play in the commodities and stock markets, help some of us escape isolation and stave off melancholy, and hunting is regarded as sport among people not bothered by bloodiness. Don't mistake me—I enjoy games. Certainly better them than war—that other antidote to the frightening stillnesses of anomie. But there's no enduring cure for despair in playground conquest.

DURING THE HOURS of his original ride, John Glenn became, as I imagine his situation, a man winging on the edges of nothingness (or death). Suffering a long-term anxiety attack that seemed the onset of craziness, I was morbidly frightened by news that a man was out there tethered to what I understood as all of actuality by no more than the ropes of gravity—a man on an invisible trapeze.

That notion was more terrifying when I began to see photographs of the blue sphere of earth, our only possible home, alone in the black endlessness of space, floating, the surface swirled with tracings of cloud. My situation on my blue planet would lead inevitably, uncontrollably, to death; I knew that for sure, and I could no longer see the comforting and often glorious intricacies of actual life. Those days were semi-unendurable.

In September of 1968, I was in Eugene, Oregon, watching on television the aftermath of the uproar surrounding the Democratic National Convention in Chicago. At that same time, although I would not know it for years, Michael Heizer was digging a square-bottomed trench 120 feet through the dusty alkaline playa of Massacre Lake in northwestern Nevada, near where my family once ran cattle. He named his trench *Isolated Mass/Circumflex (#2)*. The ninth and last of a series of earthwork installations, it wasn't very subtle work; the trench looped around a circular segment of undisturbed playa (the "isolated mass," so far as I can tell), the whole of it also resembling an abstract flying creature and a symbol of unity with all things. I suppose it was intended to dramatize both that unity and the transitory nature or extreme long-term futility of endeavor, which is for many of us a tough message to swallow.

Kicking back in a golf course café, enjoying a can of Dutch beer, I listened to a man at the next table take time from his club sandwich to talk about legalizing drugs. This was in Green Valley, Arizona, one of those old-fart Sun Belt communities to which the semiwealthy retreat from snowy winter afternoons in the Midwest. "That's where their money comes from. It's all drug money. They've got money enough to buy anybody, even the president. The reason they breed so much is they've got the money, so they can afford it. And we have to pay for it. Then they say we should pay them welfare?"

His talk reeked of hatred, and he seemed threatened, and to feel excluded from the workings of his society. Perhaps he was addicted to enjoying life as a contest; what he thought of as real may have forced him to believe that life is inherently a battle in which the winners are justified in their disdain for the losers. Or maybe he was so angry because he was bored with his ease and seeking excitement, which would then make him feel significant. Or maybe he just felt trapped.

Many experience loss of freedom like a loss of sleep; in constraint, they become drowsy. Others become furious, hyperactive, and climb the walls. In thirty years, violent crime in the United States has increased 500 percent and divorce rates have quadrupled. Teen suicides are up 200 percent. In a stratified culture—feeling cut off, and greedy to possess *things*, isolated from evolving "natural" possibilities—both jailers and jailed go crazier.

My *American Heritage Dictionary* defines the word *anomie* as the "collapse of social structures governing a society, a state of alienation or disorganization resulting in unsocial behavior." Don DeLillo, in "The Men's Room of the Sixteenth Century," writes of twentieth-century New York: "The men's toilet reminded him of one of the bathrooms in the railroad station in Venice, not cleaned since the Renaissance, an extremely poignant spot, the fecal confluence of many cultures.

"Preadolescent boys for sale. Militant forestry students. Harbingers and importuners. Jackbooted Chinese bikers. Hardrock guitarists in Vietcong sweatshirts. A teenaged girl sat on a suitcase sniffing a handful of oxidized camphor pellets through a long plastic straw."

The story features a deviation bookstore, a guns and ammo discount center, a homoerotic wax museum, a leper clinic. This antiromantic litany is another lyric of plenty. "We burn slowly and unknowingly. . . . Hell is the living electricity." Everywhere is made of fire.

In "The Indian Uprising," Donald Barthelme writes of Comanche (chaos) attacking New York City (our citadel of make-believe). The narrator says, "I spoke to Sylvia. 'Do you think this is the good life?' A table held apples, books, long-playing records. She looks up. 'No.' " The good life, we are led to think, cannot be defined in terms of commodities, however ripe and red, well written or long playing.

New York defends itself against "red men" by barricading the streets with "window dummies, silk, thoughtfully planned job descriptions (including scales for the orderly progress of other colors), wine in demijohns, and robes . . . two ashtrays, ceramic, one dark brown and one dark brown with an orange blur at the lip; a tin frying pan; two-litre bottles of red wine; three-quarter-litre bottles of Black and White, aquavit, cognac, vodka, gin, Fad #6 sherry; a hollow core door in birch veneer on black wrought-iron legs; a blanket, red-orange with faint blue stripes; a red pillow and a blue pillow; a woven straw wastebasket; two glass jars for flowers; corkscrews and can openers; two plates and two cups, ceramic, dark brown; a yellow-and-purple poster; a Yugoslavian carved flute, dark brown. . . . "

In the late 1960s, W. S. Merwin wrote of tasting foods and identifying them after reading just "that part of the label or container which enumerates the actual components of the product in question." As in: " 'Contains beef extract, wheat and soya derivatives, food starch-modified, dry sweet whey, calcium caragean, vegetable oil, sodium phosphates to preserve freshness, BHA, BHT, prophylene glycol, pectin, niacinamide, artificial flavor, U.S. certified color.' "

Feeding ourselves artificial substances, commodified food constructed with chemical ingredients, is a start down the road to inhabiting contrived, rather than evolved, environments, mind-numbing simplicities and cooked-up quasi-complexities. Merwin finishes:

"Guess how completely you become what you eat. Guess how soon. Guess at the taste of locusts and wild honey. Guess what the rivers see as they die. Guess why the babies are burning. Guess why there is silence in heaven. Guess why you were ever born."

We put up barricades against fear, failure, complexity, despair, and death with walls of social detritus and junk. As a consequence, we often live in versions of exile, in subcultures dedicated to forgetting, hoping to be continually diverted and never satiated or anxious.

FOR NINE DAYS, I traveled down the Grand Canyon of the Colorado on an inflated raft with Annick, friends, and guides. We put in at Lees Ferry, a few miles below the abominable Lake Powell. Soon we were deep in shadows, sliding through easy rapids and getting used to the vast silences in the narrow depths of Marble Canyon, four- and five-hundred-foot red-rock rims above us, the sky perfectly blue. It took days to get beyond the bookish boy of myself. If this was sport, which was the game? Or if it was theater, as in ways it clearly was, how to venture outside my run of endlessly prerehearsed routines?

What I managed was to turn my attention to the layers in time. We were making our way down, the river gradually falling through depth after depth of colored, textured stone, eventually halfway to the beginning of things on earth (parenthetical long-winded thinking is, of course, another route to staying abstract and out of the moment). I was counting layers. Or so I thought. More likely, I was tranquilized in the presence of infinities suggested by the movement of sunlight over the glazed or fractured, shadowed or glowing surfaces of reddish rock, stack upon stack.

We camped on a sandbar below a stonework granary that very ancient people had constructed in a rocky overhang where the scree-slope jumble met sheer cliff. According to archaeologists' dating of the tiny deerlike figures made of driftwood and reeds and found in nearby caves, Anasazi lived in those canyons more than four thousand years ago.

In a poem called "Seeing Things," Seamus Heaney wrote "the stone's alive with what's invisible." The canyon of the Colorado, when we were quiet, echoed faintly with what sounded like other voices. And the world seemed alive.

Vasey's Paradise—named by John Wesley Powell, who first boated the canyon, for a botanist accompanying him—is an abundant spring of bright water splashing out from cracks in the cliffside after making its unimaginably complex route through four thousand feet of fractured stone from the snow-fields of the Kaibab Plateau. The sandstone was vividly red in the morning air and contrasted vividly with the ferns, mosses, poison ivy, and thick-tasseled grasses. It resembled constructed grottoes in romantic, so-called natural European gardens such as that of the Farnese family on the Palatine Hill, above the marble ruins of the Roman Forum. Ideas of paradise often involve a place to camp.

The next cliffside spring was finer, tiny, its water falling inside a sheath of luminous travertine, a reddish porous calcite deposited from solution in water of the sort that drips down and forms stalactites and stalagmites in caverns. This was absolutely new to me, a beauty not imagined, built up over millennia, gleaming like porcelain, water splashing down inside like a secret about the goodness of things.

Water springing from stone: Why do we respond so powerfully and positively to certain natural constructs? Perhaps because they so clearly remind us: For a thoughtless instant, we are in the fast old endlessness, where we can build up a fire and dance and sing and tell our stories and value ourselves and one another like the children we always are, safe against the tigers of the night.

Before noon of the third day, we stopped on a sandy beach at the place where the Little Colorado flows into the big river. We were deep below the surface of earth, but the shallow Little Colorado was a pale, lurid blue, nothing subterranean about it; more like water come from the sky, having painted riverbed rocks vivid limestone white. This, again, I could not have imagined.

Some miles upstream on the Little Colorado, so I am told, an enormous uplifted travertine bowl has, through centuries of accumulation, formed over the great spring where the blue water of the Little Colorado comes surging up out of the earth. White sky, the red stone-fall walls of the canyon, at the bottom a river of blue soft water, elegant white rocks—it's easy to understand how the Hopi came to regard that great spring as the place where humans, their people, emerged from the earth, along with life and significance.

I don't know if they believe this literally, or metaphorically, or both. It doesn't matter. What does is that in some distant time their forebears located a place worthy of all the reverence they could muster, which in itself was sustaining, and that over generations they have been willing to travel great distances to visit and acknowledge their reverence. At least that's what mattered to me: We didn't go see that blue-water spring rising inside its travertine bowl; to us, it meant nothing but spectacle. That place should belong absolutely to the Hopi, whose whole story as a communal people begins there.

Near the mouth of the Little Colorado, some of our party sported in mud baths, and I was reminded of mud-headed figures in Hopi ritual who hang around sacred doings, mocking, hooting, playing the fool. Without frivolity, we are stuck in the muck of our own selves, and less than what we could be; fooling around is maybe our central method of learning. Others in our party tied orange life preservers under their asses like pontoons and scooted through rapids like newborns, which of course was the point of things right then.

But I sat on a white rock like a sunning turtle, dangling my feet in the water, listening to my companions, unable to get rid of my preoccupations, to some degree resenting the ease with which my friends found their pleasure, trying to console myself by thinking high intellectual thoughts about pilgrims, and the degree to which they are acting much of time, playing roles. What we most ardently want seems at times simple: a home where we can feel healed, together with ourselves and one another, and not have to think about it. Locked in my mind and listening, I was busy as the old thinker inside worked at untying knots.

That night, I lay on the sand, studying stars we never see from inside the ambient light of cities. I thought, Well, out there you got your infinity and today we were swimming in sacred water. At last I smiled. My body and mind were trying to be parts of the same fellow.

In what is called the Inner Canyon, we drifted between close walls of water-polished Vishnu schist, 2 billion years old, fluted and black, convoluted. Clarence Dutton, a nineteenth-century scientist and explorer who named geologic features, tried to capture the canyon's mystical grandeur with names from Eastern religions—thus Vishnu schist and Zoroaster granite. Travelers have complained of claustrophobic feelings in those depths, the primal mass of the canyon crowding around. Instructed by friends, I discovered the pleasures of examining tiny green beetles in their iridescent splendor; with the help of good fortune, I looked up, to find myself eye-to-eye, as we drifted by, with a big-horned mountain sheep that had come to water at the river.

For these reasons, maybe, those walls of blackish water-polished stone seemed to me simple and gorgeous, not there to remind me of my own mortality but, rather (if only I'd look around), to remind me that I was always, everywhere, part of and surrounded by precisely elegant phenomena. Finding ways to locate ourselves in new territory serves our need to think we are secure even at the bottom of things. For a while, I was nearly at ease with such intricacy, but in the end, I was glad to quit the river. Maybe, I told myself, I'm only another ecotraveler riding the winds of pointlessness. But in truth, I was frightened. Too much actuality might make me crazy, so it was time to turn my back on this flirtation. What a vastly foolish notion. We are nothing if not mystified amid glories.

WE SAW PARIS, Venice, Florence, Rome, Ronda, Madrid, the bull ring in Pamplona, Lascaux, châteaux along the Loire, and the cathedral in Chartres. The romance of oncoming spring was everywhere. Driving north from Italy, we drifted up narrow roads into the hills above the flower fields of Grasse. Mimosa bloomed vivid yellow and the air was weighted with the odor. We pushed on to Aix-en-Provence and went to eat without unloading our Peugeot. After a seafood dinner, we found the car had been ransacked. Suitcases were gone, English-language books, a laptop computer. A pain in the ass, it seemed, but not any mortal sort of disaster.

Wrong. Soon I was seriously dislocated, having under-estimated my dependence on the everyday making and remak-ing of paragraphs on that computer. I was irrevocably overseas. Annick and I were to live three weeks in an apartment in a château on the plain between Nîmes and the salt marshes of the Camargue, where the Rhône flows into the Mediterranean. And we did. But I felt naked without my props. Stolen baggage precipitated a minor death. Foolish, but true.

Knowing only perfunctory French, unable to buy sweet rolls except with mispronounced words, grimaces, and gestures, I tried diverting myself by reading a sad-hearted biography of the British poet Philip Larkin, whose life seemed focused around his obsessive fear of death: "the solving emptiness/that lies just under all we do." Missing the point of Larkin's work, which is courage, I reacted like a man about to suffer death himself.

Samuel Johnson writes in "On the Death of a Friend" that

these are "calamities by which Providence gradually disengages us from the love of life. . . . The dead cannot return, and nothing is left us here but languishment and grief. I have made no approaches to a state which can look on it as not terrible. Let it alone. It matters not how a man dies, but how he lives. The act of dying is not of importance, it lasts so short a time." Johnson wanted to keep his distance from thinking about "that last bad fifteen minutes," as someone called it. I was right there with him.

But the cure for melancholia involves the rediscovery of possibility. Montaigne speaks to himself in his final essay, "Of Experience," which I take to be about making the best of what we get, quoting Seneca, "The life of the fool is joyless, full of trepidation, given over wholly to the future." The wisest of us make it our business to recognize the value of life within the moment. I knew that, and tried. But after buying a pen and blue notebook, I found that in this fractured state, I couldn't make a sentence, much less a string of paragraphs. I got up at daybreak and drove a dozen kilometers to buy the English-language *Herald Tribune*, which I read avidly, holding on to it like a shipwrecked sailor in an exotic sea, in which, I felt for certain, with considerable panic, that I was drowning.

We are electricity, and possibly only manifestations in the life of bacteria. Thinking like that can sound silly, but, as we know, it isn't. The news that the order we perceive is a construct and doesn't necessarily spring directly from sequences in the world can cause our minds to shut down. The intertwined webwork of consequence and meaning that we inhabit dissolves, and we're left in free fall. I tell myself this is a sickness, like flu, or a chemical problem, that I must get a shot for it, and go on jollying myself down the road, wondering if this is melancholia or "deep depression." I doubt it. As Hemingway said, "Many must have it." Mostly, I think, it's an accurate response to what is irrevocably the mortal situation.

This time, my cure began when Annick led me into the swamps in the Camargue, where the sight of pink flamingos in flight at sunset comforted me as had the infinities of waterbirds I saw so commonly in childhood, although not much since. We played golf on first-rate local courses with Max Crawford, a novelist from Texas and an old pal. He was leading an expatriate's existence down the road in Pézenas. He introduced me to the virtues of wandering the countryside with detailed local maps, as if they might be used in locating a sense of who we are. With oysters and fish soup on the quay in Mèze, hours on the golf courses, and the maps and waterbirds and friendship, trust in life came flooding back. I realize this sounds like my recovery hinged on privilege, and I think it did. To be as privileged as possible, I believe that's a sensible societal goal, taken in the broadest sense.

Avoiding traces of panic, I drove Annick north on narrow roadways lined with plane trees to the blossoming little town of Saint-Rémy, where we saw an elephant in the square. (Why mention the elephant except to suggest that the world is magical, or at least able to confound our expectations?) We toured the white remnants of the medieval town of Les Baux, built on the heights of a great natural cliff, and Annick stood near the edge on a bright, windy afternoon. This "attraction" had once been a refuge where wandering singers and poets congregated to recite stories of romance to the lords and ladies, reinforcing their belief that they were gracious and of consequence. Ezra Pound called their singing a literature. By evening, I was wind-burned and relearning the trick of seeing home and travel as versions of the same thing. Eventually, the commonplace world came home, tail wagging like that of a dog that had stayed out overnight.

MEANWHILE, a majority of the humans on the earth are struggling to feed themselves and their people. They want to raise healthy babes, and experience the dignity of knowing they can care for themselves. D. H. Lawrence wrote, "Men live by lies." But not altogether.

Colin Turnbull's classic anthropological study, *The Mountain People,* tells of the Ik, who live in arid mountains near the northern border between Kenya and Uganda. They drift with the seasons, forming and re-forming in bands on defined hunting-gathering territories. Turnbull writes:

> Hunters frequently display those characteristics that we find so admirable in man: kindness, generosity, consideration, affection, honesty, hospitality, compassion, charity, and others. This sounds like a formidable list of virtues, and it would be so if they *were* virtues, but for the hunter they are not. For the hunter in his tiny, close-knit society, these are necessities for survival; without them society would collapse.

But when the Ik were forced to settle in mountain villages and farm nearly untillable land, starvation and poverty drove their society into collapse. They became "unfriendly, uncharitable, inhospitable, and generally mean as any people can be." They laughed at the misfortunes of others; young people literally dug food from the mouths of old people. "People ate when they got food, gobbling it like hungry old hens, running as they gobbled, often so as to escape others and have it all for themselves." Selfishness dominated Ik society. Acts of selflessness became risible.

It's easy to see ourselves in the Ik. But enfranchised citizens like me are overfed in any number of ways; at bottom, greed is our sport. The Ik were starving; for them, greed meant survival.

ANNICK AND I once lived in the French Quarter of New Orleans, across the street from the Voodoo Museum and surrounded by stories that seemed neither revealing nor relevant to any troubles we had. Old mysteries were functioning as a tourist trap.

Preindustrial cultures ran on human energies; ours runs on internal combustion engines, telephones, fax machines, aircraft that can't be flown without the help of computer chips, not to mention simple electrical circuits. The walled cities Annick and I walked through in Europe were illuminated by electric lamps unimaginable to the founders. Bankers in Burundi stay in hour-to-hour touch with the London exchange by messages sent via satellite. Meanwhile, just upriver in the jungles, Japanese loggers level the ancient forests and displace the tribal peoples who have lived in them for millennia, and these people then move to the teeming coastal cities, where their purposes and cultures often dissolve in acrid homelessness.

The First World and the Third World coexist in Jakarta and Manila, Tokyo and Cairo, Mexico City and Berlin, São Paulo and New York, and Moscow and Vancouver, intermixed and segregated in the same taxicabs, driver and driven. As we move toward a global culture, which languages will survive? Which birds? Can we even dream of the future? Can we understand the possibilities?

It's becoming commonplace to think we face crazy-making overcrowding, environmental disaster, and chaos. We hear talk of a "complexity catastrophe," in which processing systems like human minds have to deal with more information than they can handle. A result is fibrillation, the quivering and purposeless state that results in collapse of the entire system. The end of the Soviet Union, as I understand it, was perhaps not altogether the result of a dysfunctional economic system, but was also caused by information overload in their bureaucracies.

The interlocked network of governmental, institutional, and corporate entities that is presently calling the global shots could be on the edge of collapse, capable of averting the end of business as usual only by refusing to think or operate except within a system of belief based on predictable response to every situation—namely, institutionalized greed. Any other response is considered irrational. It is a simplifying strategy, designed to ignore overload, to weed out information and settle for being ultimately destructive but organized, filtering in just the right amount of data to fit the system and thus maintain control.

In *Player Piano* (1952), Kurt Vonnegut envisioned First World societies splitting into elite clusters of secure, well-off, and well-educated citizens while millions of have-nots plotted revenge and revolution in a *Mad Max/Blade Runner* world outside the fences, where happenstance rules. This is a prediction that might be confirmed by the fibrillation scenario.

In 1994, there were 5.6 billion people on earth. That number is increasing at 90 million a year, 7.5 million a month, 250,000 a day, 10,500 an hour, 170 a minute. Population control confronts one of our most profound yearnings, built into our genetic heritage, which is to create more of the life we so revere. But as William James said, we are not "fatal automatons."

We can make choices. Social developments often bring down the birthrate: education and economic opportunities for women, health care for women and children. In 1955, the average number of children born to a woman in her lifetime was five, far above the 2.1 needed to keep populations stable. But that rate has been falling. Presently, it is estimated to be 2.8. In Italy, a *Catholic* nation, the figure has dropped to 1.7. By 2060, it is predicted that Europe will have lost 24 percent of its people. Since the early 1970s, the rate in the United States has averaged 1.9, and in all developed nations, even lower, at 1.6. Projections show a global fertility rate of about 1.85 children per woman in 2050, with total population topping out at about 8.5 billion people and beginning to decline. Far too many people, but supportable.

Or is it? While perhaps contained globally the population explosion is still going to be booming along in the underdeveloped world—in central Africa, Brazil and Mexico, India and Indonesia—resulting in disease, crime, scarcity, refugee migrations, unpredictable outbreaks of violence, and the collapse of social structures as our organizing abilities and environments prove no longer able to bear the load.

Robert Kaplan, a journalist who has spent two decades traveling in parts of the world where chaos is already beginning to flourish—Afghanistan, Somalia, the Near East, and the Balkans—points out that the entire idea of a nation-state system is unnatural to many ethnic and tribal peoples and was imposed on them by colonialists. Boundaries of Third World nations invented when the European powers pulled out often were inappropriately defined, grouping together ethnic populations with ancient animosities (as in the Balkans), while leaving other cultures without a homeland. (The Kurds, for example, number 20 million and live in Turkey, Iraq, Iran, Syria, and the former Soviet Union.) Add to this the stress caused by exploding populations, and our old friend chaos looms.

And, worse, from the point of view of the developed world, Kaplan suggests that the unrest might prove contagious, a disease sweeping our way. We could be experiencing the first symptoms of "general system breakdown," he says. The fiction or story called civilization could very well collapse if no one believes in it anymore. It happened to the Romans and all the old empires. The long-run result, Kaplan says, might be "a rundown, crowded planet of skinhead Cossacks and *juju* warriors, influenced by the worst refuse of Western pop culture and ancient tribal hatreds, and battling over scraps of overused earth in guerrilla conflicts that ripple across continents and intersect in no discernable pattern."

We are presently evolving, certainly, into a culture based on distance. First World societies evolve in the direction of electronic chat rooms. Defining ourselves in purely economic terms, we ignore the necessary role of generosity in our lives. Economic anxiety is killing the mantle of life on earth, and we find ourselves in a double bind, in which consumption promotes peace of mind, which in turn leads us to destroy the basis for our very survival. We despise ourselves for our involvement. Acting out this scenario, we suffer a pervasive sense of powerlessness and alienation from ourselves and thus our societies. We find our problems become irresolvable, personal, and suicidal, and we move out to a land where diversion and selfishness are queen and king, finding ourselves even further removed from any willingness to sacrifice for the earth or future generations, lost in anxieties we can't whistle away with ironies and wit. We are like those increasingly featureless statues standing in the acid rain outside cathedrals all over Europe, dissolving.

Our knowledge expands as our invention continues. Our most fundamental questions involve aesthetics, understanding our own creations. Too much information and compexity generates fearfulness and subsequent attempts at walling off much of what is possible. We set up defenses, hoard our riches and powers, even the power to do good. Paralyzed, we invent and inhabit stories in which we imagine we cannot be hurt. These defensive postures are as important to humans, and as real, as walls and weapons. They often are narratives designed to excuse cruelties; humility and humane emotions are thought to be beside the point when avoiding weakness and death, when brute survival seems the only point. We try to tell ourselves that a breakdown won't ever really happen to *us*. We're wise and too rich. We'll get our shit together.

And maybe we will. We have the advantage of knowing that enduring societies don't just happen; that they evolve over time if people from diverse backgrounds are educated to believe in mutually acceptable solutions to problems. We also know that societies stay stable only when their populations have a strong emotional and economic stake in that stability, enough so that many will sacrifice to sustain it.

Developing nations will need generations to produce large numbers of people educated to act on their understanding that both injustice and oppression weaken and undermine their situation as surely as economic fragility does. Even then, some of those nations won't cohere; some fractures and hatreds run too deep to heal. Some nations would be better dismantled and then reinvented according to models as yet uncertain, but ones intended to honor their cultural components while encouraging them to take part in the oncoming global economy. We must give them the time and freedom to evolve, recognizing that their evolution can take place only in a coherent economic *and* moral setting.

Development as practiced by the World Bank and the International Monetary Fund will not even approximately get the job done. Endless time—and quantities of money that corporate economists will hate to think about—will be required for a vast sequence of long-range projects designed to save both cultures and their environments. It must be accepted that there will be failures and setbacks, that effort and wealth must be expended not in a despotic, from-the-top-down manner but both responsibly and generously among all classes, particularly to women and the poor, that education and health care are utterly fundamental to the endurance of any society, and that funds will often be spent to little effect, and should be given freely again.

Peaceful order will never be securely established in the world until it's based on freedom, and citizens everywhere are economically secure and enfranchised, educated, and healthy. Achieving those goals will involve the patience, generosity, and wealth of generations. Otherwise, stunning disorder may prevail. Which will, if nothing else, be very bad for business.

But meanwhile, the most valuable United States export, in dollar volume, is entertainment. We act as if we don't know what to do with ourselves. And certainly we won't until we can identify what it is we value and will sacrifice to preserve. In "Realism" (translated from the Polish by Robert Hass), the Nobel poet Czeslaw Milosz holds:

> *We are not so badly off if we can*
> *Admire Dutch painting. For that means*
> *We shrug off what we have been told*
> *For a hundred, two hundred years. Though we lost*
> *Much of our previous confidence. Now we agree*
> *That those trees outside the window, which*
>   *probably exist,*
> *Only pretend to greenness and treeness*

And that language loses when it tries to cope
With clusters of molecules. And yet this here:
A jar, a tin plate, a half-peeled lemon,
Walnuts, a loaf of bread—last, and so strongly
It is hard not to believe in their lastingness.
Thus abstract art is brought to shame,
Even if we do not deserve any other.

Part Four

Generosity

I had been my whole life a bell and never knew it
until I was lifted and struck.
       —ANNIE DILLARD

Outside the open window
The morning air is all awash with angels.
       —RICHARD WILBUR

AN ENDLESS DIET of cautionary tales, diatribes, and
anger won't move us to sustain ourselves. Annick's son
Alex heard W. S. Merwin give this advice to younger writers:
"Watch animals. Know words as stories. Memorize poems."

THE GREAT PROJECTS have to do with freedom from
want, ignorance, disease, and despotisms, with a peaceful
homeland thick with the textures of what is most beloved, and
with tearing down barricades between ourselves and liberty,
pleasure, enfranchisement, release, and play.
    Sometimes we think there's not much point in behaving

other than selfishly, since the world is going to kill us anyway. On the other hand, it might be more satisfying to be generous. Which aggrandizement do we wish to choose?

Trudy Gunderson called me from Oklahoma. I hadn't seen her in thirty years. When we both lived in the logging-truck and cowhand country of southeastern Oregon, Trudy tended bar in an establishment called Hunter's Hot Springs, with hot pools to bathe in and no questions asked about your companion or companions if you rented one of the rooms. This time, like always, Trudy had her mind on the main sparrow. "You must be getting old. Do you miss it?" She was talking about a version of the world where keeping score was a joke.

Paul Finnegan (a fictitious name) was, as is said, an Irish drink of water. But he was never interested in water, or irrigation, either. Paul drank gin all summer, scotch in the winter. He was always drunk, although never too boring, as he told anecdotes about the drinking trade—none of which I can recall except for one about a man who bought a seventy-thousand-dollar logging truck and never used it except to drive into town and get the mail and maybe another couple of cases of beer to ice down for the afternoon. Paul would act it out and do everybody in different voices. We wasted long stretches of time on stories like that, splendid hours all.

Among the photographs I've managed to keep, there's one from a Lakeview rodeo, a black-and-white shot taken in a photo booth at a traveling carnival—a merry-go-round, a Ferris wheel, something called Loop-the-Loop, bumper cars, and cotton candy—which set up on a vacant lot down from that row of taverns where, at age thirteen, I was privileged to drink beer like a man. Three boys are crowded together in that photograph, eyes furtive and lighted by expectations of God knows what. One was me; one was my brother; the third was a boy off a ranch down the road in Warner Valley, someone I haven't seen in thirty years now. We were children, thrilled to be inventing ourselves.

We possessed a continual willingness to revise our opinions, to break patterns, to forgive and reconcile, which is perhaps the only sound foundation for civilization. Frivolities are celebrations of freedom, and time out from necessity. Everywhere in history, carnivals have been enactments in which public sentiment comes to the surface. Trudy Gunderson was still laughing her way down the old corridors, taking responsibility for herself and enjoying her days, sans ambition. Me, I embraced all this defining and went the other way. It kind of breaks my heart.

THE RANCH HANDS and camp cooks who worked for us in Warner belonged to a pretty powerless working class. Cowhands may have believed they rode with the men in my family, the owners, as equals. But that was never true. Various of those working people became my friends. Isolated and wanting to be liked, I needed them. Besides, I couldn't get the work done without them, as they understood, although they never made me feel guilty over the inequality of our situations. I loved them because they were willing to stay humorous while shouldering the labor, and I ignored the fact that I had great power to affect their lives, trying to pretend we were pals together in a communal enterprise. It's an old ruling-class strategy: I wanted to be understood as sympathetic, and I told myself that I was too powerless to change anything.

Many of them died alone in bad hotels. Their ability to endure and stay humane, to take care and do the work as well as possible, no matter how degrading the circumstances, led me to revere them. And, unconsciously, to despise myself. Before leaving the ranch, I'd worked that system for most of a decade, ordering people around, exercising my inherited powers. Deep into the trickery of dodging moral responsibility, courting a classic double bind, I closed my eyes and never turned from our purpose in Warner, which was, we said, creation of the finest ranch west of the Rockies. Eventually, I was sort of no one, deep in blind-eyed equivocating, close to paralyzed. It can make you crazy. So, when people ask if I wish I were still on the ranch, the answer is always no.

Late in the fall of 1967, I helped ship our cattle from the Klamath Marsh. Our ranches were sold and that life was over. I was determined to try college again at thirty-five and learn how to be a writer. Sounded crazy even to me, but it was what I had.

The peaks of the Cascades were snowy and white against clear skies. The meadows were frozen and slick under the hooves of our horses, hard as iron, and true horsemen rode with swift, fearless balance. I hung back. I had another life, filled with books, before me. I'd started writing because my life was going haywire and I was desperately searching for a purpose. Do this, I told myself, each day, if it comes to anything or not. As for topics, I knew only that I loved the life I'd grown up in. I had no way to end most of my stories, because I was without much notion of what they were getting at other than reverence.

A lifetime cowhand who was married to a cousin of mine, disgusted with our horseback ineptitudes, summed it up. "Shit," he said. "You're good for nothing but reading books." I didn't answer—I was already gone—just trotted off, leaving him to go on taking the risks. I never saw him again and have never seriously ridden on horseback since. But in moments like that, I began to know that I would have to redefine and acknowledge my allegiances.

THE IDEA that backlands America had a cultural history was new to me when I went to teach at the University of Montana in the fall of 1969. I loved Richard Hugo, and his stories about Theodore Roethke and running the bars in Seattle. Hugo's poems about driving across Montana and sleeping in ramshackle motels under stands of cottonwood, the sounds of a little creek mixing with music drifting out the open doorway of the only bar in town as night settled, led me to believe I had come to the right life at last.

This was Hugo's message: Honor the disenfranchised and powerless more than anybody, because they have no choice and must survive poverty and injustice or else give up and fall down into the solace of early death. Acknowledge that women have had as much to do with inventing what culture we have as any dream of life cooked up by men. So have the old Blackfoot people who live out the last winters of their lives in the hills near Heart Butte, and the rheumy-eyed, hungover fellows clustered outside a liquor store in Browning in a cold wind at opening time, and Hutterites in communal farming colonies on the prairies, and Chicano sugar-beet farmers along the streams south of Billings, and ranch hands hitchhiking to some rodeo with their saddle in a burlap sack, and quick-eyed youngsters leaving the bedrooms provided by their families to go sleep with one another under the bridges in Missoula and snort badly processed speed.

Give everybody their freedom and their due—not only their just rewards but any reward you can provide. Dick Hugo's message—as it came across to me—was that we are equal in our fundamental powerlessness, and that error begins with some dumb failure in our capacity to imagine the sufferings of others.

In the early 1970s, trying to act on what I understood as my responsibilities, I wrote about Native Americans, conveying my sympathies. As it turned out, I was mostly full of bullshit. I carried the manuscript to a downtown tavern and showed it to a student, Woody Kipp, a Blackfoot man home from the Marine Corps in Vietnam, who patiently pointed out my subconscious racisms.

Such failure ought to be instructive, but I didn't get much from it. Life in taverns was most of what I took to be of significance. The essential arts, I thought, were floating and communality, which here could be practiced at the same time. On hot summer evenings, when the door to Eddie's Club on Higgins Avenue in Missoula stood open to the street and the last sunlight fell in slants over the worn linoleum, I'd settle at a rickety table, hands around a fresh Cutty ditch, and think, This is it. For me, that was the actual world.

Days began and ended in the Eastgate Liquor Lounge and the Trail's End, joints Sam Thompson ran on Broadway in Missoula. Sam was an outgoing man who grew up tending bars in the legendary railroader and ranch-hand taverns along Woody Street in Missoula, a stock car and speedboat sort of guy. Bartenders didn't issue bad-conduct discharges. Tolerance was the game. Sam Thompson loaned us money and persuaded the most damaged to eat a meal now and then, and he never sent us home. That would've been betrayal. With everything forgiven, it was possible to think we were bulletproof and invisible.

But no. Some chemicals proved toxic; some behavior, while not exactly unforgivable, proved fatal. Showing off for a woman, running his speedboat under summertime stars over Flathead

Lake, Sammy hit a drifting log. The woman said they hung on to that speedboat's hull until sunup. Then Sammy slid underneath. His funeral wasn't a place I wanted to be. Somebody had torn up the dance floor. Maybe it was the man in the moon.

ANNICK AND I packed in a few miles to Wall Lake in British Columbia, just north of Glacier Park, at the foot of a great cliff with midsummer ice at the top. In the morning, we saw a creature that resembled a dark reddish badger—in fact, a wolverine. Implacable, feverish, quick, and absolute, foraging on a gravel bar near the water, it was there, then aware of us, then gone. That is the only wolverine I ever expect to see. They have been almost exterminated from the tame world. I want to think that wolverines cannot be coerced or co-opted, that they're emotionally untouchable and belong to no one but themselves, and proof that everything alive isn't bent to our will, and I do think it's good for the soul to encounter creatures so utterly unavailable to human agendas, to see that going at life as a free wolverine is still possible.

Winning and subduing can be so affirming that they move some of us toward an interest in nothing but continued conquest and domination, hierarchies and hegemonies. Usually, the result is isolation, virtual death before actual death. Like trout, our connections die out in the rechanneled stream.

Maybe we should feel capable of existing like the wolverines, honoring joy and food, sex in the night and the hunt, and the kill and a good sleep. Or maybe we shouldn't.

IN SEPTEMBER 1982, some of us were in Glacier Park, working on a film featuring Doug Peacock, whose reactions to his time in Vietnam—working as a Special Forces medic and caught in what he eventually understood as beserk craziness— had brought him, once back at home, to find a kind of refuge in valuing the sane dignity of the terrible old roaring grizzly bear.

Joan Churchill, a wonderfully empathetic cinematographer, spent a morning interviewing a few of the vets whose lives circled along a string of bars they called "the trap line." A whiskey bottle was passed around the table where we sat in a yellow-painted kitchen, and the eventual consequence was a lot of candor. One ruined-looking fellow spoke of wrecking a village irrigation system, a sophisticated network of bamboo tubing that channeled tiny streams of water around the faces of white cliffs to terraced gardens, the bamboo tubes spreading like a spiderweb over the cliffs, a bright pale yellow against dark green foliage. "We tore it down," he said. Wrecking that irrigation system was the most vivid thing he remembered from Vietnam, at least that he was willing to talk about. Obviously, he thought of it as a violation of a primary contract, a transgression that worked against even the possibility of order and decency and the chance we might be able to create a safe place. Destruction of gardens. Maybe it was the whiskey, but he seemed awash in grief, and I believed in his emotion.

IN FIRST LIGHT over wheat-field hills south of Pullman, in eastern Washington, Bob Helm drives away in his 1969 Dodge van. These drives incite his imagination to wake up. It's his way of starting to be an artist for another day. Helm reminds me of old blacksmiths I've known who went down to the shop at daylight just to rap a hammer against the anvil, steel ringing off steel, before they took their first cup of coffee. Later, there would be fire, and sparking metal to be worked, reworked, and tempered.

Helm says he's looking for beauty in unnoticed places he often returns to, such as an alley in Spokane where Concord grapes drape new growth over a fence, retangling year after year, in ways that seem striking. "Artificiality makes people crazy," he says. Helm doesn't think there's much wilderness left. The Ross Cedar Tree Grove, on the Bull River, below wilderness in the Cabinet Mountains in Montana, left him cold.

"Too many boardwalks. We're about out of wilderness, and we need a fallback position." Helm finds his wildness in neglected places like the tangle under a railroad trestle. "No one has looked at the undersides of those trestles since they were built. Nobody's watching," he says.

"I'm interested in places where people spent their energy, and the way those places are repossessed by nature." He goes back to visit a 1930s pickup truck, abandoned amid lilacs on a farmstead in Colton Canyon, by the Snake River. "It's been shot so many times, the steel looks like lace." Utterly about western habits of violence, it's also abstractly lovely.

Helm courts accidents. "I use a map, I pick a road and a mileage, then set the speedometer. My mileage comes up and I stop. I try to get some feel for the place. It's a chance to see things people don't see so often. It's like when your car breaks down. You're stuck in a piece of the roadside world you didn't pick." Accidents trick us into seeing.

IN JANUARY 1992, Annick and I were in Umbria, visiting the Pulitzer Prize–winning poet Jorie Graham and her husband, the poet and memoirist James Galvin, at their home in the hill-top town of Todi. All this, to me, was very exotic from the get-go; their very threshold was a paving stone laid by Romans. So my sensibilities were wide open when Annick and Galvin and I spent a day in Assisi, wandering the narrow streets with Fran-ciscans in their brown robes and studying Giotto's frescoes depicting the life of Saint Francis inside the basilica. Still, I was mostly confused. I sensed these things should add up, and reveal to me something I could take to be true, but they didn't. I understood that Francis had thrown down the trappings of wealth to embrace universal love, that he preached to animals, that his friend Giotto broke with the stylized traditions of medieval painting to depict men and women as he saw them in their physicality, but I couldn't connect their striving to mine. The example of their work seemed merely exotic, and the day like a tourist excursion, another trip to the cultural zoo. Back in Todi, when I complained about my thickheadedness, Jorie said, "They were reinventing innocence. It's what we're all try-ing to do, isn't it?"

Jorie grew up in Italy. I respect her opinions. But reinvent-ing innocence? I went to take a nap. While resting, I began to see, like a sunrise on that Italian afternoon, some connection between previously disparate things.

We are, many of us, particularly in the privileged classes, trying to reinvent possibility and live out a story involving the pleasures and the rewards of giving. Saint Francis and Giotto broke free from the mind-set so pervasive in their times that it seemed like the only reality, and everything thereafter, from then until now, was changed. By "reinventing innocence," I believe Jorie to have meant something as simple as trying to relearn the arts of responding to life with all our socially learned blinders off, then being willing to acknowledge our responses, and speak out about what we really think, instead of what we're suppposed to think.

A few days later, the streets of Florence stank of wintertime petroleum. So it was a fine pleasure to climb the wide stairway into silence on the second floor of the Convent of San Marco, where there is a hallway sided with forty four meditation cells. In each cell is a fresco showing a singular moment in the life of Christ. The frescoes were painted at least in part by Fra Angelico, in the years between 1438 and 1447.

In each cell, there is also a small high window. Once a monk was seated for his meditation, it gave a view upward to nothing but open sky. Think of retiring to a cell with only the glories and agonies of Christ and an open, endless sky, the light fading as the day dies down, and having not a thing to think about but dying, or not dying, and the thickets of each. I think I'd much rather walk north of the city into the wooded hills, where you'd stand some chance of encountering crows in a bare-limbed tree or a muddy-footed woman whistling for her dogs. But even so, I was moved by Fra Angelico's echoing insights: Forgo pride and vanity; our appetites are insatiable; cultivate restraint; turn your life into a gift, and then pour it out to others and thus to yourself as you prepare to vanish.

But it was the fresco Fra Angelico had created on the off-white wall beside the entryway to that hall that stunned me most each time I saw it. A luridly winged angel has come to tell Mary she's pregnant with the son of God. The angel is poised, a finger upraised. Mary looks to be justifiably thunderstruck, as terrified as we might be if some apparitional creature came to us with such news. There is more to life, the angel's presence implies, than you imagine. Confronted by a creature so utterly undeniable as that angel—absolutely palpable before

Mary and yet strange as snow on the moon—we are struck by the power of uninvited news that simply announces itself.

A FORMER lady friend and I, along with another couple, spent a July week one summer vacationing in a rented cabin in an orchard overlooking Flathead Lake. We got up early every day and caught our limits of kokanee salmon. We'd crank the little motor on our rented aluminum boat, then head for a place we thought of as our fishing hole, where we anchored, opened cans of corn, and commenced chumming (an immoral practice by any sportfishing standard). Then we settled in for a day of sandwiches and Coca-Cola. We killed every fish that came over the side and cooked them up in the evening, wrapped in foil with a slice of lemon, then placed on the grill when the coals were perfect. We ate with our fingers, without saying much at all.

We had a lot of history among the four of us, and there was no sense in drinking booze at all, not with the trouble that could start, so we didn't. We'd seen difficulties, and for that time at least, we weren't having any. We were at peace, going out at sunrise to the task of catching supper. After we said good-bye, we were never all of us in the same room together again, ever.

Years later, hanging around the Seattle Public Market in rainy twilight, the streets glistening and washed with yellow reflected light, the other fellow and I were talking about James Salter's novel *Light Years,* a story about elegance as purpose and just how far that will take you, which both of us loved, in part because it displayed for us a possibility of graciousness we envied and suspected we would never quite realize. At one point, a woman says, "The only thing I'm afraid of are the words 'ordinary life' "—as if they implied calamity.

"We've got it," my friend said, meaning the upscale life around us in Seattle, and he smiled. "Who would have ever guessed." Looking out to darkness, sipping espresso, we thought we saw hotshot possibilities coming our way. But two of those friends from that week on Flathead Lake are dead. For that few days of fishing, we were happy inside, like ordinary animals. We took care of one another, though by then we were moving on to other lives. We knew it. Such losses were part of that game, if you understood the rules as I did in those days, and you cut your losses. Now I grieve for the dead, and for myself. We let go of one another so easily. It was a terrible failure.

ON A COLD January noontime, walking north from my hotel on Thirty-eighth Street in New York City, looking for warmth and quiet, I stepped inside a Japanese bookstore and leafed through picture books of Zen gardens, mossy greenery, tiny arched bridges, and immaculate raked enclosures. Then I went to visit a successful woman in her office above Fifty-seventh Street. A window behind her looked over rooftops and bare-limbed trees in Central Park. I stammered about the Japanese bookstore and finding hideouts from the city. "We value nature the same way you do in the West," she said in her firm way, slicing directly through my bullshit. "We want things to be fair. Why wouldn't we?"

Like Buddhists, we dream of pure lands, raked sand and symbolic rocks, flowering enclaves designed to enclose us and imply that both energy and calm are benevolent. In my mind's eye, I see photographs taken in Java of blossoming rice terraces stacked on hills, and I imagine traveling a Chinese scroll through shadows of pine on mountain trails above flowing rivers, studying the fish in the waters while crossing bridges to the floating islands.

Memories move in the brain like little fires. The electricity is always flowing through us like blood. We are like trout in the dazzling stream of what is. Transformative moments that cannot be ignored come to us once in awhile. The world *insists,* demanding that we see. We love things that preserve us (for instance, on this winter morning as I try to write, Bach's cantatas).

But most often, we discover what's absolutely essential only because we've been lucky enough to be paying attention when something unexpected came down the road. Attentiveness is the first move. The world tells us its simple message over and over: All the fear you can manage to drum up won't get you much beyond sick with anxiety. This time on earth is it, so far as we know. We might as well pull up our socks and enjoy it, because that's what we get.

In Montparnasse, in May, under trees along boulevard Edgar Quinet, just across from the cemetery where Baudelaire and Samuel Beckett and de Maupassant are buried, the grave shared by Simone de Beauvoir and Jean-Paul Sartre had me wiping my eyes. Later, Annick and I eased along in a street fair, walking through a dream of abundance and order across from fields of the dead. This is what I mean by annunciation. Love it now, goes the message.

> There my mind awoke to the sense of men as brothers.
> —PABLO NERUDA, "The Water Song Ends"

WE HAVE ALL stumbled across particular truths. We may, for instance, discover that we are no longer loved. Or that we are, inexplicably, truly loved.

In 1962, in *The Structure of Scientific Revolutions,* Thomas Kuhn developed his celebrated theory of "paradigm shifts," starting with the obvious fact that scientists ordinarily accept explanations when they work and discard them when they don't. Not only scientists but also artists, hunter-gatherers, farmers, lovers, toolmakers and teachers, midwives and merchants— most of us, that is—proceed through reformulations generated by discoveries. We're all intellectuals, insofar as intelligence is our tool.

Roman artists, as their culture grew more urban, reevaluated peasant life. In the *Idylls,* Theocritus wrote of shepherds pursuing love and song while tending peaceful flocks in the countryside, and Virgil suggested that everyone could escape the corruptions of civilization by settling for lives amid natural, preexisting harmonies.

Pastoral thought reappeared during the eighteenth century in response to the Enlightenment. Thinkers from Descartes and Locke to Newton and Voltaire contributed to the idea of an Age of Reason. Between 1751 and 1772, the French *Encyclopédie* was published in twenty-eight volumes, and by 1780, a supplemental five volumes and a two-volume index were added. In 1771 came the *Encylopaedia Britannica,* from a movement known as the Scottish Enlightenment. Each set was dedicated to justifying the notion that reality is an ultimately predictable mechanism—a concept that drove the beginnings of the scientific revolution, then the industrial revolution. It still drives contemporary economic and political theories.

But soon, certain European intellectuals rebelled as the fortunes of the poor and vagrant, and the mentally deficient and handicapped, went increasingly sour. Such people had customarily been kept through charity; but as materialist market economies began to thrive, ideals of efficiency sent many of those unfortunates to hospitals or workhouses, or to forced labor. Privileges like the use of common fields were increasingly denied, and the relationship between lord and peasant grew increasingly unjust. Workers in the "dark satanic mills" of industry were regarded as no more than machines.

Rousseau called for freedom from restraint and want, a new order, in which the will of the people would be sovereign and not that of any despot, however enlightened, or the rich. "What wisdom can you find," he wrote, "that is greater than kindness?" The poet William Blake, protesting the received truths of his age, wrote:

> *May God us keep*
> *From single vision, and Newton's sleep!*

Thus the Romantic movement was born. Blake held that complete liberty had to be the first step in restoring individual hopes, writing, "Every living thing is holy." These ideals informed the American and French revolutions—France was the leading intellectual center in Europe—culminating with the revolt of peasants and urban poor in the summer of 1789. On August 4, feudal privileges were abolished. French historian Fernand Braudel writes that "the 1789 Declaration of the Rights of Man and of the Citizen remains a landmark in the history of freedom, a fundamental fact in the development of European civilization."

As a young man on the ranch, I read the poems of William Wordsworth, written in his late twenties, the age I was at the time. "Have I not reason to lament/What man has made of man?" He, along with Coleridge, his early ally, reinvigorated the pastoral. I wonder how I responded more than forty years ago, whether I understood those words were more than a literary artifact, that they were relevant to my own situation, as well, that of the owner's son, who had inherited his ration of power and was ordering his farmhands around.

Wordsworth formed his sympathies while traveling in France during 1790 and 1791, when he was passionate in his belief in the Revolution and the republican ideal of equality. But he was soon shocked into disillusionment and depression by the Reign of Terror. Well he might have been.

In September 1792, mobs took helpless royalists from prison and slaughtered them. In April 1793, the Committee of Public Safety was empowered to try all enemies of the Revolution. Maximilien Robespierre took over its leadership in July. On September 5, the revolutionary government adopted a slogan: "Let us institute terror as the order of the day." The Law of Suspects was passed on September 17. Virtually anyone could be arrested, and they were. Prisons overflowed. Those convicted were directly executed in place de la Révolution, by beheading. Carts carried away the heads and decapitated bodies while crowds of peasants and workers sang and danced and drank to the murder of more aristocrats and priests. A law passed on July 10, 1794, denied suspects any right to present evidence or even have a trial. Virtually everyone accused was killed.

"Heads," an official said, "fall like slates." But at last, opposition to Robespierre developed. He was arrested and executed on July 28, 1794. Seventeen thousand had been killed. Between 300,000 and 500,000 people had died in prison of disease or abuse.

Wordsworth turned his admiration for the concept of revolution to reverence for "common life" and private intimacies. By 1798, in "The Old Cumberland Beggar," he was using the poor as a mirror.

Let him be free of mountain solitudes;
And have around him, whether heard or not,
The pleasant melody of woodland birds.
Few are his pleasures. . . .

As in the eye of Nature he has lived,
So in the eye of Nature let him die!

In *The Western Canon,* Harold Bloom writes, "Freedom cannot be more than the freedom to suffer and to die out in the open." While "human dignity is indestructible, the will endures. Wordsworth's originality can hardly be overestimated here." Is Bloom claiming the disenfranchised can't be helped? Or intimating that help isn't the right idea?

Wordsworth, in the preface to *Lyrical Ballads* (1798), published when he was still a young man, age twenty-eight, wrote, in a single famous paragraph, that he wanted to find his poems in "incidents and situations from common life" and to write "language really used by men" in "low and rustic life," where "passions of the heart find better soil in which they can attain their maturity, are less under restraint, and speak a plainer and more emphatic language" and "the passions of men are incorporated with the beautiful and permanent forms of nature."

No mention of justice. As a young man, I began to see as Wordsworth saw: This our luminous world was a cradle of natural innocence, ordered, harmonious, and inexorable, though not always, or even often, fair. Fate is the result of forces that care nothing about justice or fairness. I admired certain workingmen and workingwomen in Warner Valley and tried never to trouble myself over matters of justice—a profound mistake, that escape from responsibility. Those evasions in my background led me at first to disagree with

Bloom's statement that Wordsworth's poems depicting "the sufferings of the English lower classes are masterpieces of compassion and profound feeling and only shallow ideologues could reject them on political grounds."

In Wordsworth's poems, as in my own career as a work-camp manager, the problems of acting responsibly on behalf of the disenfranchised were not confronted; the plight of the poor is recognized, while they themselves are left to meager devices. We could provide more lasting comfort, along with independence, with a medical plan and a monthly retirement check. Wordsworth, in his embrace of rural people who spoke the common language, seemed primarily interested in healing himself and putting a lid on his anxieties. Which does not make him a bad man or poet. My discovery that wading a fishing stream usually cured my free-floating craziness was a move toward nurturing. Still, patching up the self doesn't go far toward helping anybody else.

Nevertheless, in the end, I'm inclined to agree with Harold Bloom. The poems are surely masterpieces of compassion and illumination, and invaluable as such. The first duty of the artist is to help us see freshly, and that is often, in turn, an active step toward doing something about justice.

John Clare, born in 1793, writing just after Wordsworth published his early masterpieces, was a country Englishman raised in rural poverty, and a natural genius. But after brief success in London, he and his work were largely ignored. This was in great part due to emotional problems; Clare ended his life in a home for the insane, institutionalized from 1837 until his death in 1864. In *The Redress of Poetry,* Seamus Heaney says of Clare that what "crowns the lifetime's effort is the great outpouring in his early middle years of short verse about solitary figures in a landscape, or outcast figures, or threatened creatures, or lonely creatures, or birds or bird's nests, or dramatic weather changes, all of which manage to convey uncanny intimations of both vulnerability and staying power."

About childhood, Clare wrote:

> I was never easy but when I was in the fields passing my sabbaths and leisure with the shepherds & herdboys as fancy's prompted sometimes playing at marbles on the smooth-beaten sheeptracks or leapfrog among the thymy molehills sometimes running among the corn to get the red & blue flowers for cockades to play at soldiers or running into the woods to hunt strawberries or stealing peas in churchtime when the owners were safe to boil at the gypsies fire who went half-shares to our stolen luxury we heard the bells chime but the fields were our church & we seemed to feel a religious poetry in our haunts.

It's easy to see what Heaney means by saying Clare had "a gift which is tutored by the instinctive cheer and courage of living creatures."

Clare's life was specifically hitched to the so-called system of commons in England, unimproved grazing lands devoted to use by the entire community, a local bioregion where he felt "religious poetry in our haunts." The commons gave citizens a proprietory sense of rights. Their identity and independence depended in part on shared use of that commons, shared emotional ownership, and the belief that they were capable of overcoming the injustices that threatened such ownership. Their economic claim gave them a liberating sense of rootedness, individual autonomy and collective responsibility.

In John Clare's work, we see that open countryside is not a simple retreat, but a home. For the poor, it is a source of emotional stability and whatever power they might manage to have. Clare's work says, Never forgo your connection to things that give you sustenance and freedom, or forget your duty to resist oppression. About the pointless blood-sport killing of inedible hedgehogs, Clare wrote:

> *They hurl with savage force the stick and stone*
> *And no one cares and still the strife goes on.*

About badgers, he said:

> *Some keep a baited badger tame as a hog*
> *And tame him until he follows like a dog.*

The badger is a metaphor for the poor, and the intention of the poem seems to be furthering preservation of such virtues as work, compassion, honesty, humility, reliability, and an absolute regard for truth. Written with an insider's knowledge of the rural dislocations brought on by "the enclosure," the nineteenth-century parceling out and fencing of common land, it's against ruining local communities, and the consequent disenfranchisement of local citizens.

Is the seeing through, the hope of generating a revitalization of the individual and society, enough? Doesn't help of any kind become coercive? In old age, Norman Maclean agonized over the thought that true "help" was impossible and that his family had let themselves in for relentless guilt by believing the world is lovable only when being good, or at least manageable in human terms. Which justice? Which freedom? At what cost? These questions can be paralyzing.

LOST "NATURALNESS" was of particular interest to writers in nineteenth-century America, and yet nature was so easy to encounter—Thoreau at the pond, Emerson in the woods outside Concord, Herman Melville and his great white whale, and Whitman, so clear in his admiration for animals:

> They do not sweat and whine about their condition,
> They do not lie awake in the dark and weep for their sins,
> They do not make me sick discussing their duty to God,
> Not one is dissatisfied, not one is demented with the
>   mania of owning things,
> Not one kneels to one another, not to his kind that lived a
>   thousand years ago,
> Not one is respectable or unhappy over the whole earth.

In March 1842, aged twenty-three, a working-class hustler and self-schooled newspaperman already publishing his poetic sketches, Walt Whitman heard Ralph Waldo Emerson lecture in Manhattan: "The poets are thus liberating gods. The ancient British bards had for the title of their order, 'Those who are free throughout the world.' They are free and they make free." Whitman had his marching orders: Make free. With the publication of *Leaves of Grass*, thirteen years later, writes Gay Wilson Allen, Whitman "created a new epoch not only in American but also in world literature."

The epoch also created him. In January 1863, Whitman settled into Washington, D.C., and the role of "wound dresser," a title he invented for himself. In this he was distinguished, as he so often was, by his willingness to recognize and accommodate what he truly wanted, which was to be of service, a desire that was driven by his openness to imagining the suffering of others, another way of being "natural." "People used to say to me, Walt, you are doing miracles for those fellows in the hospitals. I wasn't. I was doing miracles for myself."

Whitman went to the hospitals twice a day, six or seven days a week—in the afternoon, following his part-time work at the Paymaster's Office, and then for some hours in the evening, often sitting up with the sleeping or the dying so they would know they weren't alone. He went to the hospitals some six hundred times in three years, visiting with more than eighty thousand wounded men. Whitman spoke of "The Great Army of the Sick." His love of them overwhelmed him, to the point of seeming foolish. It was his idea that wounded men, often coerced into the bloody war, far from home and isolated from family, needed evidence that they were not forsaken or forgotten. He gave some of them small coins, fifteen or fifty cents, or envelopes, stamps, and writing paper, or tobacco and figs, oranges and blackberries and boxes of lemons, and sugar for lemonade, ice cream, and canned peaches for the entire hospital. We could say he was a brokenhearted old fool in love with dying young men, yet he was only forty-three. It would be more sensible to say he had the courage to look death and his own emotional frailties in the eye and go on being the generous, openhearted creature he'd taught himself to be.

"We go for the largest liberty," he wrote. Whitman claimed that the poet, not the president, should be the nation's "common referee" and that the "largest liberty" was something so simple as insisting on our right to help preserve one another, and refusing to be turned away.

Whitman dressed himself like a workingman, preferring to appear unbuttoned and relaxed. In photographs, he's looking directly into the lens. Writing was for Whitman a performance, the entire man devoting life to public purposes. *Leaves of Grass* was the turf upon which he showed that art could have a powerful influence on society.

Whitman regularly invites readers to share in the making of meaning. His poetry is political, self-reflexive, and multi-voiced, part of a dialogue among his various selves—in a word, democratic. Whitman seemed to hope that his work would initiate talk among all of us, and that a poetry of citizenship might begin. Whitman's example bears witness to the usefulness of insisting on universal inclusion, openness, acceptance, and justice.

Our most necessary preoccupations, obviously, ought to be taking care of one another, of every other person, and of the sweet world and discovering the joy of giving part of one's life away. How to proceed is the question. Well, I think, start with the man in full, from his work.

> *The sun and stars that float in the open air . . . the*
> *appleshaped earth and we upon it . . . surely the*
> *drift of them is something grand;*
> *I do not know what it is except that it is grand, and that*
> *it is happiness,*

Or:

> *The early lilacs became part of this child,*
> *And grass, and white and red morningglories, and white*
> *and red clover, and the song of the phoebe-bird,*
> *And the March-born lambs, and the sow's pink-faint*
> *litter, and the mare's foal, and the cow's calf, and the*
> *noisy brood of the barnyard or the mire of the*
> *pondside . . . and the fish suspending themselves so*

> *curiously below there . . . and the beautifully curious*
> *liquid . . . and the water-plants with their graceful*
> *flat heads . . . all became part of him.*

Or:

> *This is what you shall do: Love the earth and sun and the*
> *animals, despise riches, give alms to every one that*
> *asks, stand up for the stupid and crazy, devote your*
> *income and labor to others, hate tyrants, argue not*
> *concerning God.*

"Whitman's poetry," Octavio Paz wrote, is a "prophetic dream, but it is a dream within an even greater one that feeds it. America is dreamed in Whitman's poetry because it is a dream itself." Old Walt, perfect reading for this aging child of the American backlands, so utterly willing to reveal all he knew of who he was, revering himself, too, as part of things. Whitman, for Octavio Paz, is "the only great modern poet who does not seem to experience discord when he faces his world."

IN LATE January of 1992, wandering the Alhambra on a chill, bright morning in southern Spain, it was clear that the desert people who built these gardens valued flowering nature and rills of running water as much as I had the oasis valleys in the Oregon deserts of my youth. Later, in Ronda, the bullfighting town southwest of Granada that Hemingway used as a model for the place where dead fascists are thrown into the river in *For Whom the Bell Tolls,* I was sipping a breakfast brandy with the old people in a café perched alongside the bridge over the great barranca that separates the new town from the old—

thinking of Hemingway, and of Lorca, and how they had also, maybe, at different times, enjoyed morning on this balustrade.

What they liked about Ronda, I wanted to think, was what I liked, the amiable and forthright flow of talk, and the stink of pipe smoke and cigars and brandy in the sunlight of another luminous morning. Beyond the barranca were green fields and distances where we could walk beyond the hills and out of sight, out of mind. Nobody would miss us, or vice versa.

Annick and I had lunch in the old Hotel Victoria, built in the 1890s to house British railroad workers. Annick had been there before, in the 1960s, with her husband and children and our friend Richard Hugo, to visit the life-sized statue of Rilke in a cliffside park along the town's western border, looking over the countryside to the white towns perched on hilltops and the scruffy forests beyond.

Rainer Maria Rilke lived alone in the Hotel Victoria from December 1912 through January or February 1913. (Room 208 is a little Rilke museum.) After early success, his work seemed frozen. In Ronda, he wrote of "the herd, penned in its stalls," which "accepts with a long slow sigh the darkening departure of the world." And he yearned "to make the Thing, Lord, Lord, Lord, the Thing," for the glory of an insight that would free humans from their stalls, and from their fearfulness before death. But he had no such insight. Over the next decade, Rilke would blow in the wind of his seeking.

Which makes him sound both arrogant and purposeless, and he was neither. At an art colony near Bremen, Germany, Rilke had befriended a young woman named Paula Becker, a blond, warm-eyed painter. The interest was mutual. But Rilke never followed his heart, and, to provide for herself, Paula soon married an older man named Modersohn, a painter of nature scenes. Paula was at least an intermittent presence in Rilke's imaginings over the following years. In 1907, Paula died of an embolism three weeks after childbirth. Rilke responded with one of the world's great poems on betrayal, saying, "I accuse all men," each escapee, himself included, who failed to take responsibility for the freedoms of those they cherish.

> *For this sort of suffering has gone on long enough and no*
> *one's learned to bear it.*

And:

> *For this is wrong, if anything is wrong:*
> *not to increase the freedom of love*
> *with all the inner freedom one can muster.*
> *We have, where we love, only this:*
> *we must allow each other to grow great; diminishing*
> *comes easily to us and doesn't need to be learned.*

It is a profoundly political poem. The world should give each of us every possible freedom. But the fortunate or enduringly willful, the selfish, seem to collect more than the rest. But that's as far as indignation and sorrow, even self-loathing, could carry Rilke. Unwilling to dwell on the subject of injustice, he wandered the worlds of European aristocracy, often living off the rich. Rilke insinuated himself, then mooched his dinner. What he found was mostly himself, emotionally isolated while he waited, despite infatuations and love affairs. The voice of an angel was what he was waiting for.

In *Reading Rilke,* William Gass gives us a swift evocation of those years. "It is a life of packing and unpacking, of smiling at new friends, looking out of different windows, sitting in trains, trying to write at odd and irregular hours, signing books and behaving like a literary lion, having ideas, getting used to strange dark hallways, guest beds, always cadging and scrounging." Alone and wandering, always looking through glass, encased in academic hierarchies and aristocratic bureaucracies. Living in Kafka's dark vision. And living that way, so it seems, on purpose.

Why does Gass seem to care so much? No doubt because Rilke's daily rounds embody the risks confronting someone who devotes his life to waiting for insights. "When you have no daily work to go to," Gass writes, "to stabilize your life and make it useful, especially when you are like a ghost caught in daylight, when there is no protective routine with its reassuring tedium to lull the nerves, and no one about to get on them either; then you go to hell instead, and Rilke found himself in rooms full of his previous pacing." Reading that passage, I worry about myself and the long periods when nothing comes and I sort of dissolve into nobody, a being without purposes other than the vaguest political intentions.

Rilke, waiting for insight, guards his time as if he were busy with much besides anxiety, saves himself for himself, his work and his potential (an excuse used over and over by writers and intellectuals); Rilke is the user, averse to risk, and selfish. He knows this about himself, despises it and goes on with it. Learning and waiting turn out to be his lifetime job. Rilke is stoic, given to reliquishment and asceticism. The true generosity is patience while awaiting a gift to pass along. Is that the message here?

Artistic activity works a lot like evolution. Some mutations succeed; others fail. Artists seek epiphanies, moments when they can "see through" experience and find an order. Some of those insights are useful; most are not. But artists must first prepare—know all they can about the principles governing their work, and become capable of making informed choice after informed choice, thus becoming what is called "intuitive." This is true for poets, farmers, dog trainers, steelworkers.

Artistry comes in stages, Gass tells us. "Work. Blockage. Insight. Verification. Followed by the orderly development of the new idea." Or these: "initial talent, life preparation, focus, failure, distraction, revelation." Can a lifetime of studying how to get the work done be called useless? Certainly, an attempt to relive Rilke's life without his genius and luck, resulting in failure, will usually earn you the label of perpetual loafer, a loser.

In February 1922, after decades of preparing, Rilke's endurance was rewarded when he finished his masterwork, the *Duino Elegies,* in a single burst of productivity. "For beauty is the beginning of terror. . . . Every angel is terrifying." Because we so fear death, we hide and wall ourselves away from communion with life, from even the possibility of love and intricate giving and taking. We blind ourselves, tear and wound and remake ourselves into orphans. Rilke reminds us that we have no choice but to accept our mortal condition and revere what we have, always attempting to fear not. From the "Ninth Elegy":

> Once *for each thing. Just once; no more. And we too,*
> *just once. And never again. But to have been*
> *this once, completely, even if only once:*
> *to have been at one with the earth, seems beyond*
> *undoing.*

FEDERICO GARCÍA LORCA was a natural, and he came to revere Whitman. A handsome young man who was never allowed to grow old, he was shot one August morning in 1936, at the age of thirty-eight. A child of the Spanish ruling class,

Lorca grew up in countryside towns north of the ancient Moorish city of Granada. A friend from those years, Angel Del Rio, said Lorca was "what the Spanish call 'simpatico'—playful, full of humor, almost histrionic in his gaiety." He loved nights of Gypsy music and his own poetry, and wine and talk and laughing; he despised the patriarchal and elitist society of official Granada. "Paradise closed to many, garden open to few."

At the age of twenty-one, in 1919, Lorca went to study in Madrid, where he lived in the famous Residencia du Estudiantes and enjoyed a highly privileged life within a remarkable circle of artists, which included the poet Antonio Machado, filmmaker Luis Buñuel and Salvador Dalí (whom, because Dalí was older, arrogant, and eccentric, Lorca regarded as a kind of second father).

In June 1922, just twenty-four, Lorca returned to Granada and participated in a festival in celebration of *cante jondo,* or Andalusian "deep song" (spare medieval song and poetry on themes of passion and suffering). Andrés Segovia played his guitar and Lorca recited his poems. *El Defensor de Granada,* a local newspaper, gave him a rave the next day. "Granada has a poet. This boy, a dreamer who loves what is beautiful and sublime, will achieve greatness." *Romancero gitano (Gypsy Ballads)* was published in July 1928. Lorca was suddenly the most popular poet in Spain.

But soon, twilight. Lorca slipped into a depression, which was exacerbated by a break with Dalí. But primarily, he was depressed by the breakup of an affair with a young man, and—we have to speculate—by anxiety about his homosexuality, which he'd kept secret (particularly from Buñuel, who hated homosexuals). Lorca's life was the subject of gossip in middle-class Granada, among the provincial crowd he detested. "One must be happy, it's a *duty* to be happy. . . . I am going through one of the saddest and most difficult times of my life," he wrote.

Lorca called this his "sentimental crisis," and it led him, in an attempt to distract himself, to go with his mentor and friend, Fernando de los Rios, a teacher at the New School for Social Research, on a trip to New York in June 1929. During the Atlantic crossing, he wrote, "I don't know why I left; I ask myself a hundred times a day. I look in the mirror of the close little cabin and don't recognize myself. I seem to be another Federico."

Dogged by depression, and perhaps aware that he must throw off the spoiled-child trappings of privilege, Lorca, who knew little English, lived in a dorm room in Furnald Hall at Columbia University and walked incessantly through Harlem, the Lower East Side, and the Battery—gathering impressions that would form the core for his dark semisurrealist *Poet in New York* (unpublished until 1940, four years after his death). In New York for the stock market failure in October 1929, and reputed to have witnessed six suicides, Lorca was thinking of Whitman on the streets where Whitman himself had learned to think he should be useful.

Poet in New York is an inquiry into dehumanization in what Lorca understood as the city of unfulfilled possibility, a mercantile nightmare where people were estranged from natural cadences in life and their own first sympathies. Parts of the book—"Landscape of the Vomiting Multitudes, Coney Island Dusk" or "Landscape of the Urinating Multitudes, Battery Place Nocturne"—sound like easy, simple-headed disdain. But according to Conrad Aiken, reviewing Rolfe Humphries's English translation, "Lorca devoured all the properties of surrealism, stuffed his cheek with them, blew them out of his mouth again as poems—but so he did with everything else that he fed on." This poetry, Aiken wrote, was preoccupied with "pain, pain and suffering, fear of death and suffering. . . . He hated us, and rightly, for the right reasons."

Which right reasons were those? For Lorca, New York was a walled enclave of total artifice. For a corollary, I have to think of Dante's descent into a whirlpool of citified passions, or Yeats's homemade golden bird upon a golden bough, and Goya's ravished dreams of warfare and death. America frightened this poet, and broke his heart. From Keats, we hear that illness must be answered by soul-making. The soul Lorca found to admire in America, as he began his efforts at recovery, was Walt Whitman.

> *Not for a single moment, beautiful old Walt Whitman,*
> *have I ever ceased seeing your beard full of*
> *butterflies.*

But finally, despite Whitman:

> *America drowns under engines and tears.*

By midsummer of 1930, Lorca was home in Spain and insulated again, surrounded by his friends and family. In 1935, he wondered, *asked*, "What would become of little rich children if it were not for their servants, who put them in contact with the truth and emotion of the people?" But he never had the time to find out.

THAT IS NOT TRUE of his friend Pablo Neruda. Revolutionary intellectuals often flaunt emotional homelessness like a flag, but Neruda went the other way. A world traveler all his life, Neruda was continually relocating himself in Chile and wrote of himself as "perpetually Chilean."

Born Neftalí Ricardo Reyes Basoalto, he was raised poor in Temuco, a railroad town on the rain-forested frontier in south-central Chile, most of whose forests have since been logged to the ground. Son of a railroad worker but always the singular child, he collected snail shells and beetle carpaces, read his books, and wrote, as he said, "with the sweep of rain on the roof." At thirteen, he read *Les Misérables,* and the works of Cervantes, Gorky, Rimbaud, and the French encyclopedists, and he finally went to see Gabriela Mistral (an eventual Nobel Prize winner, who was then teaching in Temuco) with his own poems. She pronounced him "a true poet" and rewarded him with a lifetime of friendship. At seventeen, he was an anarchist affecting a black cape at the university in Santiago; he took to the bohemian life, fell in and out of love with various people, and renamed himself Pablo Neruda.

The early masterpiece, *Twenty Poems of Love and One Song of Despair,* was published when Neruda was twenty. Thus he was launched. In his twenties, he served in Chilean consuls across the tropical Orient—Rangoon, Batavia, Singapore—writing romantic poems in seaports, mooning, marrying unhappily. Then in 1935, he was appointed to Madrid and waltzed into a golden age of Spanish creativity. Lorca was at its center.

"The only true rivers in Spain are its poets," Neruda wrote in his *Memoirs,* and Lorca was "popular as a guitar."

By the next summer it was over. "A million dead Spaniards. A million exiles." Fascists began their conquests. "For me," Neruda wrote, "it started on the evening of July 19, 1936." He'd talked Lorca into accompanying him to a wrestling match. "Federico did not show up. He was at that hour already on his way to death. We never saw each other again; he had an appointment with another strangler. And so the Spanish war, which changed my poetry, began for me with a poet's disappearance.

"What a poet! I have never seen such grace and genius, a winged heart and a crystalline waterfall, come together in anyone else as they did in him."

Lorca had gone home to what he thought was safety in Granada. He was arrested on August 16. On the nineteenth, he was shot at dawn, near a spring known to Granada's Muslims as the "Fountain of Tears," and buried by Franco's fascists in an olive grove north of town, near the village of Viznar. We think of Lorca confronting last things, the fields where he wandered as a child, and real birds, ravens in the oak trees, which got to go on living. Neruda wrote, "If one had searched diligently, scouring every corner of the land for someone to sacrifice, to sacrifice as a symbol, one could not have found anyone or anything, to the degree that it existed in this man who was chosen, to demonstrate the essence of Spain, its vitality and its profundity."

IN *Translating Neruda*, John Felstiner writes, "Neruda entered history." He endangered himself in the role of a witness speaking against the forces of coercion and was soon removed from his consulate for his efforts on behalf of the Republicans. His first work was literary—starting a magazine, signing manifestos. But Neruda was reimagining his role. In Madrid, on July 1, 1937, he published "I Explain Some Things."

> *You'll ask: And where are the lilacs?*
> *And the metaphysics matted with poppies?*
>
> *and in the streets*
> *the blood of children*

flowed easily,
like children's blood.

He was writing with a new purpose, a sense of what to speak for and whom to speak to, a vocation. He'd joined what he saw as the common struggle. In 1938, Neruda was called home to Chile. That summer, he read to porters in the common market in Santiago. When he finished, one of the men said, "We are forgotten people, I can tell you, we have never felt such emotion." Then he broke into tears. Neruda called it the most important event of his career. "I felt I was in debt to my country, to my people." In 1939, he wrote, "The world has changed, and my poetry has changed."

On the last day of October 1943, after traveling from Mexico to Peru, Neruda rode a horse up to the Incan citadel of Machu Picchu. Built around 1440 and never discovered by the Spaniards, Machu Picchu was not subjected to the destructions of conquest but was abandoned to the jungle and then rediscovered by the American Hiram Bingham in 1911. No one knows exactly why Machu Picchu was built, or how it was used, but it is beyond doubt one of the world's transcendent stonework constructs, at the edge of vast highland cloud forests that reach off to the east, gazing down thousands of feet into the twisting rain forests of the Urabamba River valley.

In *The Heights of Macchu Picchu*, Neruda reminds us that civic glory is often a result of inhumane exploitations. In the poem, he imagines speaking to the men and women who worked to fit the Incan stones so seamlessly together: "tell me everything, chain by chain,/link by link, and step by step." The poem ends with the line "Speak through my words and my blood."

My own experience at Machu Picchu, colored by my reading of Neruda, was complicated. The flooding Urabamba River had recently washed out the narrow run of railroad tracks, so we were forced either to walk or to travel expensively by helicopter (used and formerly Russian, piloted by smiling Peruvian adventurers). We chose the risky move and came in like proper colonialists, looking down on precipitous mountains terraced centuries before by the Inca, many of them still farmed. I imagined climbing a muddy path to a high stack of fields, sleeping up there under a pile of straw for weeks, hoeing and hoeing. Making a go of it.

Intricate, marvelously worked, Machu Picchu was glorious in the slanting sunlight that dappled through mists as we walked the paths and touched enormous stones that had been fitted precisely one into the other so long ago. Machu Picchu is that rare thing, like Lascaux, a tourist attraction that's better than advertised. Those stonework harmonies couldn't, I think, have been created by people who were not at least trying to believe in what they were doing. I'm inclined to agree with Neruda that the work at Machu Picchu was driven by oppression, but not altogether. I saw perfect scale, each thing fitted to use, irrigation water flowing in tiny channels cut in the fundamental stone by unknown hands over five hundred years ago. But the question remains: Is this beauty and harmony worth the cost?

ON JULY 8, 1945, Neruda formally joined the Chilean Communist party, and that summer he read before 130,000 people in a soccer stadium in São Paulo, Brazil. After that, he lived as an icon; he built himself three Chilean houses with barrooms, one in Santiago, one overlooking the sea at Isla Negra, and another high in the hills above the port city of Valparaiso. He wrote his poems, called his friends around for one happy hour after another, and involved himself in Chilean politics. He bought figureheads off sailing ships, along with antique doors, and installed them in his houses. When he won the Nobel Prize for Literature, Neruda bought a first edition of Diderot's *Encyclopédie,* a luminous assortment of seashells to put beside his collection of mounted beetle carapaces, and a narwhale's horn. His themes constantly involve complexity and energy, whether in tides flowing on the beaches, or in politics, or between men and women (he was given to romantic adventures).

In 1970, Neruda backed the Marxist presidential candidate, Salvadore Allende Gossens, for whom millions marched. In *Memories of Fire,* Eduardo Galeano writes that they "were breaking the custom of suffering." Allende won, and he promptly nationalized the Chilean copper, iron, and nitrates industries, as well as the banks. Hopes of social justice rose like a sun over Chile. But in corporate and governmental meeting rooms around the world, the people in charge of international trade decided this would not do; ultimate matters were at stake. They dealt Chile out of the international economic game, stopped buying Chilean products, and soon the nation went bankrupt.

When Chilean military officers demanded Allende's resignation, he refused, took up a rifle, and spoke on the radio one last time. "Rest assured that, much sooner than later, great avenues will once again open up through which free mankind shall pass to build a better society." When Allende was killed in the presidential palace, a reign of terror began. Thousands were executed by command of a military junta led by Gen. Augusto Pinochet Ugarte. Chilean copper reappeared in world markets.

Neruda was suffering from prostate cancer. After Allende's farewell speech on the radio, Neruda fell into agony. On

September 23, 1973, less than two weeks after the Popular Unity government was overthrown, Neruda died in Santiago. His houses were ransacked by the military—tables splintered, mattresses and books burned, seashells smashed. The house where his body rested in Santiago was flooded. But the people of Santiago, defying machine guns and armored cars, took Neruda and carried him through the streets. Singing "The Internationale," this multitude took their poet to his burial.

While it's necessary to deplore Neruda's decades in support of Stalinism, it's just as important and useful to understand the aura of possibility Neruda cast into the often hideously oppressive public life of South America. The systems of repression in place in Chile, Argentina, Bolivia, and Peru for centuries seem now to be slowly withering. My sense of that, based only on a brief period of traveling in those countries, is that the emergence of a merchant class with economic leverage will in the long run prove a good thing in the lives of the peasants. More teachers, hospitals, doctors, and nurses, more concern over clean water—that's what I hope will evolve. And gradually, maybe generosity will accumulate and inspire political changes that will help to alleviate the misery of impoverished millions. But maybe nothing is changing at all.

Neruda's influence was insistent everywhere we went in South America. His story was taken as undeniable proof that men can devote their lives to acting on behalf of justice. Problem is, it's always someone's brand of justice and very apt to turn into another coercion.

INDIGENOUS PEOPLE and working classes are normally close to powerless in the game of revolution. Who will liberate them? Owners say they provide marginal citizens with the means of survival—jobs, food, health care, a context in which to live. Intellectuals say they give groups who are out of power the ideas and leadership their members need to enlarge and enfranchise their lives. Both sides are to some degree correct.

Intellectuals, of course, are often interested in taking status, privilege, and power for themselves. And, like anybody, in their statements, they find reasons to applaud their own virtue, thus making themselves emotionally comfortable while often deferring actual risk taking and action. Sentiment comes easy. Intellectuals tend to sympathize and point in dismay. But there's always the exception, like Gandhi.

The poet Garrett Hongo and I were driving the Vermont countryside in late summer, going home from the Bread Loaf Writers' Conference. We got to talking about writing and politics, and he told me about the frustration among the youth in the Japanese-American community after World War II because the older people wouldn't speak out against injustices they suffered in internment camps like the one at Tule Lake. This silence, Hongo said, was the result of the older generation's belief in detachment, charity, and forgiveness. "All we wanted was to know what happened. We wanted to know the stories." The new generation needed to hear the stories so they could discover their own feelings and devise their own responses. That's where a great part of intellectual usefulness lies— in telling stories, helping individuals and communities to remember their experiences and to reevaluate them.

IN THE SLABLIKE buildings that house the University Center for Atmospheric Research on a hillside above Boulder, Colorado, whose staff found the holes in the ozone layer, I listened as John Cobb, a theologian from the Claremont Graduate School, outlined an order he saw in European history. For more than a millennium, Christianity was the principal ideology until, after vastly destructive religious wars, papal powers were taken over by kings. Nationalism became "the real religion." But then nationalism generated its own grand procession of inhumanities: colonialism, slavery, trench warfare, Nagasaki and Hiroshima, the Holocaust, the gulags. That faith has faded, gradually replaced by belief in economic activity and growth as a source of worldwide social coherence. But institutionalized greed has proven to be both inhumane and irresponsibly destructive of the environment. So lately, there has been a widespread public acceptance of an ideology Cobb called "earthism," which began with the insight that we are personally, each equally and primarily, responsible for both the environment and one another.

Polls taken in the late 1990s indicate that 40 million United States citizens, up from roughly 10 million in the 1970s, might be called "earthists." Citizens in Bolivia, Indonesia and Brazil, Honolulu and Ann Arbor work locally to act out a core of widely accepted social and environmental ideas in a decentralized movement that resembles the "village revitalization" advocated by Gandhi in that the focus begins with neighborhood. Called NGOs, short for nongovernmental organizations, this crowd includes groups such as the Florida Panther Society; Adopt-a-Watershed, from San Francisco; the Calgary Zoo; the Land and Water Fund for the Rockies; the Maine Farmlands Trust; and the Allegheny Defense Fund. People with earthist sentiments are getting wind into their sails worldwide; they are likely to command enormous political power in coming decades—without, one hopes, evolving into bureaucracies.

Henry Kendall, winner of a Nobel Prize for the discovery of quarks, gave up physics in order to devote his life to the environment. Nature, Kendall explains, will put an end to our problems if we don't, and brutally. We are, he said, in a race against oblivion.

Having irrevocably refashioned our place to live, thus distancing ourselves from biological diversity, having embraced selfishness as an operative ideology, we don't enjoy listening to the likes of Henry Kendall and John Cobb. We want to take pride in ourselves and our society, and believe in progress. We don't want somebody telling us that we're mindlessly ruining the world.

We hear arguments in bars and banks. My dentist talks about floodplain problems as he works on my root canal. We see starving people, regularly, on nightly television. Politicians sell themselves and equivocate; citizens turn away in disgust. Nobody is responsible; damage accumulates. We look to the clouds or at our feet. This, we say, will pass. And indeed it will. It already is.

THE FOOD SOURCE for all animals is the energy green plants bind into organic molecules through photosynthesis. Per year, this comes out to about 225 billion metric tons of organic matter. Humans now use up almost a third of the total.

The production and distribution of food is a multitrillion-dollar business, the world's largest global economic activity. Increasingly, it is controlled by enormous vertically integrated corporations that raise seeds, plant and harvest, package and distribute. Du Pont buys the world's largest seed producer, Pioneer Hi-Bred. Continental Grain combines with Cargill. It's possible that four conglomerates will eventually control the food industry in the United States (the Midwest is the world's largest tract of class A agricultural land) and in much of the world. Small farmers in North Dakota or northern India can't compete with them, so they go broke or sell out. We're being forced into a centralized world food system that was never voted for by anybody, that rarely operates with humane interests in mind. Its existence is an insult to the possibility of world economic and political equality—not to speak of the well-being of small-time ag producers everywhere, from Java to France, North Dakota to Argentina.

For more than a century, in the United States and around the world, professional agriculturalists—experts working for the Department of Agriculture, faculties from the land-grant colleges and research staffs and field technicians from international chemical and seed corporations—have advocated food production models that attempt to imitate the efficiencies of industry—mechanized farming and livestock rearing and fattening expedited by chemicals—as well as the use of fertilizers and pesticides that are ofttimes harmful to all species, those they're meant to "help" or "improve" as well as those indirectly contaminated.

These professional agriculturalists seem willing to abandon a heritage that has evolved over millennia in localities from Umbria to the highlands of Mexico and New Guinea, an ancient tradition of on-the-land responses to the particularities and whimsies of local climates and ecologies. They attempt to design crops and creatures that will thrive anywhere given the proper chemical fix, and they teach farmers, both in agribusiness and those working barefoot in the Third World, to believe that only professional answers to their fertility, pest, and disease problems are valid. Over the last century, we've seen a commitment to single-species monocultures, whether endless acreages of wheat, rice, and corn or cattle, chickens, and hogs in intensive feeding operations, all doctored with chemicals. It's a system designed to benefit the corporations that sell science in agriculture for enormous amounts of money, and eventually, if we don't watch out, it will fail to feed us.

Indigenous varieties are allowed to go extinct as they are replaced by those developed and sold by multinational seed companies. Third World farmers are given stocks of chemically dependent seeds developed in research labs and told to forget their old seed stocks, which they then eat. Thousands of years of local genetic adaptation are thus lost. Diseases and insects soon evolve and thrive amid the chemicals. But by then, the local seed stock is gone. All this in service of what is called the "green revolution"—another colonialism, this time on the part of those corporate entities that took over the imperialist exploitations manifested in the nineteenth century. Over seven thousand varieties of apples were grown in the United States in the last century, of which more than 85 percent have been lost; 87 percent of the pear varieties are extinct. They represent a trail of experimental decisions, millions of them over thousands of years, involving all domesticated plants and animals. Each loss of genetic diversity erodes our ability to breed plants and animals that can respond to future adversities. Sanctioning this, and treating foodstuffs as a commodity, is nothing less than catastrophic. Biological diversity exists only in species, which exist only in their genes, which we cannot create. We recombine genes, but whatever's lost is gone for good. Agricultural corporations respond by buying rural seed companies that have hoarded indigenous species for use by regional farmers, acquiring their stocks to use in breeding commercial food crop variations. But this program cannot persist much longer, since the number of small seed companies is finite.

A system of "real-cost" pricing in which social and environmental expenses such as the costs of lost diversity are added to
the cost of what these corporations produce might shock us.
What does it really cost, in terms of topsoil and petroleum fuel,
to produce a pound of grain-fed beef? In the United States, it's
estimated that it takes about $2.70 worth of oil-based input
(fertilizers, etc.) to produce $4.00 worth of corn. Feed the corn
and the petroleum and topsoil involved in raising the corn to a
steer for a winter and you've got a choice rib steak the world
can't afford. We ought to occasionally eat grass-fattened beef
and raise all the corn we can, sans fertilizers and pesticides, as
human food.

We could demand that the interwoven system of coercive economic institutions that dominate so much of life these
days reinvent itself, act on behalf of everyone or cease to exist.
The idea that humans, because of population pressures, face
inescapable starvation, is a tactic promoted by the major agricultural corporations to sell petrochemicals. The miseries of
starving people around the world are to a great extent the
result of inhumane choices within the market system, while
the agricultural corporations pretend this is the very tragedy
they mean to prevent.

If we stop applying the chemical fixes that drive industrial agriculture, how will we feed ourselves? Do we face, as
world population rises toward 8.5 billion in 2050, a "system
collapse"—widespread starvation?

The answer is a simple no. We can raise plenty of food by
hand, each of us focused on his own garden. How to fix the
world? Garden by garden. Traditional practices—natural pest
control and fertilizer and attention to the health of individual
plants and animals, growing complementary crops that will
mature at different times in the same plot, which is more

productive but difficult to cultivate or harvest with large-scale machinery—can feed everyone the world is likely to hold, and feed them well. Gardening in this sense is everybody's responsibility.

The population explosion, if the projections are real, will have been controlled over much of the world due to millions of individual choices on the part of people who want better lives for themselves and their children—because they *have* choices. Falling birth rates, of course, are both a result of planning—available contraception and legal abortion—and social change—education, higher incomes, delayed marriage, easier divorce, and more economic opportunities for women. Bottom line? Humans are capable of managing their collective fates.

But sub-Saharan Africa is currently home to 770 million people. In Nigeria and Ethiopia, the reproductive rate remains high, and population growth reinforces the poverty. Demographers estimate that the populations there could double in the next half century. Pakistan is projected to grow from 146 million people in 1999 to 345 million in 2050, and the population of India, about 1 billion at present, to gain another 500 million.

And the wells all over the world are running dry. Aquifer depletion may reduce grain harvests in Africa and Asia by 25 percent. Under the northern plains of China, which produce 40 percent of the grain harvest, the water tables are falling by five feet per year. Crops will inevitably fail. Those people can be fed, but not, at least as we presently proceed, by the produce of their homelands. Will they be fed? Twenty million starving "ecohomeless" people recently roamed sub-Saharan Africa in misery. We occasionally saw them on television, cadaverous children carrying one another on dusty trails, flies crawling their eyelids. Nearly a billion people are at present hungry and malnourished. The suffering represented by these statistics is unimaginable. Meanwhile, in 1995, corporate plantations in Africa inherited from the colonialist period went on producing cotton for export, while far less human food was produced than in 1965. Our economic and political thinking is leading us to hideous policies. We're capable of feeding those people, but our politicians and bureaucracies just don't seem interested in getting the job done. Maybe they think we're too distracted to notice, or that we don't really care. Maybe they're right.

Tribal people venerate stories. Experienced elders carry tribal memories with them in the form of narratives about appropriate responses to the waves of drought and abundance that flow across their homelands, and they are treated as kings. But they don't know how to turn the hearts of the long-faced men and women who sit in corporate boardrooms. Sophisticated cultures become extinct and the loss of their detailed local understandings and languages is a loss of feedback possibilities within the human community. Actual loss. Nothing theoretical about it. We are diminished.

Carbon-based fuels and the consequent accumulation of carbon dioxide in the atmosphere causes acid rain; "greenhouse" gases cause average temperatures around the world to soar; the global ice caps are melting, and insurance companies have begun to panic; the great warming is real; sea levels are beginning to rise, and heavily populated coastal areas around the world will very likely be inundated in another fifty years. And by then, the petroleum era will be history, the world supply 80 percent gone, never to be replaced.

Can we put a stop to these destructions? Certainly. Generate energy without using petroleum or coal. In response to oncoming coastal flooding—the harbors of New York, Singapore, and Tokyo underwater for the foreseeable future—and the very strong chance of disastrous consquences to insurance companies, banks are beginning to finance solar-powered facilities. Money protects money. However, better late than not at all.

By 2050, nearly half of the approximately 1,390,900 species on earth may be extinct. Lose enough, and the global ecology of genes in interacting systems will cease to function. Allowing such a die-out is unthinkable, but not, apparently, undoable.

Generating the will to rethink entrenched procedures entirely and implement change will be enormously difficult. Financial and governing bureaucracies are populated by people—hundreds of thousands around the world—who've been educated to believe in the system they serve. They've devoted themselves to its success, and they will profoundly resist abandoning it. Deep-seated revision of that system is unlikely so long as they continue believing that accumulation of wealth is in itself progress, until they become individually convinced that their mission lies in servicing communities and habitats. Or until the seas start rising dramatically.

And they metaphorically are. Twenty-six percent of the adult population of Zimbabwe is infected with HIV; in Botswana, it's 25 percent; in South Africa, with 39 million people, the infection rate is 22 percent; in Namibia, Swaziland, and Zambia, 18 percent. In Tanzania, with 32 million people, the rate is 9 percent, as it is in Ethiopia, with a population of 59 million, and Nigeria, with 106 million people. And as yet, many Africans don't know that they have the virus. Zimbabwe, Botswana, and South Africa are likely to lose 20 percent of their adult populations to the disease within the next decade. Losses will equal those due to the bubonic plague, which wiped out 25 million, one-fourth of the people in Europe in the four-teenth century, or smallpox among Native Americans in the sixteenth through the eighteenth centuries, from 10 to 20 million dead. To what degree are we responsible? For the HIV virus, not at all, but for the plague and its consequences, to the degree that they can be controlled, for mitigating the suffering, absolutely.

Can we conjure up the will to care more about plagues and starvations and ecosystems than gross national products? Can we plan at all without forfeiting freedoms? Scary sequences of thought come to mind:

- Technologies like computers are tools used to manipulate and control "nature," and ours are sophisticated to the point where it's possible to imagine the end of "nature" as unmanaged and independent, which leads to thoughts of . . .
- Living in planned, managed, semivirtual habitats, our desires continually manipulated, which leads to thoughts of . . .
- Genetic engineering and personality-altering drugs— will it be possible to create better minds in better bodies in a better world?

Who owns the future? The answer, in evolutionary terms, is simple. Whoever owns the genes. The terrible box is open. Sheep and corn can be biologically reconfigured. Genes can be owned and sold, possessed and doled out. Are these unthinkable enterprises? Or a good idea? Who gets to decide? This is not some sci-fi dream. It seems proven, for instance, that a gene triggers nurturing behavior in female mice; without that gene, they allow newborns to die of neglect. Maybe altruism, too, is a genetic trait, and it may be possible to breed altruism out of warriors. Passivity is likely to be a genetic trait; perhaps we can breed passive citizens who are both politically inert and highly susceptible to advertising. Or else brain-dead altruism can be engineered in and we could enjoy a race of happy servants. Probably we can influence aging, and certainly we can weed out the infirm before birth. Cloning isn't even so complex. Can we make humans to order and use their bodies as replacement parts for the ill and the aged? Or—dream of dreams—breed an entirely humane and environmentally responsible citizenry. Which is unfortunately a very bad idea of the Nazi sort. In any event, human cloning lies in our future. Count on it. Would I like a new heart if mine fails? Indeed I would. But no matter how gifted and immortal those biological creations might be, they will not be us. With no plan anyone can enunciate, what are we creating?

COMMONS are everywhere, whether blighted or elegantly organized, wild or gardened or ravaged. Bright skies are a commons, and so are whales and spawning salmon at the headwaters of our great rivers, and the children who live across the street, none of which we define as owned. And there is the man-made commons: streets and telephone lines and airfields and the water flowing from kitchen taps. For thirty years, I taught school, hired to care for that commons.

In Missoula, the small city where I live in Montana, the economy is not exactly thriving, but citizens have voted to spend millions in tax dollars to purchase steep mountainsides in order to prevent development, residential or otherwise. They did so because they understood what they wanted. Even with a supply of good automobiles and television and take-out hamburgers, they were looking up. The mountains were there every morning, snowy or flowering, and impossible to ignore, the sight of them of great value. People began to meditate about how much those mountains mattered in their lives. In winter, we stand on downtown sidewalks and gaze up at herds of elk in the snowfields. In summer, we walk there among nesting birds. From the mountains, we can look down into the sweetness and defeats of our lives while wild mice rustle nearby. In Boulder, Colorado, citizens voted to deny fire protection to houses built above a prescribed level on the slopes above the city, so no one built on those hills. People in Oregon voted for zoning that prevented urban sprawl from spilling into farmlands. Trying to ensure that their communities evolve in connection to humane sympathies and ecological rhythms, through openhanded public acts, citizens deliberately create commons. They *plan,* and do so on purpose.

We eat and breathe commonalities. Native people in the Bitter Root Valley of Montana burned hillsides to provide grazing for horse herds. They were caring for and re-creating a commons. In the Italian hills west of Siena, a man gathered roadside greens for our dinner, and we felt included in his ancient hospitality, another commons.

Beyond the biosystem, concepts like order and peacefulness or constraint and liberty are common-pool resources. They're our responsibility, and thus a limitation on freedom. Highways are a commons. We aren't allowed to drive when we're drunk. Overpopulation, crime rates, nuclear weapons control, the AIDS plague, and fragmented cultures and anomie—name your poison—are also part of our commons. Generosity is part of our commons, as is greed.

In a 1968 issue of *Science* magazine, environmental theorist Garrett Hardin suggested imagining a pasture "open to all." Though each herder directly benefited only from his own herd, the costs of overgrazing were shared. "Therein is the tragedy. Each man is locked into a system that compels him to increase his herd without limit—in a world that is limited. Ruin is the destruction toward which all men rush, each pursuing his own best interest in a society that believes in the freedom of the commons." Hardin also wrote that "Mutual coercion mutually agreed upon" could restrain people from destroying the resources life depends upon, but many immediate wants would have to be denied. That, Hardin wrote, "is preferable to total ruin."

Each person, however, is not "locked into a system which compels him to increase his herd without limit." While all creatures are driven to succeed, there are many definitions of success; and if we're often indifferent to outsiders, we are equally often openhanded within our band. Citizens using a commons are not entirely driven to exploitation by their natures. They're also driven by stories, ordinarily embodied in customs and laws, which tell them how to proceed, how to use. And they can always reinvent their stories—for the common good or otherwise, unfortunately. We do it all the time. It's part of planning for the future.

People's sense of their own best interests vary widely, and properties held in common have been successfully managed all around the world, if indeed usually in compliance to "mutual coercion mutually agreed upon." Strategies evolved to sustain lobster fisheries in Maine, mountain pastures and forests in Switzerland and Japan, irrigation cooperatives in Spain and the Philippines, and flood-control management on the Mississippi River watershed suggest models. The same problems come up over and over again, and it's common knowledge among resource managers that solutions require at least three elements: individual commitment, institutional flexibility, and compliance, with monitoring.

These problems have historically been controlled in stable communities with a shared past and the expectation of a shared future, usually in a system that includes a reputation for keeping promises, honest dealings and reliability, a willingness to preserve and democratically revise the system so as to endure, along with fair application and obedience to agreed-upon rules that are enforced by public law and more so by public will, by shaming. Common-interest communities, small and local inside the regional and national, each talking to the other, negotiating in a framework of widely understood democratic etiquette, offer about as much freedom as we are likely to realize anywhere within the restraints of civilized life.

Obviously, it's possible to expect fairness from our fellow citizens. Successful cultures usually instruct their members about proper treatment of one another, in a defining mythology coded into law. Disregard for that code is usually a route toward exclusion from the benefits enjoyed by society—by shaming, deportation, fines, imprisonment, or death.

We are surrounded by cautionary tales about what can happen when societies institutionalize selfishness. The conduct of the conquistadors in Mexico and Bolivia seems sufficiently inhumane to make me wonder if they were not an extraterrestrial species. "Ethnic cleansing" of aboriginal lands in the Americas and Australia and by the Nazis throughout Europe, and nowadays by various parties in the Balkans, in Rwanda, in Ireland, and in the Near East provides further hideous evidence. The world has little trouble cooking up totalitarian pathologies; fighting back without becoming as coercive as those you resist is the trick.

But most of us understand the importance of at least occasionally putting personal desires aside in favor of acting for the good of others in our family or community. Generosity at that level is ordinary, and can also grow wild, like roses in the fencerow.

IN SITKA, we watched bald eagles flying out of rainbows as a trio played a Mozart oboe concerto—two versions of beauty. On a gray afternoon, we went out in a yellow oceangoing rubber raft to see humpback whales. We wanted to hear them sing, to witness their rising, but we didn't. We did sink into vivid ankle-deep moss as we climbed over intricately layered timber on a tiny island inhabited by deer and an occasional bear that swam out from the mainland. From a stony beach, we watched an eagle watching us from a snag while tearing at the flesh of a twitching salmon.

The anthropologist Richard Nelson, having lived for years with the Koyukon Indians in central Alaska, helped me see how people imagined life during the 99 percent of human existence in which they were hunting and gathering. "The natural and supernatural worlds are inseparable; each is intrinsically a part of the other," Nelson writes. He says that the Koyukon believe we must treat plants and animals with humility, as kin, never to be exploited or treated in harmful ways. We are mutually dependent on shared order. Restrained, respectful interactions with life generates "biorhythmic harmonies." Which helps cure stress, as the doctors tell us. Nelson says he wants to be eaten as soon as he dies. "I want to get back into circulation." He laughs, but it isn't a joke. We have no choice but to harvest one another. But the natural order of things is not warfare.

Bruce Chatwin wrote, "A leopard at the kill is no more violent or angry than an antelope is angry at the grass it eats." Hunters thank the game; farmers thank crops; herders thank the sheep and hogs and cattle. Cultures without such rituals find butchering repellent.

The Chumash Indians on the Southern California coast

would light the countryside afire in the dry late fall, climb in their boats, and go out to spend the winter on the Santa Barbara Islands. They'd come back in springtime, to find the countryside in vivid renewal, the game animals well fed for another year. It was a method of gardening.

This began as a book about paradise. The word comes from ancient Persia and denoted a garden, a cultivated sanctuary, a watered and fertile oasis where beasts, actual and metaphoric, could lie down with one another—like the Garden of Eden, or the walled garden and sanctuary of the Alhambra. Most people are attracted to knowable neighborhoods in which people strive to live in harmony, trying to get along with one another while resisting the urge to regulate and oppress. Where cooperation is taken to be imperative. The blue earth floats in the black sky. We might think of it in its entirety as both garden and commons, the only one we'll ever be privileged to inhabit.

The unruly creature we are hungers for a sanctuary. Stories about gardening tend to stress sanity and satisfaction, acting out our common dream of organizing ourselves to care for and defend life. But forays into generosity can sometimes drift off into sappiness. For that reason, the bargaining world often succeeds in ignoring intensely practical thinkers like the Buddha, the radical Jesus, Saint Francis, and Gandhi.

Travel, for me, runs on a desire to visit gardens. I want to know why people revere their particular order of life, how it works for them, if it might help me find solace. By traveling, we court adventure, but also hospitality and a sense that people are working patiently and willingly at life-enhancing arts.

My friend Beverly, from the hippie bar scene in Missoula, told me about the day she got ten thousand ladybugs from a mail-order house. Ladybugs eat garden pests. "The box said

'Refrigerate until needed.' But those ladybugs were alive. How could you put ladybugs in the refrigerator?" she asked me.

So she didn't. She opened the box and put the ladybugs in a spare bedroom, where by the next morning they covered her walls and ceiling. "They were beautiful, but I had to do something. I got a spoon and saved them one by one." Those who knew her in the old days find this remarkable. "But it was all I could do," she said.

Beverly's mother married the fellow who owned the Oxford, a workingman's joint in downtown Missoula, where Senator Mike Mansfield used to show up and spend an hour or so staying in touch with his electorate. (You have to think it was a sweeter world.) "I was a wild-assed five-year-old," Beverly says, "with the run of the bar. So they sent me up Pattee Canyon to the farm where Julianne Daniels took care of kids. We had cows. I loved the garden because I loved her, and I'm back to it. I'm living my memories." Beverly's garden is elegant and purely organic. She makes a little money selling catnip to pet stores, and fruits and vegetables at the Saturday-morning Farmer's Market down by the Northern Pacific railway station, but she's not in it for the money. Standing beside her compost pile, she says, "This is the answer. Using shit."

Sandra Perrin was reaping yellow tomatoes the size of marbles on a mid-September afternoon in Missoula. They radiated warmth as she dumped them into my hands, a Siberian variety that does well in Montana. A brisk, graying woman, Sandra was a girl on a farm in southern France, near Toulouse. "We raised what we ate. With free manure, organic was the only way. We supplied Paris in the wintertime. The best food in the world. So eat." I felt that I should.

Those yellow tomatoes were not what I had been educated to understand as attractive. My idea of tomatoes came from ads for those big juicy red and tasteless objects of the same name that I bought in supermarkets. The jubilation with which my body greeted them was shockingly physical, a flooding of surprise. I hadn't known I was so deprived. These tomatoes tasted of dry weeks on a gravelly slope at the mouth of Pattee Canyon, and a genetic story extending garden to garden over centuries from Siberia to Montana to me. As I gobbled tomatoes, lost in pleasure, Sandra regarded me, the poor starved creature, with sympathy. How did we allow ourselves to lose touch with such gratification?

"What I am," Doug Bleecker tells me, "is a kind of bowerbird." Bleecker is a redheaded giant—six foot four and three hundred pounds anyway, energized every summer morning by what he wakes up to find in his garden. "Maybe I'll attract a mate." When I first met him, Doug was a bartender and bouncer in a Missoula hippie bar called Eddie's Club, and he was terrifying late in the night when a scuffle broke out and he came vaulting over the bar. There was a lot of scurrying out the front door, with him close behind.

Because Doug's backyard was once an old automobile junkyard, and untillable, the soil mostly river rocks and gravel and chunks of broken castings, his garden consists of 556 steel drums filled with soil and set on end, an old tire around the rim of each, and more than 400 baskets strung on wires between the cottonwood trees, all of it hooked up to drip irrigation lines. The barrels work like raised beds. "I can stand up to my work. Like a big boy," he says. He showed me twenty-three kinds of colored peppers, with names like Blackbird and Cardinal, a wall of scarlet runner beans, and vines thick with huge half-hidden red Delicious tomatoes (only one of his three dozen varieties). Ripening cantaloupe were suspended high above the ground in old bras donated by women friends, and blossoming flowers, including seventy-five varieties of tulips, were interplanted with vegetables in abandoned urinals and bathtubs; the compost pile supported a thicket of blue morning glories.

MAYBE THERE should be a poetics of gardening. There's obviously a relationship between gardening, managing what we have in a nurturing manner, and responsibility. Planning a garden is a matter of cooperating with nature, honoring intertwined systems, instead of some design we've cooked up. But some say gardens are not really nature. On the other hand, people build trout streams from the dry ground up, with riffles and deep holes and mosquitoes and evolving aquatic life, the works—as they would a garden: They're not reclaiming ruined streams, but creating new ones, attempting to start the complexities and then let them run. While it's easy to dismiss engineered streams as jerry-rigged and unnatural, they're also utterly fishy and wet. Mayflies evolve in them, and we could fall in and drown. Maybe they're natural enough.

Annick tells of a recurring dream in which she climbs the stairways of a Victorian house, until at the top she finds the bedroom that is hers; it has always been hers. "I thought it was a real house and wondered where it was, until I realized that it existed only in my dreams." After her husband died, she again found herself climbing the stairs to her bedroom, resting on a padded seat built into a bay window, looking out to blossoming trees in a flowering garden. Her husband sat high in the limbs of the tree, smiling across at her without speaking. She awoke feeling comforted. No doubt there are many points to this story, depending on who's thinking about it. For me, it has to do with finding rest in a warm interior space, from which she could see out to blossoming trees, and beyond that to fields, and beyond the fences to wild forests and then mountains on the horizon, and how that expanding sequence of enclosures—clear to the stars if you want, and beyond again—is home, where love is located, and how those enclosures are always there, what we have, and sometimes enough.

The yearnings built into our DNA, which evolved in wilderness, are for us the imperishable world. One of the things we're likely to love is freshness at table, produce straight from the garden plot or mushrooms dug among the cottonwoods lining the river. In creating gardens, from vegetable plots to wild parks, we nurture ourselves by taking part in living physical harmonies, organizing spaces that put us at ease. Some of our gardens are primarily places to grow food, whereas others are places where we can rest and reconnect to life. The fields below the limestone cliffs along the Vézère River near Lascaux are a perfectly tilled farmland that was never intended to be a park, though it is anyway. Scaled to dimensions that allow us to feel comfortable, placed, safe, and at liberty, this land that's been farmed continuously for three thousand years also shows us it's possible to use the world's productivity without being profoundly destructive.

A central concern—which all our plans must allow for—is intimacy. Walled cities, islands, homes, and oasis ranchlands—neighborhoods—each is an emotional habitation. Each answers our need for intimacy with what the old animal within senses as the "natural" rhythms of life, and is a place we can respond to physically, in what's called a "body-related" harmony with nature: a feeling of community in a domicile or homeland that is in balance and is a source of physical and emotional well-being. Gardens are fashioned to make us feel we're in an organized world. In this, gardens resemble narratives, which invite us to develop expectations and give our own responses. In Japanese Zen gardens, stones often stand alone or grouped into archipelagoes in expanses of raked sand, imitating a homeland of islands.

Milton said that as Adam and Eve made their way out of paradise, "the world lay all before them." In this imagined world, animals lie down together to symbolize the interactions of evolution that produce abundance. Berries fell to the hand and animals gave their lives so humans could eat. Milton's version of Eden is another dream of the natural golden age, in which no creature, however powerless or insignificant, is oppressed, a land where we might all be native.

Europeans and then Americans tried for a long time to convert the continent, this new paradise found, into a garden, a symmetrical haven where chaos was walled out. Jefferson promulgated an imaginative act that had much to do with the conquest of North America, the grid survey, by which the length and breadth of the United States were measured into square, mappable entities, thus quantifying phenomena like deserts and mountain ranges, not to speak of watersheds and intricate ecologies. Naming with numbers, staking claims. The grid survey was a fundamental step toward both emotional and physical ownership, toward rendering space into a commodity, as on Manhattan, usable and salable—partially stripping the continent of mystery and dangers, and leading us directly to the asphalt dreams of city-lot ownership that are Los Angeles and Phoenix.

By the late nineteenth century, however, urban areas were perhaps too quantified, and a cautious movement toward the reestablishment of wildness began. A key practitioner was Frederick Law Olmsted, who hoped that people would "enjoy beautiful natural scenery" and that they might "obtain occasional relief from the nervous strain due to the artificiality of city life."

Olmsted was devoted to creating democratic pleasuring grounds. After touring England in his late twenties, he wrote, "The great beauty and the peculiarity of the English landscape is to be found in the frequent long graceful lines of deep green hedges and hedge-row timbers, crossing hill, valley, and plain, in every direction; and the occasional large trees, dotting the broad fields, either singly or in small groups, left to their natural open growth." He loved the play of streams and ponds and "the clean and careful cultivation, and the general tidiness of the agriculture." He had found his vision, and it was pastoral. But it was tempered by his distaste for what he saw of social injustice in that same setting, the worst being the conditions in which farmworkers were expected to live. Their "mode of life," Olmsted wrote, "was like that of *domestic animals.*"

The development of parks, part of a broad set of social reforms to improve conditions in the industrial cities, was just beginning in England. Olmsted had found public lands being used to promote the refreshment of all the citizens, not just the wealthy, and he began to think that creating such parks could be a prime aspect of social responsibility in America. His first design was Central Park, inspired by the parks he'd seen in England, and based on notions of the pastoral—meadows, avenues of trees, ribs of stone, and glimpses of water. A place to walk on trails (if now dangerous at night), the great park was built in the interest of helping citizens feel at home and at ease in the greater creation, the desensitizing vastness of New York City. In the late years of the nineteenth century, parks in cities from Chicago to San Francisco were engineered in this tradition (often by Olmsted) and became models for suburban landscapes—the enclosure, and inside that, the home and refuge, whose picture windows look out over lawns to curving tree-lined cul-de-sacs, all the elements of the primal prospect-and-refuge landscape. The appeals are obvious, but so are the limitations. Parks are meant to be safe, engineered havens; we escape to them.

By 1858, when Olmsted was at work on Central Park, an alternate tradition already existed. The first notable voice was Ralph Waldo Emerson's. In *Nature,* published in 1836, he celebrated naturalness as a source of emotional solace. In an 1862 essay entitled "Walking," Henry David Thoreau wrote, "Hope and the future for me are not in lawns and cultivated fields, not in towns and cities, but in the impervious and quaking swamps. Life consists of wildness. Not yet subdued to man, its presence refreshes him. . . . In short, all good things are wild and free." Finally, and most famously: "In wildness is the preservation of the world." Together with Whitman, these Transcendentalists were outlining the spiritual case for what was to become the American conservation movement: Save our emotional and spiritual selves by preserving the natural sources of glory, the mirror in which it's possible to witness deity unfolding.

This core message was already at work in the world. On the night of September 19, 1870, a group of people, including Nathaniel P. Langford, a Montana investor interested in promoting tourism on the Northern Pacific Railroad, camped in the Yellowstone area. Someone proposed preserving its "wonders" and "curiosities" by creating a national park. By 1872, after intensive public-relations efforts by Langford, Congress set Yellowstone aside "as a public park or pleasuring-ground for the benefit and enjoyment of the people."

The need to preserve areas of the world in their natural state was reiterated by nineteenth-century Americans like John

Wesley Powell and John Muir, as the conservation movement began gaining acceptance. Aldo Leopold—in *Sand County Almanac,* published in 1949, a year after his death—called for a "land ethic," in which citizens would see themselves as integral parts of nature. "That land is a community is the basic concept of ecology, but that land is to be loved and respected is an extension of ethics."

In *A Timeless Way of Building* (1979), Christopher Alexander proposes planning for emotional comfort. He writes of what he calls a "pattern language" based on habitual activities and events. By "patterns," I take Alexander to mean the common movements of people from solitude to intimacy, from public arenas back into the home, while doing something as simple as carrying firewood. Children at play in water is one of the 253 patterns Alexander identifies. All of them mirror ordinary, biologically driven activities. We enact them over and over in places designed to accommodate these commonplace psychic transactions.

It's inevitable that our planet is mostly going to be a vast garden, tended by humans. But in order for that garden to be a truly functional place for our kind to live, it will have to include enormous tracts of wilderness where various species can go on evolving without supervision or scrutiny, areas where we have given up all possibility of manipulation. To keep hands off is a difficult lesson to internalize. At some point, we have to say enough with the improvements, draw lines in the sand, and declare that certain entire ecosystems, regardless of short-term economic value, to the degree that we can ensure it, are and will remain wilderness, wild.

That's because thinkers in the modern environmental movement have revealed to us that the complex biological exchanges that are absolutely necessary to continued adaptive evolution, without which life on earth will eventually be dead in the water, can take place only in extensive tracts of wilderness. This is not sort of true; it's scientific fact, the practical reason for supporting wilderness.

And then there's that spiritual argument. Paradise, the safe, flowering haven, lies deep in the dreams of every culture. But heavens on earth tend to be creations orchestrated by imperialist egos, works of art built with somebody's money. The Alhambra, with its rilling waters, and Hadrian's Villa near Rome and the formal lawns at Versailles each express the pride of those with the power to cause monuments to be created; and as Neruda reminds us, great projects tend to be erected on the bones of the oppressed. Wilderness reminds us of our actual situation and what we are, and in doing so, it reawakens our old animal.

Even so, I listen up when folk wisdom says I won't have lived a whole life until I've built a house for myself. It's no doubt a sign of aging and wanting to reimagine myself one more time. I daydream about building my house amid flowering fields in a mountain enclave, and a porch where visitors would stand and look out to the canyons across the river before they entered sunny public rooms. We might send our overnight friends to sleep on covered verandas out by the raised flowering beds of a thickety garden. Or in winter, they could sleep under down comforters on porches along the sunrise side of the second floor, fields below them at twilight like a snowy blue universe and icy with new snow at sunup, already tracked by some creature. But I don't act on that impulse because Annick's log house on a meadow in the mountains outside Missoula is entirely home enough, and much like the one I dream about.

Evenings, as we grow older and are inclined to celebrate the cocktail hour at home, Annick and I gather in her kitchen, and her sons, too, when they are home. We drink decent wine out of good glasses, compare recipes, and get serious with mixing and stirring. The kitchen is the center of the household, where food, the central metaphor for communality, is prepared so we can eat, laugh, and enjoy such abundances as suit us and that we can afford. Gatherings of the same kind take place, of course, in taverns and cafés, at wakes and ceremonial feastings all over the earth, from here to Timbuktu, every day. Cheers, may you have joy.

The stone pathways and canals in Venice are like veins and arteries in a body or leaf. In India, people enjoy garden houses called *baradari,* where they can catch the breeze and watch the churning of thick black clouds as they enjoy listening to falling rain, sort of like people in Tucson, who go out to stand in the streets and get wet when the monsoons hit in July and water runs deep in the sandy arroyos. Awakenings are like blossoming.

HUMANS ARE clearly capable of both selfishness and generosity in the same gesture. We give in order to feel good, or in an attempt to ensure successful lives for our progeny and species—all of which can be thought of as an ultimately selfish motive. But excessive giving is taken to be a sign of weakness unless we are very secure; throwing our advantages away can also indicate our sense of casual strength and superiority. Most of what we do, in fact, is both sweet and sour. Potlatch ceremonies among tribal people on the northwest coast of North America were based on the notion of giving away all you owned, occasionally to the point of killing slaves. During Mardi Gras in New Orleans, citizens ride floats through the crowded streets, throwing coins and strings of beads to the masses as if (almost) making fun of their own rank. Other giveaway ceremonies, like buying rounds of drinks in a crowded bar, indicate economic power, a willingness to grasp life, and an indifference to our commonplace fear of mortality and, of course, wealth.

Because such behaviors are a result of both our genetic makeup and social conditioning, institutionalized generosity the idea that generosity should be a primary consideration in making all of our most urgent private and public decisions will be a tough sell. Most of us have lived our lives committed to win-lose models of economic behavior and social justice, and we are in thrall to the idea that we control our own fates, and that *power*—over people, life, nature, *things*—will quiet our uncertainties and fend off our most profound fears. It would be silly to claim that many of us would voluntarily act against our best interests. Still, we could manage to rethink our strategies, maybe even understand generosity as both an individual and societal route toward survival. Can we and the rest of our citizenry learn to enjoy the pleasures of caring for the entire world as if it were a commons? Can we plan for amplitude and freedom? Can we understand that generosity toward others is also a measure taken on behalf of ourselves?

Humans are largely defined by what they long for. The yearning for intimacy, lover to lover, flesh to flesh, and mind to mind, is built in. People enjoy strangeness, escape, secrets, and adventures, laughter and open simplicity, both reassurance at home and prowling in the night before forgiveness in the sunlit warmth of morning, quick complicities and perversities and abandon in the same rough wet sack with innocence and abundance. Most of us find comfort in repetitions, like meals at established hours and sleeping through the night and freedom on weekends. Most of us ordinarily agree on the value of family, health, prosperity, and security. We *can* reformulate our ideas of how to get those things. We do it all the time.

While the organization of societies, like gardens, grows in an organic fashion and our responses are often predictable—clear morning light makes me happy every time, and sleeping on airplanes drives me crazy—we aren't "genetic victims." We routinely transcend inclinations such as greed.

We find fulfillment in caring for whatever it is we take to be naturally invaluable. We care about our people because we are genetically wired to love someone, if only ourselves. Most of us want to take part in giving, at least in situations where we feel secure, because we want to feel we are useful, maybe even powerful, and because we intuit that our kind is most likely to survive in benevolent circumstances.

Some of us, the privileged third of humankind, have the time and resources to cultivate elaborate desires; we demand to participate in the lyric of plenty, the feast, the decorative and flowering life. We enjoy fine cheeses and wines, rafting on rivers and playing on the best golf courses. Our urge to play derives from our urge to participate in activities so dense and complex that we can sense but not really fathom their order, such as billiards or a run of metaphor about melancholy from Montaigne to Sam Johnson to Beckett, such as winds behind our sail or the lucky streak on the craps table or in the stock market.

But sadness is everywhere, along with hunger, injustice, and violence. A majority of the world's people live in coercive circumstances. Many thousands will die this year in prisons or of starvation. Incessant cruelties, injustice, inequality, and disenfranchisement are normal on downtown streets, and out on the flowering prairies and in the suburbs and elementary school classrooms. Fearfulness drives hatred. We want to say it is not our fault. But it is.

There's no law of man or nature that says it has to be like this. We can think of other lives, and have them. In the hope of improving ourselves, we might attempt naming what beyond ourselves we take to be invaluable. Maybe sidewalks in our major cities, crawling with extraordinary poets? Or the laughter of citizens suffering only the ancient, basic troubles, meanwhile getting along with mothers, fathers, children, and lovers in the thickets of those attachments? We need stories that encourage us to think that being good is giving nourishment *and* taking all possible responsibility. What do we mean by *proper* ambition? Which creature do we want to be?

A culture based on institutionalized selfishness is going literally insane. Are we pleased by the fact that the most powerful forces in ours work on behalf of relentless economic progress and not much else? Should we insist they take strong, expensive, and immediate efforts to ensure the success of human and other ecologies? Should we insist—to our fellows and our governments and corporations—that greed and nothing else simply will not do? Should we force them—by law, and through citizen disapproval—into conduct focused on public generosity and caretaking? Probably so. Governments and corporations are ours, after all; we allow them to exist at our forbearance, for no other purpose than to serve us.

Citizens the world over wonder how they can lay hands on the power to run their own lives and call their own shots. Part of the answer lies in talking, listening, arguing, working toward agreement, bargaining, defining and redefining values, then starting over when the settlement falls apart. Despite politicians and planners, laws and legislation, standing armies and irresponsible despotisms, public consensus will in the long run rule the world. The essential act is citizen participation, the play of minds that courts a responsible society into being. When that dialogue dies, as history has shown us again and again, the result is a loss of private and public self-determination and ultimately of social cohesion. That's why we have no choice but to participate. Common goals only come of common discussion. In village squares and community halls in Kansas and Indonesia, and in cafés in New Orleans and ski condos in Switzerland, talk about who we might be and how we might live is the most important business the world is conducting.

Our discussions and opinions must be public and reported as widely as can be, in print and on the radio and television, in theaters and along the lines that link computers—constantly, everywhere, by all means possible. Public responses can then work to generate a worldwide sense of purpose. Common goals and values flow from café advocates and hippie gurus, Corn Belt pig farmers, schoolteachers, and women on the dusty streets of Alto La Paz, and they will prevail no matter what public and private power structures might dictate. Public will is relentless when powered by a common purpose.

Planning involves understanding how things are, where we are, and how things could be. But efforts to entirely manage the future never work except in confined environments, and even then not for long. Planning must allow for evolution. Sanctuaries designed to embody particular visions usually drain life dry, then turn it into an entrapment. History demonstrates that no lid stays in place for long. To imagine we can define specific solutions to future problems is profoundly foolish. Solutions are always contingent. Evolution will always have the best hand.

A Gabra elder explained what happens to people who do not give in the Gabra way: they end up dying alone, under a tree. "Even the milk from our animals," he added, "does not belong to us. We must give to those who need it, for a poor man shames us all."

—DAVID MAYBURY-LEWIS, *Millennium*

. . . however so selfish a man may be supposed, there are evidently some principles in his nature which interest him in the fortunes of others and render their happiness necessary to him, though he derives nothing from it except the pleasure of seeing it.

—ADAM SMITH, *The Theory of Moral Sentiments*

A YOUNG BOY brings half a dozen cows and calves out of the rimrocks toward his father's home fields in the isolations of the sun-blasted country north of the Black Rock Desert in Nevada. He dreams of girls by the Humboldt River in Winnemucca throughout his day.

While snow blows across highland Nevada, a redheaded woman feeds juniper firewood into a stove made of a fifty-five-gallon fuel barrel and listens to zydeco music on National Public Radio, then goes all dreamy as she braids a perfect rawhide riata. That woman and her husband grow a huge garden the next summer, and the woman trucks the produce to some town and just gives the food away. She will mark her rough signs to say FREE FOOD.

That redheaded woman and the boy who's helping her stand before cardboard boxs of carrots and snapbeans and corn and beets in the dusty light of a Saturday morning on the streets of Lovelock, and people study them as if they might be crazy or dangerous. Then another woman, maybe a school-teacher or a single mother run off from a seaport like San Diego, comes forward to accept a dozen ears of corn, a gift that has meaning primarily because it is a gift and adds to the beauty of things. One act of the imagination, then another. Think of faraway ice beginning to break, shattering.

JESUS ADVOCATED sharing the wealth. "Go, sell everything you have and give it to the poor, and you will have treasure in heaven."

We hear legendary stories about the Buddha and Saint Francis throwing down their rich-man robes and going over to the side of the poor. There are thousands and thousands of stories from around the world about awakening, casting off custom to reinvent society on a humane model—stripping down, nakedness as metaphor. We value these stories, accumulate them, and focus our lives on what we make of them and what we imagine they tell us about who we are supposed to be, or, if we believe in notions of fate, what we are meant to be.

MY FRIEND, the artist Robert Helm, maintains a fermenting, rotting compost pile. "It's my friend. I think I'll go out and piss on it right now."

While it is no doubt impossible to define a specifically "natural" way of being, we are often happiest when intimately connected to a flow of passions. In the laughter of their children, mothers find reasons for laughter, even when wandering the gutters of uttermost poverty. A broker in his perfect shirts may love the run and flow of his market with an equal fervor. Is one kind of joy more valuable than the other?

Maybe we should put together a catalog of revered places and people and the stories that make them invaluable, a listing of the things people have acknowledged they cannot live without, whether it's clean water in the tin bucket, a certain grove of yellow pine on warm late-summer afternoons after a rain shower, a living wage, freedom, or just one another. Lascaux and the windows at Chartres and the garden above the homesteader's orchard behind the house in Warner where my father planted strawberries in rows laid out with a spool of string, blue water surging up from the spring at the Hopi emergence site on the Little Colorado—for me, these are sacred places. My regard for them is built of intuitions I can only approximately articulate, but it has everything to do with the value of complexity.

YEARS AGO, I heard a chemist speak to a group of humanist academics. "Our discipline is not like yours," the chemist said. "Our questions have answers." Everybody laughed.

But certain scientific questions—for example, How does consciousness arise from chemistry?—do not, at this time, seem to be answerable. The same applies to the question, Where did we come from and why are we here? No one knows, and no one's likely to provide verifiable answers in any foreseeable future. We have no choice but to go on about our business while remaining utterly uncertain about ultimate matters. We tell ourselves stories in an effort to ameliorate this uncertainty, yet it remains. One result is chronic divisiveness. Still, pressed hard enough, given a choice between preserving one's beloved or otherwise being faced with enormous loss, people can find ways to agree. And we may be pressed very hard over the next several decades.

No one I know wants our species transformed into a different kind of creature, or even purged of selfishness. We're likely to continue being commercial, trading and dealing as much to our own advantage as possible. But maybe we need to rethink our ideas about "advantage." The infrastructure of world markets can be rethought and reinvented, if only incrementally. At the same time, intimidating questions about what we should be doing to ensure a reasonable future for our species can be answered—at least to a degree that makes certain conduct seem far more sensible than the alternatives. So, if desire is controllable, or at least manageable, if we believe we can actually think in terms of long-loop altruism, what can we sensibly ask of the world economic establishment?

In *Natural Capitalism: Creating the Next Industrial Revolution*, Paul Hawken, Amory Lovins, and L. Hunter Lovins have outlined a set of reasonable objectives. Ecosystem degradation should be considered a real business cost, and it should not be passed on to future generations. Natural resources should be used completely, down to the least valuable part, as Koyukon hunters do in Alaska when they kill a deer. Pollution should be eliminated and all waste returned to nature as a nutrient or used in manufacturing. Industrial models should be based as much as possible on biological processes, as with a leaf turning sunlight into energy. A premium should be placed on reinvesting in natural capital—restoring ecological and social damage and preserving resources. And people in business should act as brokers of social services, entering long-term relationships with their customers, rather than simply delivering one-off products on a onetime basis.

In *Development as Freedom*, Amartya Sen tells us that human capabilities are the key to economic success. What's most crucial is freedom, and practical support by a society that wants to see those capabilities developed, both of which encourage individuals to play, explore, and learn, to educate themselves. Societies that have safeguarded both liberty and tolerance and promoted the powers of individuals are the ones we ultimately envy for their stability and wealth. Widespread trust and openness—transparency, full disclosure, and lucidity—are of intrinsic moral value and of instrumental value to economic success. They should be thought of as primary social tools, which lead usually to the expansion of human abilities and citizen involvement in seeking out the common good. Given elementary capabilities—education and literacy, civil rights, health care, access to information through free media, the chance to work and earn a reasonable income, and the freedom to participate in politics through elections—people often achieve humane and generous solutions to social problems. There has never been, Sen points out, a famine in a modern democracy. Freedom from oppression, ignorance, and poverty—it's a matter of giving the genius of our species a chance.

But democracy as it is understood in nations like the United States will probably not thrive, for instance, in Africa just south of the Sahara until the cultures there have had time to invent political environments in which individual free choice is primary. Such a reinvention is not likely to take place until a middle class has evolved—a local culture with persuasive moral power that is for selfish reasons interested in orderly problem solving and a role in the inevitably developing world economy. Over the decades in which the political institutions that will ensure freedom are evolving in those cultures, the First World will, in self-interest, as a stay against chaos, be obliged to extend them extensive generosities. There is no other sensible choice. It's imperative for the future of people everywhere that disenfranchised cultures all over the globe be free to develop without being exploited or oppressed, that poverty be alleviated, that people be well fed, healthy, and schooled in both their own traditions and languages and in those of the First World. Then, eventually, they may be able to become full participants in the humane, self-respecting world-wide culture that could evolve. Otherwise, chaos looms. Again, it is a matter of giving their genius a chance.

In order to realize such agendas, we have to rethink some basic notions. Stories help us to locate ourselves and our values, to define who we are and what our purposes should be, and they should be continually rethought, over and over, particularly at present, a time of widespread alienation, anger, and hatred, with suicidal furies raging in societies around the world.

THE SWEETEST, most reassuring, and most peaceful stories can be recipes for singing ourselves to sleep. People need to hear cautionary tales. We need to remember, no matter how decent the majority of us may be, that we're dependent on a pattern of abuse that is ravaging the earth, rendering it uninhabitable for our race and most every species this side of cockroaches. We must know what it actually, physically means when we say that genetic loss through extinction is likely to be literally catastrophic for our children.

We're capable of thinking our way past biological imperatives, and we often stay true to those we love, despite all temptation. We want to believe in our freedom, and much of the time we do. (For instance, I can daydream about catching tiny trout in the little late-summer holes on Deep Creek whenever I'm awake; it's my choice, even if I can't choose to live forever.)

And most often we demand that other people act as if they are free even when it's clear they exist as patterns in a matrix. If we aren't really running our lives or controlling our fates, this news is often mitigated by our ability to feel free.

While we know that much of behavior is ultimately determined by our genes, we still ordinarily demand that people take responsibility for their actions (unless they are constrained or incapacitated by disability or craziness), although the degree of responsibility we demand varies from situation to situation and from culture to culture. In Japan, for instance, drunkenness excuses violent acts that nowadays would seem beyond the pale, or be severely punished, even in the wild American West.

Are the fish left in the stream valueless to a fisherman because someone might get to them before he returns? Not if communality counts more than accumulation. Genetically, we're wired to win, and, by extension, to survive, but that doesn't necessarily involve excluding one another. Taking care of life in the broadest sense is absolutely self-concerned. This planet is our common resource and we must insist that it is not up for grabs. We think of evolution as progress—toward what? No one really knows. We would profit by learning to think of progress as a movement toward sharing, rather than accumulating, and to consider our most central values in terms of our willingness to give.

ALONG RIVER ROAD in Missoula, her bare legs already muddy, Karen Zrschke was stooping to weed her carrots. Karen and her husband own a commercial raised-bed organic garden, about a half acre, on which they were able to support themselves.

"It's one of the most revolutionary things you can do," she said. I wondered why revolution interested a handsome, vital woman. Karen grew up privileged in the hills east of Berkeley, where she gardened alongside her mother and grandmother, then went on to an upscale life, managing a gallery in Seattle. "But something was missing," she said. "I remembered my mother's garden. So I set out to make a life around gardening. We raise enough food to feed about one hundred and thirty people. I'm proud of that." The revolution she spoke of is a people's movement aimed at caring for the world.

NIKOLIA VAVILOV was a Russian geneticist, and his work represents the first systematic attempt to locate the regional origins of the world's major crops. In 1940, T. D. Lysenko—the renowned crackpot Stalinist geneticist, who maintained that acquired characteristics can be inherited—blamed Vavilov for the failure of Soviet agriculture after collectivization. Nikolia Vavilov was arrested, interrogated, and sentenced to execution. He starved first.

The Vavilov Institute of Plant Breeding in Saint Petersburg, which preserves food-crop seeds to ensure genetic diversity, survived him. In 1942, during the German blockade and siege, people in Saint Petersburg ate dogs, cats, rats, and grass. Six hundred thousand people starved to death. The thirty-one people who worked at the Vavilov Institute, surrounded by seed potatoes and bags of rice seed, were each given a ration of 120 grams of bread per day, a quarter of an American loaf. Fourteen of them died of starvation in December alone. But they didn't eat the seed stock, an irreplaceable genetic resource.

Is such dedication crazy, or is preservation of our genetic heritage an absolute duty? If people everywhere understood that the weave that constitutes life is under attack—and, as in war, suffering great losses—would we be irresistibly moved to nurture it and one another? What would we be willing to forgo on behalf of future lives? We yearn for kisses and miracle cures, elegant cooking, incessant blossoming, and laughter in the fields and streets. So how do we plan our garden?

Epilogue

Jitterbugging at Parties

... between grief and nothing I will take grief.

—WILLIAM FAULKNER, *The Wild Palms*

And now the haunted
uprisen wailing call,
And again, and now the beautiful sane laughter.

—DAVID WAGONER, "Loons Mating"

MELVILLE WROTE, "We become sad in the first place because we have nothing stirring to do." Cut off from the most insistent practicalities of animal survival, we suffer what is called "postmodern existential melancholy." We search for significant, or at least diverting, things to do.

Thinking about our planet as it coasts on the fringes of a minor galaxy is like gazing into the fun-house mirror of mortality. Equipped to apprehend only what we can see, we see ourselves looking back, with all our distortions intact.

There were no answers as I stood gazing down on my mother's powdered face, eyeing the gates of nowhere. She was any number of light-years away. Nothing ended that bright morning, though everything did. No hope remained of calling to her again. All of us encounter sorrow that will not, in our minds, bear speaking about, and we weep, in truth, for ourselves.

We should've talked about death. I should have asked her how she felt, what she could tell or give me, but I was afraid. I should've said we had to talk about this now—and then it was too late. The primal loss, for the child, is so often the caregiver, the mother, to whom we were literally connected, who would never turn against us.

Rehearsals begin in childhood. Afflicted at five with polio, I spent months in hospitals. My father carried me off the train we rode to Portland, then went back to his farming. This was only natural; masculine abilities were expressed in work. In my hospital room, as I howled in the night, I was most grieved by the absence of my mother. The most important promise seemed broken.

Two photographs of my mother as a young girl study me in the room where I write, reminding me that my anxieties and my angers are mostly homemade. After she died, I'd think I wanted to call and tell her some particularly vivid line of gossip, just the sort of thing she loved at the end.

Uninhabited bodies wait at the end of our garden. We have no hope of progressing beyond them. The order of things is not our fault. In that sense, we are entirely innocent. We dream of perpetuity, yet an unimaginable transition awaits us—into what? We ask for truth, and what do we get? Candor.

In "The Speed of Light," W. S. Merwin writes:

> ... the brightness we could not touch
> and the air we could not hold had come to be there all the
>   time
> for us and would never be gone. ...

Merwin concludes:

> . . . *we began to listen for what*
> *might be escaping*
> *us and we hear high voices ringing*
> *the village at sundown*
> *calling their animals home*
> *and then the bats after dark and the silence on its road.*

When I was a boy, I believed the morning brightness would indeed never be gone. This was something the light told me, and the light would not lie. But in not so many years, this very life will have been a dream. So why should I care for anything but my own fears and loves and loathings?

Such thinking releases us into affectionless behavior. We kill what we cherish and cherish what we kill. Humans seem capable of acting out marvelously rapacious behavior, or any other social agenda we can imagine as a stay against anxiety. We seem incessantly willing to sacrifice for wealth or power. Like Cortés, we destroy white cities floating on the lake, along with their citizenry. We can create Zen gardens with mosses and pools, bridges, and sand raked around rough stones to remind us of mountain ranges or constellations, but contemplating infinity doesn't keep us from killing all the singing whales in the seas, every last one, for profit. We are confronted with the possibility of personal and social chaos, and our civility collapses as we watch.

I'm tempted to think that it's possible for people to dream their way into a world community in which it's understood that everyone's interests would be served by pursuing the common good, engendering feelings of both affection and responsibility for the blossoming world, for one another, and for all of us. But I wonder. We long to transcend the fact of our inevitable death through acts of the imagination, yet we must be vigilant, since ideologies so often lead us into monstrous indecencies. There is no transforming story. There's no one to be but who we are. It's impossible to describe perfection as anything more than a marginally better version of what we already have, or to take part as anything other than what we've always been, an evolving creature in an evolving situation. Though we'll never be able to re-create our biology or brains more than marginally, it might be useful, as an exercise, to think of the earth as a communal and ever-changing garden, even the parts that are left to wilderness. We might just hedge our bets, and pass whatever's ripe and tasty around the table.

If I had my way—this is a wish list—the world would embrace these ideas.

- That biological diversity and cultural diversity are aspects of the same complex, fluctuating system from which we sprang.
- That we must live in terms of the rhythms evolution-ary history has built into our nervous systems.
- That some settings and proportions are comfortable and others are not, for emotional reasons that are bio-logically driven.
- That we must resist the impulse to simplify and weed plants and creatures and people into monocultures. Complexity is what's elegant and alive.
- That our physical conquest of the geographic world is over, and that we have nowhere else to go; and that movement between domesticity and wandering is natural, just as adventuring and exploring provide a balance against comfort, work, and meditation in a secure situation we call home. In any case, our cultural challenges are primarily emotional and intellectual.

- That many of our categories and cultural constructs do not really exist. Nothing is inherently "natural" or "wild," as opposed to "unnatural" or "tame," except in degrees.
- That we have to reexamine many of the manufactured, commodified desires the society drills into us.
- That we can do much to reimagine desire, and understand home as interwoven, manifold activities and relationships, rather than as a simple place.
- That metamorphosis is our most important topic as we seek to exist in harmony with the evolving patterns of those things that surround us. Verbs, as Ezra Pound said, but no nouns.

This is what I've come to believe: The world is luminous with significances. I'm born to revere those I love, to sorrow beside my mother's open coffin, to wish I could talk to my father one more time, to despise the injustices I've sanctioned. And I have no idea why I exist. Never will, not in this life.

Our cultures are based on accumulated information. Rather than biologically adapting to environments, we use the powers of our heritage to refit our various locations. People plant seeds, direct water to crops, and wait out the summer for the harvest; they breed animals for slaughter, to drag loads, and to carry riders; they build skyscrapers, then travel on rockets to the moon and walk around up there. But they never escape.

We see from a specific point of view, and think of ourselves in the third person, talk about ourselves as if we were objects, and think about thinking. Some of us even wonder if we ourselves are imaginary. What we need to do, however complex the working out, is simple enough: Face up to what's going on and figure out how to develop both sustainable and just communities for ourselves on what's clearly a transmogrified planet. Meanwhile, we should acknowledge that survival of the fittest doesn't mean survival of the violent, or the cruelest, or the selfish. We are not genetically driven to kill, to warfare, or even to games of accumulation. We are driven to survive, and in the long run, that is likely to involve altruism. Such are my dreams. It's easy enough to deplore the poetry of slaughter. But how to name those aspects of life we take to be most valuable?

AS WE IDLED through the bookstore in the National Gallery in Washington, D.C., Annick bought me a massive book entitled *Beyond Representation: Chinese Painting and Calligraphy, 8th–14th Century,* which helped me escape the anxieties generated in my country person by the rationalities typified in the huge abstraction of the National Mall. China, it seems, is a land of rivers, the Huang and the Yangtze, and mountains. What first attracted me to that book were the reproductions of landscape scrolls, towering peaks, intertwining waterways, empty distances. The tiny human figures were wrapped inside mists and sunlight and snow and rainfall, surrounded by trees and birds rendered precisely, each unique and distinct in the fluidity of things. Mountaineers and rock climbers claim concentration is central to finding joy. "You're absolutely there on the face. Daydream, and you're in trouble." Focus on the particularities of your work and surroundings, and eventually you'll be in the world. Abstractions will run off the slopes of your brain like rain. At least that's what they tell me.

Wildness is not background but essence, and humans are a part, like butterflies or clouds. Journeying and crossing over bridges is a fundamental situation, traveling without definable destination, each of us sustained by the whole, the other, and one another. No beginning, no end, no hierarchy or teleology.

The pulse of significances moves through life in riffles like water, its pools and underground seams, which suggests that the center of the cosmos is everywhere and that our actions ought to proceed from reverence for all, including ourselves. Mortality, then, is the ultimate wedding ring.

Annick strides up the Pacific beaches, eyes up, watching for dolphins. The waves are shot through with sunlight. Dark illuminated strands of seaweed inside the water are lifting with the roll, and falling. In summer meadows, the fragile odors must be meaningful; birds sing before sunrise. The world will kill us, but in the meantime we can pull up our socks and take pleasure in thoughts of flight and water in constant play.

The Japanese revere a quality of mind they call "aware," with which a pleasing sadness can be derived from confronting the transience of life. To me, it has come with the smell of wet sage and oranges being peeled. Traveling through highlands in the West, Annick and I often pick some sage to carry with us. One noontime, she peeled an orange. I was startled and almost disoriented, lost to a rainy afternoon in my boyhood on the deserts of southeastern Oregon, sitting on my bedroll in a tent at Sagehen Springs and eating a sweet section of orange. For that instant in our automobile, I was exactly in love with the long-ago stench of wet sage and cow shit in that tent with those bored horsemen who were dealing cards and getting ready for the fistfight that came along an hour or so later, and with this woman and her orange.

In 1919, Wallace Stevens wrote:

> *I placed a jar in Tennessee,*
> *And round it was, upon a hill.*
> *It made the slovenly wilderness*
> *Surround that hill.*

> *The wilderness rose up to it,*
> *And sprawled around, no longer wild.*
> *The jar was round upon the ground*
> *And tall and of a port in air.*
>
> *It took dominion everywhere.*
> *The jar was gray and bare.*
> *It did not give of bird or bush,*
> *Like nothing else in Tennessee.*

"It took dominion everywhere." Metaphors stand as a scrim between us and what is. Stevens went to Key West, escaping winter in 1934, and got into a famous, unlikely boxing match with Hemingway. In any long run, Stevens won. In "The Idea of Order at Key West," written that same year, he writes:

> *It was her voice that made*
> *The sky acutest at its vanishing.*
> *She measured to the hour its solitude.*
> *She was the single artificer of the world*
> *In which she sang. And when she sang, the sea,*
> *Whatever self it had, became the self*
> *That was her song, for she was the maker. Then we,*
> *As we beheld her striding there alone,*
> *Knew that there never was a world for her*
> *Except the one she sang and, singing, made.*

Riding at anchor in a catamaran, rising and falling in light rain over the shallow reef just south of Key West as Annick explored just under the surface, I listened to Ry Cooder and some Cuban musicians on a CD deck, fondled a warmish quart of Mexican beer, and wondered what else I needed. Not much. Annick, as she dried her hair, was happy and excited about brain coral, lobsters, and the blue-and-orange fish that hovered like luminescent angels in occasional drifts of sunlight after the rain passed on. We love the weave of our invention, without which, single artificers wouldn't be able to make sense of anything.

Maybe all we want is clarity, varieties of light, translucent clouds reefing over the hills in Italy or moonlight on the hay fields of my childhood, but mostly just the occasional clarity of mind to think without irony or panic. *This is what I am, and these are my chances.* Most of us are delighted to see as clearly as can be managed from the inherently half-blind human situation. We enjoy an occasional dose of egoless honesty.

Lawrence Weschler writes of interviewing an Italian jurist named Antonio Cassese, who was serving as president of an international panel of judges on the Yugoslav War Crimes Tribunal meeting in The Hague, reviewing details of one inhumane atrocity after another. Weschler asked how, "regularly obliged to gaze into such an appalling abyss, he kept from going mad himself." Cassese said he liked to "make my way over to the Mauritshuis museum, in the center of town, so as to spend a little time with the Vermeers." After visiting the Vermeers himself, Weschler says, "At a tremendously turbulent juncture in the history of his continent, he [Vermeer] had been finding—and, yes, inventing—a zone filled with peace, a small room, an intimate vision . . . and then breathing it out." Breathing it out. Giving it away.

OFF SOUTH, as we flew in over Houston for an art opening and a weekend of parties, dense black smoke curled to the sun, rising from open petroleum fires burning in the river. I thought of opera, high Wagner Götterdämmerung stuff.

A friend from southeastern Oregon once sang in the Houston Opera, then gave it up and went home to manage the family ranch. On a desert highway south of Burns a few years back, I listened to Beethoven on the tape deck and drove through the morning at great speed, blowing past the alkaline playa where he died of too much or not enough. Over Houston, everything was symbolic.

For us, it was an exotic occasion, a weekend with artists and collectors, people with casual wealth. A Frida Kahlo painting studied me as I fed myself with broiled shrimp piled on a tiny white porcelain plate. Now, everything was an enactment.

Sunday morning, out seeing the sights, we found ourselves facing a vertiginous IMAX film about pollination, food, and lovemaking—enormous swooping, disorienting images. So much dizziness so far from home. "Close your eyes," a young man said. "It's the Buddy Bolden Rule." Think of funeral-march music in New Orleans, and the great trumpet master Buddy Bolden slipping without farewell into what was called craziness for life, a clean getaway.

The Cockerall Butterfly Center was closer to the bone. Who could dream this up? Maybe someone feeling deprived, tired of closing their eyes. Two thousand quasi-free butterflies, fifty to sixty widely different varieties, were fluttering away their lives within the expansive confines of a cone-shaped three-story glass tower. We walked beside waterfalls in a flowering multi-tiered jungle, and the butterflies sometimes were attracted to bright colors; they rode on Annick's loose silvery hair like fluttering decorations, and contributed, as unrestrained creatures will, to restoring our shot nerves. Maybe that's civilization's main reason for contact with other forms of life these days; we like to have them around because their presence reminds us of rhythms that might keep us sane. We go to petting zoos in order to touch and witness emergence and interconnection and rebirth; we plug into situations where we can practice dancing the big dance, the old contact sport, with animals. The creatures, alone with us amid infinities, are our only companions. As we watch, life-forms are disappearing. It's like watching our invulnerabilities vanish. Of all our myriad duties, preservation has to be central.

Late that afternoon in Houston, we walked across great lawns to contemplate another actuality, the ensemble of murals Mark Rothko created for the eight-sided de Menil chapel, fields of radiant darkness, from which there came no message but whatever each viewer called up. For me, it was the demands of acceptance. On that bright afternoon, I thought of Glenn Gould in the studio he built in the backlands of Canada, humming along to immaculate Bach and then, in between times, on the telephone to faraway friends; and then of the aged stranger Piet Mondrian, poor and exiled in New York during World War II, surely dying, but out wandering Times Square at night, infatuated with the neon and skyscrapers and with Meade Lux Lewis and Teddy Wilson and Dizzy Gillespie and Charlie Parker, with Fred Astaire and Ginger Rogers—Mondrian, an old man jitterbugging at parties.

In 1943, the year before he died, he came forward with his final masterpiece, the multirhythmic *Broadway Boogie Woogie* in red and blue and vivid yellow, which I can only think of as sprung from a soul at the end of things. Facing death, we can feel about to be cut out and excluded from the feast of being, and angrily eager to defeat loss in an effort to heal ourselves, or else we can enjoy having been included, suffering the fate of being part of everything.

Mark Rothko and Glenn Gould and Piet Mondrian gave their work as a gift. Harmony and dancing are a form of prayer. There's nothing to do but make peace with the rising flames while the house is burning, a try at joyousness, like Mondrian at some party in New York or Glenn Gould up north, humming and dialing.

In "Song of Myself," Whitman says of animals, "Not one is respectable or unhappy over the whole earth." Should we envy them and want to be like them? Probably not. Our species cannot comfortably live without intelligently defined purposes. But which?

The garden we are creating of the world can be denuded and perilous, a location where the poor and disenfranchised scrap in the night, and where the privileged dither in their selfish waltz toward death. Or it can be plentiful and democratic, a peaceful stage where citizens enact a drama centered on serving what we have and one another. The agenda I propose is simple enough. We must relearn the arts of generosity. We cannot, in any long run, survive by bucking against natural forces, and it is our moral duty to defend all life.

It's time to give something back to the systems of order that have supported us: care and tenderness. As we work on behalf of one another and the world, we begin to experience the solace of reinhabiting our emotional skins. Generosity is the endless project.

PERMISSIONS ACKNOWLEDGMENTS

Grateful acknowledgment is made to the following for permission to reprint previously published material:

HarperCollins Publishers, Inc.: "Realism" from *Facing the River: New Poems* by Czeslaw Milosz, copyright © 1995 by Czeslaw Milosz. Reprinted by permission of HarperCollins Publishers, Inc.

Alfred A. Knopf: "Anecdote of the Jar" from *Collected Poems* by Wallace Stevens, copyright © 1923, copyright renewed 1951 by Wallace Stevens, and ten lines from "The Idea of Order at Key West" from *Collected Poems* by Wallace Stevens, copyright © 1936 by Wallace Stevens, copyright renewed 1964 by Holly Stevens; seven lines from "I Go Back to May, 1937" from *The Gold Cell* by Sharon Olds, copyright © 1987 by Sharon Olds; nine lines from "The Speed of Light" from *The Vixen* by W. S. Merwin, copyright © 1995 by W. S. Merwin. Reprinted by permission of Alfred A. Knopf, a division of Random House, Inc.

New Directions Publishing Corp. and Agencia Literaria Carmen Balcells, S.A.: Six lines from "Explico Algunas Cosas / I Explain a Few Things" from *Residence on Earth* by Pablo Neruda, copyright © 1973 by Pablo Neruda and Donald D. Walsh. Rights in the open market administered by Agencia Literaria Carmen Balcells, S.A., Barcelona. Reprinted by permission of New Directions Publishing Corp. and Agencia Literaria Carmen Balcells, S.A.

University of Illinois Press: Three lines from "Loons Mating" from *Traveling Light* by David Wagoner (Urbana and Chicago: Unversity of Illinois Press, 1999). Reprinted courtesy of University of Illinois Press.

Printed in the United States
by Baker & Taylor Publisher Services